THE MACDONALD ENCYCLOPEDIA OF
AQUARIA

MACDONALD & CO
LONDON & SYDNEY

Published in Great Britain in 1982 by
Macdonald & Co (Publishers) Ltd
London & Sydney
Maxwell House
Worship Street, London EC2A 2EN
ISBN 0 356 07914 7
Printed in Italy by Officine Grafiche
Arnoldo Mondadori Editore, Verona

ACKNOWLEDGEMENTS
The publishers would like to thank John Strong for reading the
text prior to publication and for his advice, the Nuku-Nuku,
Moana Club and Ornis of Milan companies, as well as the Civic
Aquarium of Milan and the Tropical Aquarium of Syracuse for
the specimens supplied for the photographs.

CONTENTS

PUBLISHER'S NOTE

Animals in general, and aquatic ones in particular, exhibit wide color variations. Variability may be determined by a number of factors— among them, for example, the animal's environment, its age and its emotional state. It should also be noted that in the majority of species the coloring of males is stronger and more conspicuous than that of females. Such sexual dimorphism becomes more marked in the reproductive season. In addition, underwater photographs are influenced by the lighting conditions prevailing at the time a picture is taken.

For these reasons, there may on occasion be differences between the colors described in the text and those appearing in the corresponding illustration.

SYMBOLS

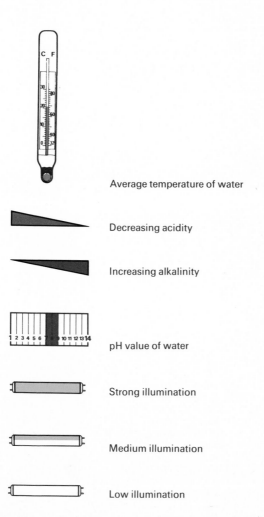

Average temperature of water

Decreasing acidity

Increasing alkalinity

pH value of water

Strong illumination

Medium illumination

Low illumination

INTRODUCTION

A pond is an ecosystem—that is, the totality of living beings and their environment. The various actions and reactions of its components are in equilibrium.

What Is an Aquarium ?

A freshwater aquarium may be planned in two different ways, through either an ornamental or a natural approach. Konrad Lorenz, one of the founders of ethology, has forcefully argued in favor of the natural type of freshwater aquarium, on the ground that it reproduces, as nearly as is possible, a natural environment tending toward biological equilibrium. But such aquaria are often not aesthetically ideal and are relevant only to natural-science studies.

Contrary to popular belief, neither freshwater nor marine aquaria constitute "samples" of natural environments transplanted into our homes. An aquarium, and in particular a marine aquarium, is an abnormal environment whose success depends largely on whether the animals are able to adapt to such different conditions. If the animals survive, we should congratulate them rather than ourselves, because they are more likely to have done so in spite of, rather than because of, us.

The aquarium environment is undoubtedly anomalous in that it is isolated from the beneficial effects of exchanges with the biosphere, and some of its biological parameters are very different from the natural ones.

In spite of these difficulties, however, it is quite possible to

keep a large number of aquatic animals in captivity. To do this, you must above all learn to detect deteriorating environmental conditions and correct them before they become irreversible. The principles to follow, therefore, derive from an understanding of the mechanisms at work in an aquarium and the realization that aquatic animals have very specific, basic physiological requirements which make them, so to speak, physiological extensions of the water they live in. Bearing this in mind, and with some practical experience, you will find that owning an aquarium can be very satisfying.

Tanks
Although frame tanks are economically attractive, they are considered obsolete, particularly for use in marine aquaria. By a frame tank we mean the very common type with a metal framework (or, more rarely, a plastic one) and glass walls sealed with putty. Even if accurately built, a tank of this type is rapidly corroded by seawater and should therefore contain only fresh water. The frame is usually made of enameled iron, a light alloy or stainless steel, but is always subject to corrosion and, moreover, liberates toxic substances into the

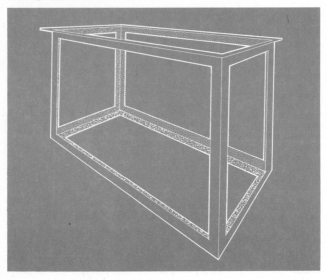

water. Plexiglas tanks also liberate small amounts of toxic substances but are aesthetically very pleasing. This type of container, even if it is built of high-quality materials, has drawbacks. Plexiglas is not particularly hard, so it scratches easily and tends to lose its clarity. It also tends to yellow with time.

Thus the best aquaria are those built entirely of glass and banded by silicone adhesives, which afford very resilient joints and yet retain some degree of elasticity. For very large tanks you can also use Eternit walls and a glass front. The Eternit surfaces in contact with water should be carefully painted with nontoxic paint and thoroughly washed in running water before the aquarium is used.

An important factor to take into account in acquiring or building a tank is the thickness of the glass. For a sidewall 40 in (1 m) high, the glass must be at least $\frac{1}{2}$ in (13 mm) thick, while the bottom must be at least $\frac{1}{2}$–$\frac{3}{4}$ in (13–19 mm) thick. You also need to keep in mind the overall weight of the tank and give careful thought to its location.

Fresh Water
Fresh water contains small amounts of salts and gases in

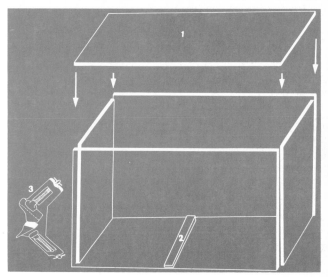

solution. Other substances, such as acids, may also be present in smaller quantities. With the aid of devices that measure electrical conductivity, fresh water may be classed as "hard" or "soft" according to the sodium and calcium it contains in compounds.

Freshwater fishes may prefer soft, hard or even slightly brackish water. In the first case, spring, well or tap water (if free of chlorine) is adequate. To obtain softer water it is sufficient to add a proportion of distilled water, whereas the addition of sea salts (measured with a hydrometer) yields brackish water. Rainwater should not be used, because it contains man-made atmospheric pollutants. Acid water, which some species need in order to reproduce, is distinguished by its amber color. It is obtained through the use of peat soils, long-submerged wood or chemical additives, such as tannic acid.

Seawater

Seawater differs from fresh water by its salt content, generally between 2 and 4 parts per thousand. This variability in salt content is very important. You must keep the salinity in the aquarium as close as possible to that which exists in the

TYPICAL FORMULA FOR ARTIFICIAL SEAWATER, SHOWING COMPONENTS AND PERCENTAGES BY WEIGHT

Components	% by weight
$NaCl$	65.2
$MgSO_4 \cdot 7H_2O$	16.3
$MgCl_2 \cdot 6H_2O$	12.7
$CaCl_2$	3.2
KCl	1.7
$NaHCO_3$	0.49
KBr	0.07
H_3BO_3	0.06
$SrCl_2 \cdot 6H_2O$	0.04
$MnSO_4 \cdot H_2O$	0.009
$Na_2HPO_4 \cdot 7H_2O$	0.009
$LiCl$	0.002
$Na_2MoO_4 \cdot 2H_2O$	0.002
$Na_2S_2O_3 \cdot 5H_2O$	0.002
$Ca(C_6H_{11}O_7)_2 \cdot H_2O$	0.001
$Al_2(SO_4)_3 \cdot 18H_2O$	0.001
$RbCl$	0.0004
$ZnSO_4 \cdot 7H_2O$	0.0002
KI	0.0002
EDTA NaFe	0.0001
$CoSO_4 \cdot 7H_2O$	0.0001
$CuSO_4 \cdot 5H_2O$	0.00002

natural environment of its inhabitants. At first glance, it may seem that seawater itself would be best for aquarium use, but because of its pollution and tendency to deteriorate, it is usually safer to use appropriately conditioned "synthetic" seawater. Natural seawater is a "living" substance, containing living organisms with which it interacts. Many commercially available sea-salt preparations will adequately sustain marine life. They also contain those trace elements which, present in low concentrations, are essential to many biological functions. Because these trace elements are consumed, half or a third of the water should be changed every three weeks. Unlike recently collected seawater, which usually contains too many bacteria, artificial seawater does not contain enough, which is its main drawback. This can be corrected by conditioning, according to the following procedure.

The salt mixture should be dissolved in water in a clean container and the mixture should be aerated for 48 hours. After the water has been allowed to settle for at least a week, soil or filtered solids from an established aquarium should be added. A technique to accelerate conditioning is to introduce highly resistant organisms that liberate organic substances and ammonia into freshly made-up water, thereby mineralizing and nitrifying the water.

pH Value

Alkalinity is an important variable in both fresh and sea water. It is expressed in pH units (hydrogen-ion concentration on a logarithmic scale). Neutral water has a pH of 7, with alkalinity above and acidity below. Apart from some particular species with unusual reproductive needs, freshwater fishes can live in pH values of 6.5 to 7.5.

Natural seawater usually has a pH value between 7.9 and 8.5 and is thus slightly alkaline. In the aquarium, the pH value of artificial seawater should be kept between 7.5 and 9.5. The optimal range for fishes lies between 7.5 and 8.3. Freshly prepared seawater has a pH value of between 7.5 and 7.7, but after a few days it tends to reach values above 8. It is essential to monitor the pH value. Commercially available indicator papers come with instructions for use. If the pH value is too low (the water is acid), one can raise it by adding sodium bicarbonate ($NaHCO_3$) or other alkalinity correctors for aquarium use. If, on the other hand, the pH value exceeds the upper limit (8.6 for seawater, which is thus alkaline), one should add potassium dihydrogen orthophosphate (KH_2PO_4). Limestone shingle or sand, which contains calcium and magnesium carbonates, has an efficient buffering effect and stabilizes the pH value.

Wastes

Living organisms in an aquarium excrete metabolic wastes (urine and feces) and soluble proteins (largely albumins) derived from decaying food. These lead to the accumulation of highly toxic nitrogen compounds such as ammonia, which must be oxidized to nitrates by bacteria. Nitrates, in low concentrations, are essential to the conditioning of water and are particularly important as plant nutrients. (Nitrate concentrations of 100 mg/l should be considered excessive, although organisms are able to adapt to gradual increases of up to ten times this amount.) Frequent water renewal and efficient filtration with large centrifugal pumps are sufficient to keep nitrate levels under control. Marine aquaria, in particular those with large numbers of animals, should contain an absorption column with a foamer, to eliminate soluble proteins before they form toxic nitrogenous compounds.

Aeration

Apart from certain bacteria, all aquatic organisms are aerobic and thus need oxygen dissolved in water for respiration. It is therefore essential for the water in aquaria to contain a high proportion of dissolved oxygen, particularly if the water temperature is high, as in tropical aquaria; this is because the solubility of oxygen in water is inversely proportional to the temperature.

A pump, therefore, is needed to aerate aquarium water. It may be either a membrane pump or, better still, a piston one. The pump will constantly blow air through a diffuser (natural or synthetic) connected to it by a tube made of silicone or a chemically inert plastic. The pump should be silent and, of course, extremely reliable, functioning continuously without breaking down. The diffuser, or porous stone, should have pores of a diameter small enough to increase the surface area in contact with water without requiring excessive pump pressure.

If a centrifugal pump is used for filtration, a venturi tube connected to the water-return tube will blow in a good deal

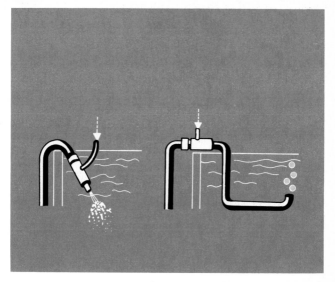

of air. Although most aquatic animals prefer still or slightly
moving water, some prefer rather more turbulent water; this is
another function of a vigorous airstream. The movement of
the water will also tend to increase gaseous exchange with
the atmosphere and will help to bring the oxygen content
closer to its optimum concentration of 50 percent. Pumping,
however, will also dissolve atmospheric pollutants in the
water. To avoid this increasingly bothersome drawback, it is
best to prefilter the air entering the pump by bubbling it
through a small volume of water, which will absorb most
toxic airborne substances.

Filtration

For an aquarium to function well, the filter is crucial, because
it retains suspended particles and decaying foodstuffs. The
filter system should be as large and efficient as possible.
Internal filters are impractical and not particularly efficient
and are not recommended. External filters with centrifugal
pumps are preferred. These have very high rates of flow and
ensure continuous mixing of aquarium water.

Ideally, the output of a filter system should be enough to
ensure a complete recycling of the water every one or two

Purifying bottle for washing out poisonous gases:
1) air from the pump;
2) purified air to the aquarium;
3) tap water.

hours. The filtering material removes unwanted substances from the water. Nylon wool acts as a mechanical filter and retains all the particles that come into contact with it. Activated charcoal acts as both a mechanical and a chemical filter, thanks to its ability to absorb a wide variety of toxic substances. Pumice or marble chips are also of great use in a filter. Pumice chips release trace elements, while marble acts as a pH buffer. Anion-exchange resins are of doubtful value. They remove soluble protein degradation products and seem useful at first sight; their defect lies in their ability to bind trace elements and thus impoverish the water.

For these reasons, it is best to install a foamer or protein skimmer in marine aquaria. This device is made more efficient when it is combined with an ozone generator and works by absorbing in a special column a foam containing a high proportion of proteins and other wastes. The wastes are gathered in a small container and may then be easily removed. It must be remembered that all drastic systems of filtering and purification should be used sporadically, and that only traditional filters are meant for continuous use. An albumin foamer should be used only as an emergency measure. All filter materials are short-lived and should be changed frequently. The filter system should be dismantled

and the nylon wool replaced regularly—more often than is usually recommended by the makers. Mixed filtering is at present very popular; it includes both an external filter and one or more easily maintained internal filters. The latter are held by special partitions on the side or back surface of the aquarium. More elaborate systems include a biological filtering compartment containing algae and bacteria. Filter-feeding mollusks may also contribute to the removal of bacteria and suspended particles.

Heating and Water Temperature

Aquatic animals from cold or temperate climates cannot tolerate a plunge into temperatures higher than those in their normal habitat. However, they may be made to adapt, within limits, to higher temperatures by means of a gradual increase in the temperature of 1–2 °F (.5–1 °C) per 24 hours. Mediterranean and cold-sea animals do not tolerate temperatures above 72 °F (22 °C), whereas tropical animals usually prefer temperatures between 75 and 83 °F (24–28 °C) and show signs of discomfort below 68 °F (20 °C). Water is usually heated by a glass tube containing an electrical heating element, whose power output is expressed in watts.

Diagram of the "classic" filter which operates through an aerator.
Its size must be related to that of the aquarium (100 l of water and
fish requires 1.5 l of filter material).

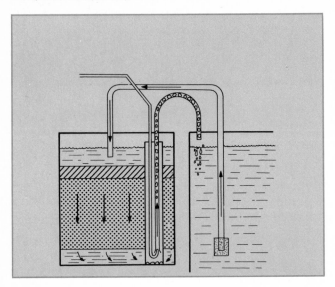

In spite of the rule of thumb of 100 watts for every 100 liters, it
is best to include a thermostat in the heating system. This will
switch the heating current on and off to maintain the selected
temperature.

Temperature readings should be obtained from a thermometer situated as far as possible from the heater. Mercury and
thermocouple thermometers are the most precise, but the
cheaper alcohol type is adequate. The thermometer should be
out of reach of aquarium animals, particularly of large fish and
crustaceans, or protected in such a way as to make its glass
parts inaccessible. A broken thermometer, especially of the
mercury type, could rapidly poison the water. To obtain
uniform heating, it is best to suspend the heater in a water
current and to avoid setting it on the bottom or burying it.

Cold-water flora and fauna suffer from high summer
temperatures and require special care. They must be kept in a
cool, well-ventilated environment away from direct sunlight.
If this is not sufficient to keep the temperature below
68–72 °F (20–22 °C) one can use a spiral glass pipe
immersed in the aquarium, connected by tubes to the water
pipe and the drain. It is possible to use thermostatically
controlled filter–pump refrigeration units, but these are
expensive. Water temperature is an essential factor in

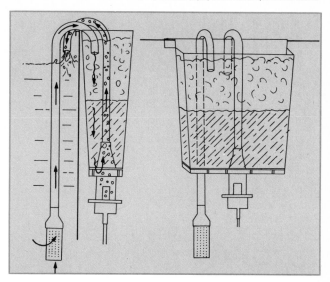

aquarium life. Since its control must be scrupulously maintained, under normal conditions and particularly in emergencies, you should buy the most efficient equipment you can afford.

Illumination

All living organisms, animals as well as plants, require a certain amount of light and a light—dark cycle. But putting the aquarium next to a window in order to expose it to natural light—dark variations is not recommended. The levels of indirect natural light are usually not sufficient, and excessive direct sunlight will raise the water temperature. Aquaria should be illuminated with artificial lights that are carefully isolated electrically from the water. Ordinary incandescent bulbs are inefficient and ill suited to the job, because of their inadequate light spectrum and their undesirable heat. Fluorescent tubes, on the other hand, are highly recommended; they are both very efficient and available in a wide range of colors that can be matched with the aquarium environment. Particularly efficient fluorescent tubes, designed to replace natural lighting completely, are commercially available. At least one of these should be used to

21

The Eheim filter system. Note how the water, after filtering,
reenters the aquarium through a perforated tube $\frac{3}{4}$ in (2 cm) above
the water surface.

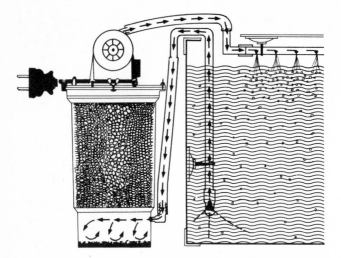

provide the quality and quantity of light needed by most
living things.

The light–dark cycle must be accurately determined,
because an excessively long light period may cause the rapid
growth of encrusting algae. Depending on the power of the
available light sources, it is best to alternate ten hours of light
with fourteen hours of darkness, gradually modifying these
values to minimize algal growth. The use of ultraviolet lights
is often recommended. These, if used with very great caution,
kill bacteria and widen the light spectrum in the aquarium.
Aquarium water, especially seawater, tends to become turbid
as a result of uncontrolled bacterial growth. In such a case, an
ultraviolet source solves the problem in a few hours.
Furthermore, ultraviolet light has beneficial effects on both
the prevention and the cure of certain skin diseases of fishes.

Accessories

A number of frequently used accessories are necessary for
daily aquarium maintenance. Mention has already been made
of the need to install a thermometer. Aquarium thermometers
are often low-precision industrial products, and it is a good
idea to use a precision, rapid-reading thermometer for

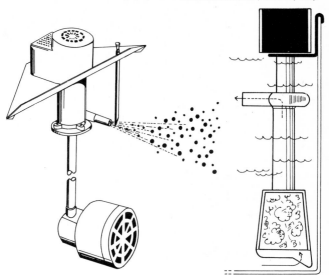

(Left) Internal turbine filter with air supplier (Zoobeko system).
(Right) Internal centrifugal pump filter (Turbelle system).

occasional checks.

Marine aquaria require a hydrometer to determine water density, which is related to salt content. Under normal conditions, pure water weighs 1 kilogram per liter, whereas seawater weighs between 1.024 and 1.029 kg/l. On the hydrometer scale these values are marked respectively as 1024 and 1029. Control of density and salinity is necessary because evaporation, proportional to temperature, tends to increase the salt concentration. Fresh water may be added to reestablish normal salinity.

Two pairs of stainless steel or plastic forceps, one long and one short, will enable you to pick up objects from the bottom, move the fittings, introduce food for sessile organisms, place plants, etc. To capture aquarium animals, you need several fishnets of various sizes. To clean the algae and dirt from internal surfaces of the aquarium you can use a blade scraper, making sure not to scratch the glass, or a pair of flat magnets covered with synthetic abrasive on one face. These can be bought or made. One magnet is placed on the inside of the glass, while the other one, covered in felt, is placed opposite, with its poles reversed, on the outside. If the external one is moved, the abrasive magnet will follow it, thereby cleaning the glass without damaging it.

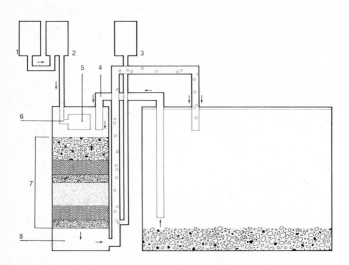

There are two reasons why aquatic animals should never be touched with the hands. 1) The mucous layer with which fishes in particular are covered is vital to their well-being. Damage to this protective coat can lead to a higher incidence of disease. 2) Many organisms are dangerous to the handler, either because they have mechanical means of defense, such as crustacean claws, or because they bear venomous spines (certain species of fish) or stings or sharp jaws, as is the case with sea anemones and certain annelids.

Aquarium maintenance operations include periodic water changes and the removal of waste materials from the bottom. A siphon made from a length of glass or plastic tubing, connected to a rubber tube, can be used in both cases. To extract sediments, you can connect the tube to the pump of the external filter, if there is one, and thoroughly sweep the aquarium with the open end of the aspirator tube. So-called rapid filters are also available and can be used in emergencies or to siphon out sediments and clear the water. Some suppliers of scientific instruments also offer filter cartridges, usually rather expensive, which collect algae and even bacteria.

Pipes, corners and tubing are best cleaned with bottle brushes, particularly the type with a long flexible handle,

A Sander system ozonizer unit:
1) foam collector; 2) reaction tube; 3) water inlet; 4) diffuser;
5) water-return tube; 6) foam-retaining grid; 7) air-ozone-
mixture duct; 8) air duct; 9) aquarium frame.

An aquarium is not just an ornament, but an inexhaustible source of observations on the life and behavior of its inhabitants. These two pages show various phases in the reproductive cycle of Betta splendens.

(Opposite : top) The female being courted by the male. (Bottom) The male embraces the female by arching his body. (This page : above) The eggs in the nest. (Below) A young B. splendens, a month old.

which is well suited to aquarium use. The various types of food dispensers (floating rings, floating sieves for *Tubifex*, etc.) are useful, if sufficiently numerous, to avoid unnecessary and damaging competition among animals at feeding time.

Furnishing the Aquarium

Once all the aquarium components and accessories are collected, you are ready to assemble and equip the aquarium. One of the most exciting things about aquaria is that, apart from some general rules, each aquarium has a character of its own and reflects the preferences of its owner. However, it is always necessary to keep in mind the physiological needs of aquarium fauna and flora from both an aesthetic and a biological standpoint. As far as possible, you should look upon an aquarium as a model environment, with all the components of a natural habitat.

The preparation of a freshwater aquarium begins with the installation of the substrate. This may be made from various materials—for example, sand or pebbles—which may be bought or collected in natural surroundings. In the latter case, you must make sure that the material comes from unpolluted areas, and in any event it should be washed thoroughly with running water before use. The substrate is then spread on the aquarium floor, sloping gently from a depth of $2\frac{1}{2}$–4 in (6–10 cm) at the back wall to 2 in (5 cm) or less at the front. This makes it easier to plant a lot of vegetation at the back of the tank, to create a denser backdrop.

After putting in approximately half the total water, you can add stones, rocks and wooden structures. Stones and rocks should be insoluble, so that they will not liberate potentially toxic salts which would give rise to a chemical imbalance. Strikingly attractive wooden objects can be made from roots, branches, small stumps, etc.; but make sure you use tough, durable wood. Pieces of wood found in water (peat-bog wood, for example) are recommended. These can be bought in special shops. Some wooden ornaments may slightly color and acidify the water, which is usually undesirable but is sometimes favorable to the survival and reproduction of certain species. When you are in doubt as to the quality of the wood, it is best to wash it in running water and boil it in water for two hours before putting it into the aquarium.

If the aquarium is to contain animals that need to leave the water at least temporarily (such as certain fishes, crustaceans, amphibians and reptiles), it is best to build easily accessible structures abovewater. For the installation of plants, which will draw nutrients from food particles and waste products released by the animals, you may use earthenware pots buried in the soil or you may put them directly into the soil itself, making sure to plant them with a short lateral movement rather than simply by pushing them in vertically. This ensures correct positioning of the roots.

Freshwater aquaria lend themselves to a great variety of ecologies, while seawater aquaria are of two main types: temperate (e.g., Mediterranean) and tropical (e.g., coral reef).

The temperate marine aquarium should have a mixture of sand and stones to provide for the needs of animals living on a soft bottom (sand, mud) and of those which prefer rocky substrates with cavities and cracks. To avoid stagnation of water in the substrate it is best to use medium-grained sand (particle size not smaller than $\frac{1}{16}$ in or 1–1.5 mm). Avoid fine sand, which is likely to reach the filter system when stirred by the animals. In contrast to the freshwater aquarium, the sand-bottomed marine aquarium requires a thicker substrate of up to 6–8 in (1–2 cm). You can distribute the sand in steps, higher at the back of the tank, and keep it in place by flat stone dikes. To facilitate water renewal in the soil, it is best to include some mollusk and coral fragments in the sand. This alone is not sufficient, however, and the water must be filtered every week, while the sand is moved to stir up the particles trapped in it. Shell fragments also tend to stabilize the alkalinity level.

"Living rocks" are of great value in both temperate and tropical seawater aquaria: not only are they beautiful to look at, but they also condition the water. These living rocks are natural rocky fragments inhabited by various plants and animals including algae, annelids, crustaceans and mollusks. These organisms present drawbacks as well as advantages, because they are fragile, as in most balanced biological systems. They may die suddenly without apparent reason, and they do not tolerate foreign substances such as drugs in the aquarium water. To reconstruct a coral environment, one usually adds the chalky skeletons of branched corals, particularly white or red, and some attractive gorgonian skeletons. The possibilities of arranging them with stones and rocks are infinite. However, it is best to ensure that tall structures are stable by resting them as solidly as possible on the tank floor or, if necessary, by using nontoxic adhesives to

join them together. Such arrangements are usually taller at the back of the aquarium, to prevent them from looking out of proportion. You can also make use of several tricks to simulate seawater depths, such as painting the outside surface of the back of the aquarium or, if necessary, adding glass or plastic panels of the desired color inside.

Like all objects that are to be introduced into an aquarium, coral skeletons should be thoroughly washed before use. Unfortunately, the appearance of these natural materials tends to deteriorate rather rapidly underwater. Their porosity gives them a tendency to retain suspended particles from the water and to become coated with brown and green algae. They therefore require periodic cleaning, including energetic brushing in running water, immersion in boiling water for at least three hours, and about five days' immersion in concentrated seawater. An equally effective method— slower, but rather less laborious—is immersion in a 15-percent solution of potassium hydroxide for a week, after which the coral must be washed in running water for at least ten days. Its chalky composition precludes the use of hydrochloric acid, even in low concentrations, because it would make them extremely fragile or destroy them outright by dissolving them.

A possible landscape for tropical marine fishes.

To summarize, then, the rules of assembly and furnishing: it is best to give this part of the construction a good deal of thought and to build carefully and slowly, experimenting with various arrangements and their maintenance needs. As for the number of animals to be kept in an aquarium, this corresponds to the volume of water. It is best to keep furnishings functional and avoid using so many as to clutter the tank. Few animals and simple furnishings usually result in fewer disappointments for beginners. The various plastic objects available have purposely not been mentioned; they are chemically inert, but their use is a question of personal taste. They certainly do not make the aquarium a natural environment.

Safety Measures and Devices
Maintaining an aquarium, whether freshwater or marine, requires certain precautions to avoid damaging the fittings and equipment. This is particularly true with marine aquaria. For example, we have already mentioned the importance of using a net to capture or restrict an animal without directly touching it. If hand contact is unavoidable, it is best to wear high-quality rubber gloves to protect both you and the

aquarium animal. Fish scales are covered with skin and mucous layers of varying thickness necessary both for osmotic exchange and for protection from pathogens (bacteria, fungi, etc.) ever present in the water. This barrier must not be impaired. Other animals have delicate, fragile structures that are easily damaged if handled without extreme care. In addition, there is the risk to the handler from many organisms' defensive and offensive structures. Besides having claws and spines that can inflict simple wounds, many aquatic, and in particular marine, animals are venomous.

A list of noxious animals would draw on all major groups listed in zoological textbooks. The aquarium owner must beware of coelenterates (jellyfish, sea anemones and living corals), annelids (burrowing or free-living marine worms), mollusks (some cones and cephalopods are notorious for their toxicity), crustaceans (medium and large crabs and prawns), echinoderms (sea urchins and starfish) and fishes (scorpion fishes and others). Not all animals belonging to these groups are venomous, but some secrete extremely potent poisons which may be fatal to humans. With such animals it is best to act prudently, but without excessive fear, keeping in mind that these dangerous devices are used to ensure survival in hostile natural environments.

It is also important to remember the presence of electricity in or near aquaria, and that water (particularly salt water) and electricity should be kept well insulated from each other. In the first place, water attacks all materials, and electrical appliances may become poorly insulated; secondly, salt water conducts electricity well and enables electrical leaks to occur. In marine aquaria, therefore, it is best to prevent accumulation of salt deposits by periodically, after disconnecting the power, washing the appliances in fresh water and drying them thoroughly. *ALWAYS REMEMBER WHEN HANDLING ANY ELECTRICAL APPLIANCES: PULL OUT ALL PLUGS FROM THEIR SOCKETS*. Turning off the switch is not enough; switches can fail to interrupt the flow of current.

Similarly, except when adjusting the thermostat, you should disconnect the power when dealing with lights and heaters. You should also periodically check the state of insulating materials—particularly plastic and rubber parts, which age rather rapidly; they should be replaced at the first sign of deterioration. When installing electrical appliances, you should strictly follow the maker's instructions and avoid submersing parts not designed for underwater use. Current leaks, often the first sign of an electrical fault, can be detected with a voltmeter. If any leaks are found, the electrical equipment should be thoroughly tested. One final rule concerning immersion heaters: do not switch them on outside water, and do not immerse them once hot; if you do, they may explode. Sudden temperature jumps are damaging to plants and animals, and also can fracture glass tanks. For this reason, when filling or washing the tank, make sure that the water added is at the same temperature as the tank water, or ambient temperature. In any event, very hot or very cold water should never be added.

Food

No living organism can survive without a constant energy input in the form of food. Plants make use of light energy to transform inorganic compounds and constituents into organic ones by means of photosynthesis. They draw their nourishment from the soil and the water.

An aquarium will be able to support plant life after it has been inhabited by animals for some time, but it is possible to shorten this period by adding fertilizers or special soils such as peat, which releases humic acids into the water. Animals pose more complex feeding problems. They may be roughly subdivided into dietary categories according to ecological criteria: herbivorous animals, whose diet is almost exclusively composed of plants; carnivorous ones, which eat other animals; omnivorous animals, which combine both the above, and scavengers (detritus feeders), which feed on decayed material in suspension and on the bottom, and on organic wastes of various types.

These varieties of animals also have different feeding rhythms; carnivorous predators feed sporadically, while all the others feed more or less continuously during their diurnal or nocturnal activity periods. Feeding times, as well as the type and quantity of food, will depend on the nature of the aquarium fauna. The best compromise usually consists of frequently adding small amounts of food sufficient to feed all the animals without leaving any food floating, suspended or on the bottom. This principle also holds for animals needing specific diets.

If the aquarium contains predators, and if problems of compatibility arise, the predators must be fed live prey or adequate substitutes, following the rhythms suggested by the species' natural habits. Providing excess food inevitably leads to deterioration of the delicate environmental balance and of the health of its inhabitants. On the other hand, although aquatic animals will tolerate extremely long fasts, one should not go to the opposite extreme and provide too little food. It is easy to reach a satisfactory feeding pattern for any aquarium, provided that competition, present in nature and emphasized by artificial aquarium conditions, is taken into account. Food should be spread uniformly across the aquarium in order to favor those animals which are somehow unable to compete with animals better or more rapidly adapted to the aquarium.

A wide variety of food for freshwater animals is available, all more or less adequate if the diet is supplemented with fresh, natural food. Freeze-dried foods are convenient and well tolerated. Among these are brine shrimps, *Daphnia* and other crustaceans, *Tubifex*, fish eggs and meat (liver, heart, etc.). A short list of natural foods, many of which are easily found in natural surroundings or in special shops, includes living planktonic animals (brine shrimps, *Daphnia* and other crustaceans), *Tubifex* and other worms, small mollusks, insect larvae and small adult insects, small fish and various vegetables (boiled rice, fresh or boiled vegetables, etc.).

In particular, young fishes (larvae and older fry) require specially prepared products, or even better, protozoan cultures (*Paramecium*) and plankton (*Artemia* nauplii); but bear in mind that larvae of oviparous fishes need smaller particles than larvae of viviparous species. Marine organisms have diets similar to freshwater ones, with the addition of fresh or frozen mollusks and crustaceans, chopped or liquefied fish and algae. Liquefied foods prepared with mortars or blenders are particularly suitable for certain coelenterates (sea anemones, gorgonians, branched corals and other corals) and for so-called filter feeders (bivalves, many crustaceans, etc.). To make the best use of frozen foods, divide them into portions and wrap each one in aluminum foil. In this way it is possible to use food as it is needed while conserving the rest in good condition.

Plankton is available in the form of *Artemia salina*; this is a small crustacean which lives in very salty waters such as salt marshes and flats that are subject to high evaporation. The small brown eggs of these crustaceans hatch better if exposed to a temperature of 77 °F (25 °C) for one hour and then immersed in well-aerated seawater (artificial or natural), at 77 °F (25 °C) in a shallow container. Depending on the

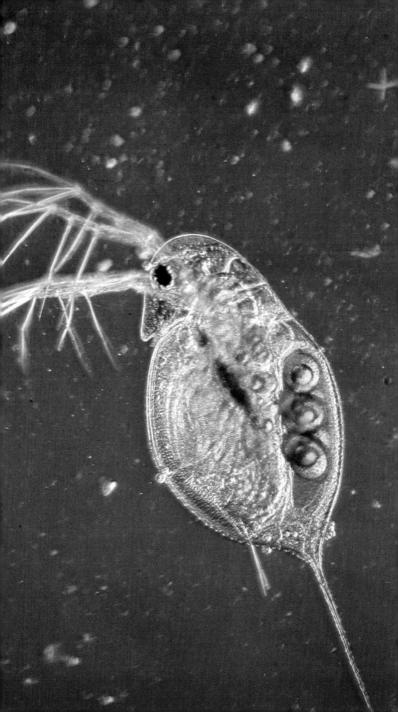

temperature, salinity and illumination, *Artemia* larvae, known as nauplii, hatch within 12 to 20 hours and swim vigorously, using their three pairs of swimming legs. Excellent *Artemia* incubators are available and will facilitate these processes. If most of the container is shielded from light, the animals will concentrate in the unshielded area and can be easily removed with a fine-meshed dipnet.

A good appetite and eagerness to feed are signs of good health and adaptation to environmental conditions. Recently acquired animals, however, seem unwilling to feed even if the food is varied. The change from a natural habitat or a commercial aquarium to the new environment often requires a long period of adaptation. Various animals, including many fishes, do not find aquarium food palatable. These animals may require painstaking adaptation periods while their diet is gradually shifted from the natural one, which may be difficult to find, to imitate or even to ascertain, to artificial ones. Fortunately, however, this is unusual, because animals bought from reliable dealers have already been adapted to aquarium life. One final point: natural foods may carry undesirable contaminants or organisms and should be washed in running water before use.

Quarantine

Quarantine refers to the set of hygienic precautions designed to prevent a newly arrived animal from infecting or infesting those already living in the aquarium. This usually applies to fishes that often carry in their natural state various diseases or pathogens as well as ecto- and endoparasites. Although there are specific regulations governing the import, transport and sale of animals, the more reputable dealers apply supplementary measures to observe and disinfect animals that are going to be sold.

These rules, however, are not always respected, and the aquarium owner should have a spare tank specifically designed for the quarantine of newly arrived animals. This glass tank, which can also be used for the treatment of diseased fishes, should contain $6\frac{1}{2}$–11 gallons (30–50 liters) of water. It should be sparsely furnished with a pebble substrate and an earthenware pot resting on its side to provide a refuge for the animal during maintenance. Tropical animals will, of course, require safe, thermostatically controlled heating as well as efficient filtration and aeration.

The quarantine procedure for recently imported tropical

An Artemia *nauplius, food for newborn fish.*

fishes is as follows. Bring the temperature of the water up to 85–86 °F (29–30 °C) and keep the fish under observation for two weeks. The high temperature causes latent diseases to emerge. If no symptoms have appeared after this time, gradually lower the temperature to 77 °F (25 °C) and keep the fish under observation for another week.

The mild disinfectants that manufacturers suggest for use in the second phase are certainly not damaging, but they are of dubious value to a healthy animal. On the other hand, one may treat the animals with antibiotics for eight hours (never more, for reasons of toxicity, than ten hours). With the filter pump switched off and increased aeration, add 200,000 International Units of penicillin per liter of water before introducing the animal into the tank. The animal must be kept under observation and transferred to clean water if it appears not to tolerate the drug and exhibits anomalous behavior.

Quarantine methods, which are the subject of a great deal of disagreement, may also include the use of drugs specifically designed for aquarium use. This, however, does not eliminate the need to adapt the animal to captivity and, above all, to aquarium food. In order to make this phase as quick and easy as possible, several forms of sedative

treatment are now being developed to reduce the stresses experienced by the more emotional types of animals. When quarantine is completed, you can transfer the animals to the aquarium without any further fears about hygiene.

Aquarium Pathology and Therapy: Diseases (Tables 1 and 2)
All living organisms are subject to diseases, and aquarium animals are no exception. Although our knowledge of invertebrate pathology is still fragmentary, fish pathology and therapeutics have long been studied. (See Tables 1 and 2 for a summarization.) You can minimize the incidence of disease in fishes by taking certain simple precautions such as using only reputable supplies, quarantining adequately, handling

Diseased Congo tetra, covered with white spots, characteristic of Ichthyophthirius *(white spot) infection.*

carefully, ensuring cleanliness and hygiene in the aquarium and immediately isolating animals suspected of being diseased. Less-than-optimal environmental conditions will lead to the emergence of diseases. Preventive therapies may be conducted in the main aquarium, but cures should be applied only in the quarantine tank, both to avoid contagion and because of the toxicity of drugs to other animals (for instance, coelenterates, mollusks and crustaceans do not tolerate copper sulfate). Abnormal behavior is the first sign of disease in fishes, and it takes various forms, depending on the species, such as floating, immobility on the bottom or odd movements. Alterations in appearance or skin color may indicate disease if the animal appears somehow crippled or discolored.

SOME DISEASES OF FISHES AND THEIR TREATMENT

Disease	Treatment
1. Viral	Avoid contagion
2. Bacterial	Avoid contagion and treat with antibiotics
3. Parasitic	
a) Fungi (*Saprolegnia*)	Avoid contagion, treat with antifungal medicine and disinfect tank with copper sulfate solution or formalin
b. Dinoflagellates (*Oodinium*)	Clean tank and disinfect as above
c. External protozoa (*Costia*, etc.)	Avoid infection and treat with formalin, copper sulfate, methylene blue or malachite green
d. Intradermal protozoa (*Ichthyophthirius*)	Avoid contagion; kill free protozoa by disinfecting tank water with formalin, malachite green or copper sulfate and increase water temperature for a few days to as high as the fish will tolerate
e. Intestinal protozoa (*Hexamita*)	Specific medicines available (e.g., Enheptin)
f. Systemic protozoa (*Myxosoma*, etc.)	Avoid contagion. There are no practical effective treatments
g. External trematoda (*Gyrodactylus*, etc.)	Controllable by bathing in solution of formalin or potassium permanganate
h. Parasitic worms (Trematoda, Cestoda, Nematoda, Acanthocephala)	Eliminate infested animals and intermediate carriers (mollusks, crustaceans, etc.). Administer Kamala orally for Cestoda and piperazine citrate for Nematoda
i. Crustaceans (*Argulus*, etc.)	Remove parasites mechanically. Bathe fish in solution of potassium permanganate or formalin
4. Other	
a. Conditions due to incorrect environment: wrong feeding, skin damage due to bad handling	Find out and eliminate cause; avoid increasing susceptibility to more serious illness
b. Tumors	Remove affected animals

PRINCIPAL MEDICINES USED AGAINST INFECTIOUS DISEASES IN FISHES

Medicine	Preparation	Treatment
Sodium chloride (NaCl, salt)	Solution in water (3% by weight)	Bathe for 30 minutes to maximum of 2 hours (for freshwater fishes only)
Copper sulfate $CuSo_4$	Solution in water 1 : 2,000 ratio (can add glacial acetic acid, about 1 ml per l)	Bathe for 1 minute
Formalin (commercially available at 37% by weight of formaldehyde in water)	Dilute in water 1 : 500 or 1 : 4,000–1 : 6,000	Bathe for 15 minutes Bathe for 1 hour
Potassium permanganate $KMnO_4$	Use solution in water diluted to: 1 : 1,000 1 : 100,000	Bathe for 10–40 seconds Bathe for up to 30 minutes
Methylene blue	Solution in water in ratio 1 : 350,000	Bathe for 3–5 days
Malachite green	Solution in water at dilution 1 : 15,000 1 : 200,000	Bathe for 10–30 seconds Bathe for 1 hour
Chloramphenicol	Add to water in the ratio 1 : 20,000	Bathe for an indefinite time
	Or, commercially available form	Orally, in food at the rate of 50–75 mg per kg body weight per day
	Or, commercially available form	One peritoneal injection of 10–30 mg per kg body weight
Oxytetracycline	Commercially available	Orally, in food, at the rate of 50–75 mg per kg body weight per day. Treat for 10 days

The Meaning of Color Variations in Fishes

Temporary or seasonal color variations are rather common in animals and serve various adaptive purposes. They are related to physiological variations (such as reproductive periods, particularly in males) or psychological states (changes of "mood"), or may serve to render the animal less conspicuous.

It is well known that the males of many species exhibit a "nuptial display" with brilliant, more intense colors, sometimes different from the normal ones. Less well known is the ability of certain types of fishes to change their color patterns with their mood, as in the case of the well-studied cichlids. Indeed, some animals have as many as ten different color displays, depending on whether they are quiet, anxious, frightened, socially dominant or submissive, defending their territory, etc. On the other hand, some fishes such as the soles change their coloration for mimetic purposes, to merge with their environment. The butterfly fishes and other species also vary their patterns according to age, so that variations of color quality and distribution are found within a species, sometimes to such an extent that they are mistaken for separate species.

The structures responsible for these color changes are known as chromatophores or pigment cells, which may be black (melanophores), yellow (xanthophores), red (erythrophores), white (leucophores) or iridescent (irid-ocytes). The chromatophores are under hormonal and nervous control and when stimulated may either contract or expand the pigment granules they contain, giving rise to paler or more intense coloring.

Transport of Aquatic Animals

Animals must be suitably transported when taken from their natural environment and when bought from a dealer. Small, square-bottomed Plexiglas aquaria equipped with battery-operated pumps were once popular, but plastic bags are now preferred for practical reasons of weight and bulk. To transport aquatic animals, insert the plastic bag in a second one of equal size, making sure that both are separately sealed when packing is finished. The water in the inner bag should not fill more than one-third of the available volume. The remaining space must be emptied of air and filled with pure

oxygen. If gaseous oxygen is not available, it is possible to use commercially available preparations which release oxygen on contact with water.

For more favorable transport conditions, animals should be thermally insulated—for instance, by being placed in boxes made of expanded polystyrene. Fishes in particular should be transported in the water to which they are accustomed, with the addition of small amounts of disinfectants, anesthetics

and antibiotics. The most commonly used anesthetic is MS 222, which should be used in a dilution of 1:45,000. Methylene blue can be used as a disinfectant when one drop of a 5-percent solution is added per liter of water. A good antibiotic is oxytetracycline, dissolved in water in a ratio of 25–125 mg/l. Fishes should be introduced into treated water only when all the drugs are completely dissolved.

PLANTS

1 DWARF SEDGE
Acorus gramineus
Var. pusillus and var. variegatus

Family Araceae.
Distribution Japan; the variety *variegatus* is of horticultural origin.
Description *Acorus gramineus* is a shrubby plant, 10–12 in (25–30 cm) in height, with long, narrow, ribbonlike leaves, slightly curved when at maximum length. It is an amphibious marsh plant which, however, can adapt to underwater life in an aquarium. Var. *pusillus*, with short, rigid leaves 1½–4 in (4–10 cm) high, and var. *variegatus*, with leaves reaching 16–20 in (40–50 cm) and bearing yellow streaks, are more common than the original form.
Propagation Through division of the tufts or the rhizome (the fleshy underwater stem) by cutting their tips and planting the base of the stem immediately in shallow water, whose depth is then gradually increased.
Environment *Temperature:* 59–68 °F (15–20 °C), best at 65 °F (18 °C). *pH:* neutral. *Water hardness:* soft. *Illumination:* moderate to normal. *Soil:* No particular requirements; clay or clay with peat.
Note The dwarf variety of *Acorus* is commonly used in small aquaria.

2 ALTERNANTHERA SESSILIS
Alternanthera sessilis

Family Amaranthaceae.
Distribution Humid or sporadically flooded areas of the Old World.
Description Perennial plant, always partly immersed in its natural habitat, but well suited to life underwater in the aquarium. Its stalks are very branched and characteristically red. The leaves are stalkless, lanceolate, up to 2⅜–2¾ in (6–7 cm) long and ⅜ in (1 cm) wide. The upper surface is variously colored from dark green to wine red, and the lower side is always bright red.
Propagation Very simple, by cutting.
Environment *Temperature:* 60–72 °F (16–22 °C), possibly somewhat less. *pH:* near neutrality. *Water hardness:* medium. *Illumination:* Normal to intense, even if artificial. *Soil:* sand and rock, possibly with the addition of fertilizer.

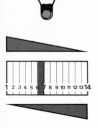

3 ANUBIAS LANCEOLATA
Anubias lanceolata

Family Araceae. The genus *Anubias* contains six species.
Distribution Tropical Africa.
Description Perennial plant with a fleshy underwater stem over 15¾ in (40 cm) high in its natural habitat, seldom higher than 11¾ in (30 cm) in an aquarium. The leaves are lanceolate, rather blunt at the tip, 4–4¾ in (10–12 cm) long and 1³⁄₁₆–2 in (3–5 cm) wide, dark green, with long stalks and leathery blades, concave on the upper side.
Propagation Very slow, by division of tufts.
Environment *Temperature:* this species requires high temperatures, between 68 °F (20 °C) and 86 °F (30 °C), best at 77 °F (25 °C). *pH:* neutral or, if possible, slightly acid. *Water hardness:* average to soft. *Illumination:* low-level. This species grows naturally in rain forests, where light levels are low. *Soil:* no particular requirements, but preferably sandy.
Note *Anubias lanceolata* is an excellent plant to use in warm aquaria. Its only drawback lies in its slow rate of growth.

4 LACELEAF PLANT
Aponogeton fenestralis

Family Aponogetonaceae. The name of the genus is derived from two Greek words—*apon* (water) and *geiton* (close to).
Distribution Madagascar.
Description Oblong leaves, 5⅞–7⅞ in (15–20 cm) long, characteristically lacking spongy tissue and therefore consisting only of a network of veins.
Propagation By division of offshoots; less commonly by seed.
Environment *Temperature:* 60–68 °F (16–20 °C) with possible extremes of 57 °F (14 °C) and 76 °F (24 °C); undisturbed, frequently renewed water. *pH:* 6–8, or neutral. *Water hardness:* soft to medium. *Illumination:* normal, preferably diffuse and artificial. *Soil:* mainly large-grained sand, and a little mud.
Note Cultivation of this plant is difficult; during the period of winter dormancy, the water temperature must be maintained around 55 °F (13 °C).

5 APONOGETON HENKELIANUS
Aponogeton henkelianus

Family Aponogetonaceae.
Distribution Madagascar.
Description Similar in appearance and form to *Aponogeton fenestralis*. The oblong and variously sized leaves differ from those of *A. fenestralis* only in their color, which is brownish, while the stalks are reddish.
Propagation By division of the offshoots, rather more difficult by seed; when done by seed, water temperature should be 68–77 °F (20–25 °C).
Environment *Temperature:* Usually between 60 °F (16 °C) and 68 °F (20 °C), with possible extremes of 57 °F (14 °C) and 76 °F (24 °C). The water must be undisturbed and frequently renewed. *pH:* neutral or, at most, slightly acid. *Illumination:* normal, if possible diffuse. *Soil:* sandy, a mixture of coarse sand and a little mud.

6 APONOGETON ULVACEUS
Aponogeton ulvaceus

Family Aponogetonaceae.
Distribution Madagascar.
Description This is probably the *Aponogeton* species most suited to aquarium use; its leaves are approximately 10 in (25 cm) long with wavy, translucent pale green blades. In turbulent water *Aponogeton ulvaceus* may exhibit a certain variety of shapes, with longer and narrower or shorter and wider leaves, depending on the current.
Propagation By division of offshoots; propagation by seeding is more difficult and rarely succeeds.
Environment *Temperature:* 68–74 °F (20–23 °C) with frequent, if partial, renewal. *pH:* neutral. *Water hardness:* soft. *Illumination:* normal, diffuse if possible. *Soil:* sandy, a mixture of coarse sand and mud.

7 BACOPA AMPLEXICAULUS
Bacopa amplexicaulus

Family Scrophulariaceae.
Distribution Atlantic coast of North America.
Description Perennial aquatic or marsh plants with a lemon scent; stem finely grooved, $15\frac{3}{4}$–$23\frac{5}{8}$ in (40–60 cm) high, often emerging from the water. The leaves are stalkless, arranged on opposite sides of the stem, fleshy, pale green, with a lanceolate-oval blade. This plant flowers abovewater, and the flowers have a near-regular, bell-shaped arrangement of blue petals.
Propagation By growth of offshoots or by sprouting.
Environment *Temperature:* 64–77 °F (18–25 °C), best around 68 °F (20 °C). This makes it an excellent species for use in tropical aquaria. *pH:* neutral. *Water hardness:* mild. *Illumination:* normal to strong. *Soil:* sandy, if possible with some fertilizer.
Note *Bacopa amplexicaulus* is usually grown initially on humid terrain and the small plants are then moved to the aquarium, where they grow without much difficulty.

8 BARCLAYA LONGIFOLIA
Barclaya longifolia

Family Nymphaeaceae. The genus *Barclaya* comprises only three species, living in Southeast Asia along the banks of tropical waterways.
Distribution Thailand, Laos, Vietnam, Burma.
Description Fairly uncommon plant. Has longish leaves which are lanceolate, with wavy edges and conspicuous veins on the lower blade.
Reproduction Asexual. Not easy to cultivate.
Environment *Temperature:* 68–86 °F (20–30 °C), best around 77 °F (25 °C). *pH:* neutral. *Water hardness:* medium. *Illumination:* medium to dim light; in the plant's natural habitat it gets little light. *Soil:* heavy soil mixed with sand.
Note *Barclaya longifolia* grows better if other species are also present in the aquarium. Although the plants compete, a good flora is eventually established.

9 CABOMBA spp.
Cabomba spp.

Family Nymphaeaceae.
Distribution North and South America.
Description Perennial aquatic plant, usually entirely submerged, but partly floating under certain conditions, both wild and cultivated. Its leaves, supported by erect stems, are arranged on opposite sides of the stem and subdivided so finely they are almost reduced to their veins; small, wide, floating leaves appear at flowering. The flowers are solitary, with long stalks and with white or yellowish petals.
Propagation By cutting. Place a six-inch length of the stem in the soil.
Environment *Temperature:* 64–77 °F (18–25 °C), best at 68 °F (20 °C), for *C. aquatica*; 53–72 °F (12–22 °C), best at 65 °F (18 °C), for other species. *pH:* slightly acid, 6.4–6.5. *Water hardness:* soft. *Illumination:* normal to intense, preferably artificial; no direct sunlight. *Soil:* Must contain a high proportion of loam: one-third loam, one-third sand, one-third garden earth.
Note *Cabomba* species are not easy to grow, but if well cared for they tend to grow rapidly.

10 CALLITRICHE spp.
Callitriche spp.

Family Callitrichaceae. The term is derived from two Greek words, *kallos* (beauty) and *thrix* (hair), referring to the beautiful hairlike leaves.
Distribution The genus includes some forty species, widely distributed throughout the world except in southern Africa.
Description Aquatic plants, soft, delicate, almost always submerged or parly floating. Leaves arranged on opposite sides of the stem. Linear, floating leaves sometimes oval. Very small, solitary, unisexual flowers. The male flowers are composed of a single stamen, while the female flowers comprise a single pistil.
Propagation Simple and easy, by cuttings, which easily take root.
Environment *Temperature:* these species are suited to cold aquaria, 50–65 °F (10–18 °C) or even lower. *pH:* neutral. *Water hardness:* soft. *Illumination:* very intense. *Soil:* no particular requirements. Even a simple layer of sand will do.
Note When grown outdoors, grow well in ponds or basins; even if these freeze over in winter, the plants survive and help to oxygenate the water.

11 CARDAMINE LYRATA
Cardamine lyrata

Family Cruciferae. The term *Cardamine* may be derived from the Greek *kardamon*, meaning cress. According to some authors, however, it is derived from *kardia* (heart) and *damao* (to tame), with reference to certain sedative properties of the plant.

Distribution Eastern China, Korea, Japan.

Description Graceful plant, with thin stems and lyre-shaped leaves with a broad, rounded tip and three to five small lobes along each edge. When the plant is completely submerged, the leaves take on a beautiful pale green color; when the plant is abovewater, the green becomes more intense.

Propagation By division.

Environment *Temperature:* 59–72 °F (15–22 °C), best around 65 °F (18 °C). This species grows well in cold and temperate aquaria. *pH:* neutral. *Water hardness:* medium. *Illumination:* low-level to normal. *Soil:* sandy.

Note *Cardamine lyrata* thrives in shaded damp and marshy places along waterways. It adapts easily, however, to aquarium conditions.

1 2 3 4 5 6 7 8 9 10 11 12 13 14

12 CERATOPHYLLUM DEMERSUM
Ceratophyllum demersum

Family Ceratophyllaceae. The name *Ceratophyllum* is of Greek origin, from *keras* (horn) and *phyllon* (leaf), referring to the texture of the leaves.

Distribution Temperate and tropical areas.

Description Herbaceous perennial plant, with branching, very fragile jointed stems; solitary flowers at the leaf base, the male ones at the top, the female ones below, both very inconspicuous.

Propagation By division of the stems. Portions of stems are anchored to the soil with a clod of earth or a stone, and soon take root.

Environment *Temperature:* 50–65 °F (10–18 °C), best at 59 °F (15 °C) in clean water. *pH:* neutral. *Water hardness:* hard. *Illumination:* very intense. *Soil:* no particular requirements.

Note *Ceratophyllum demersum* is an excellent species for oxygenating the water. It may become infected by brown algae which can cover the plant.

1 2 3 4 5 6 7 8 9 10 11 12 13 14

13 CERATOPTERIS THALICTROIDES
Ceratopteris thalictroides

Family Parkeriaceae. Belongs to the Pteridophyta (ferns). The generic name is derived from the Greek *keras* (horn) and *pteris* (wing), referring to the leaves; the species name *thalictroides* refers to its resemblance to the genus *Thalictrum.*

Distribution The genus *Ceratopteris* includes only three species, occurring in tropical areas. They are *C. cornuta, C. pteridioides* and *C. thalictroides,* the last-named inhabiting Old World tropical areas.

Description Annual aquatic fern, submerged, with soft fronds, composed of small, oblong, lanceolate leaflets and narrow, linear, forked prothallia, resembling antlers. The leaflets of the latter are covered with buds which easily give rise to new plants.

Propagation The safest and simplest method is the vegetative one, as follows: the older leaves, already bearing young plants, are severed and left to float. When the young plants have grown, they can be separated from the carrier leaves and planted.

Environment *Temperature:* 64–86 °F (18–30 °C), best around 77 °F (25 °C). Winter temperatures must not go below 64 °F (18 °C). *pH:* slightly acid. *Water hardness:* soft. *Illumination:* normal. *Soil:* if the aquarium also contains fishes which produce organic wastes, a sandy soil is sufficient; if not, a mixture of earth with fertilizer and peat will be required.

Note *Ceratopteris thalictroides* exists in diverse forms exhibiting variability in "leaf" shape, which can be narrow, wide (see photographs) or intermediate.

14 CRYPTOCORYNE spp.
Cryptocoryne spp.

Family Araceae. The name *Cryptocoryne* is derived from the Greek *kryptos* (hidden) and *koryne* (club), referring to the club-shaped arrangement of flowers on the stem enclosed in a sheath of leaves.
Distribution Tropical Asia.
Description Members of the genus *Cryptocoryne* are aquatic, perennial, stoloniferous plants (producing shoots and buds) with oblong or linear leaves sometimes chordal or oval. *Cryptocoryne beckettii* is a species that exists in several forms. Its leaves are 4 in (10 cm) or so long and ¾ in (2 cm) wide, with slightly wavy veins. One of its forms has reddish median and lateral edges.
Propagation By division of the rhizome (the underwater base of the stem).
Environment *Temperature:* 68–86 °F (20–30 °C), best around 77 °F (25 °C). *pH:* slightly acid. *Water hardness:* soft or very soft. *Illumination:* normal. *Soil:* sand may be sufficient, but one-third loam, one-third garden earth and one-third sand is recommended.
Note *Cryptocoryne* species are probably the best plants to use in warm aquaria.

15 CRYPTOCORYNE LINGUA
Cryptocoryne lingua

Family Araceae.
Distribution Borneo.
Description Beautiful small plant, at most 4 in (10 cm) high. The leaves, which resemble little spatulas, are oval, bright green and fleshy, with a round tip; the leaf base narrows into the stalk, which constitutes half to two-thirds of the length of the leaf.
Propagation Easy propagation by rhizome division. Note that aerial plants multiply more rapidly than submerged ones.
Environment *Temperature:* best around 77 °F (25 °C), but the plant will live well between 60 °F (16 °C) and 86 °F (30 °C). *pH:* slightly acid. *Water hardness:* very soft. *Illumination:* C. lingua, like all *Cryptocoryne* species, does not require too much light, and even shuns excessive light. *Soil:* the best soil would be composed of equal parts of sand, field earth and clay; however, the plant will grow in sand alone.

16 ECHINODORUS PANICULATUS
Echinodorus paniculatus

Family Alismataceae.
Distribution South America.
Description The genus *Echinodorus* contains some of the most beautiful species of aquatic plants, and *E. paniculatus* is one of the most beautiful species of this genus. It forms conspicuous tufts composed of long, pointed lanceolate leaves, with veins over their entire length, borne by long triangular stalks. It seldom flowers in aquaria. The flowering stalk produces plantlets which may take root and grow independently of the mother plant, from which they must be detached. The flowering shoot should therefore be brought into contact with the aquarium soil.
Propagation By division of the plantlets which develop on the shoot.
Environment *Temperature:* 68–77 °F (20–25 °C), best at 72 °F (22 °C). *pH:* neutral. *Water hardness:* medium. *Illumination:* intense. *Soil:* sand; rather coarse sand should be used with the regular addition of fertilizer.

17 WATER HYACINTH
Eichhornia crassipes

Family Pontederiaceae. The genus *Eichhornia* is named after the Prussian statesman J. A. F. Eichhorn. *Crassipes* means "swollen foot" and refers to the swollen leaf stalks.
Distribution Brazil.
Description Perennial, floating, short-stemmed plant, with a large rhizome. The leaves are bunched together to form a rosette and are borne by oddly swollen stalks which contribute to the plant's buoyancy. The leaves are dark green, shiny and heart-shaped. The stalk bears purplish flowers in terminal ears, 4 in (10 cm) long. Summer flowering is short-lived. Distinctive, purplish-blue roots.
Propagation By cutting the summer offshoots.
Environment *Temperature:* 60–86 °F (16–30 °C), best at 68–77 °F (20–25 °C). *pH:* neutral. *Water hardness:* soft. *Illumination:* intense. *Soil:* though *E. crassipes* is a floating species, it needs a fertile soil with a proportion of peat to ensure that the water will contain dissolved substances necessary to the plant.
Note Not recommended for aquaria, as it will soon overgrow the tank and deprive other plants of light and nutrients.

18 SPIKE BUSH
Eleocharis acicularis

Family Cyperaceae.
Distribution North America.
Description This is a rather slim plant not taller than 12 in (30 cm) with very thin stems, bearing at their extremity offshoots which are capable of giving rise to new plantlets. These in turn carry offshoots which may give rise to smaller plantlets.
Propagation By offshoots.
Environment *Temperature:* 59–77 °F (15–25 °C), best at about 65 °F (18 °C). *pH:* slightly acid. *Water hardness:* medium. *Illumination:* normal to low-level. *Soil:* sand with some field earth, not too rich.

1 2 3 4 5 6 7 8 9 10 11 12 13 14

19 ELODEA DENSA
Elodea densa

Family Hydrocharitaceae. *Elodea* is derived from the Greek word *elos* swamp.
Distribution Argentina, but also common in Paraguay, Uruguay and Brazil. Acclimatized elsewhere.
Description Probably the best species of this genus for the aquarium. The stems are up to 10–13 ft (3–4 meters) long (much shorter, obviously, in an aquarium), scarcely branching, with leaves grouped in closely compressed whorls of four leaves each (hence the name *densa*). Leaf color varies from light green to dark green, and blade shape varies from linear to lanceolate, slightly notched.
Propagation By cutting of young stems.
Environment *Temperature:* 60–68 °F (16–20 °C), best at 68 °F (20 °C). The plant can stand temperatures from 50 °F (10 °C) to 77 °F (25 °C). *pH:* slightly alkaline. In acid water the plant soon wilts, turns brown and dies. *Water hardness:* hard. *Illumination:* intense. *Soil:* no particular requirements; even sandy. The addition of a small proportion of earth composed of 75 percent field earth and 25 percent loam is recommended.
Note *Elodea densa* is well suited to cold and temperate aquaria.

20 WATER MOSS
Fontinalis antipyretica

Family Fontinalaceae. *Fontinalis* is derived from the Latin *fons, fontis* (spring), referring to one of the preferred habitats of this moss; *antipyretica* is due to an old belief in its fever-reducing properties.
Distribution Northern hemisphere.
Description Typical of cold and usually running waters; this species forms tufts of leafy stems 12–20 in (30–50 cm) long, anchored to the bottom or to a rock or stone. These carry numerous oval or pointed dark green leaves arranged on opposite sides of the stem, at most $\frac{3}{8}$ in (1 cm) long, $\frac{1}{4}$ in (.5 cm) wide and with a marked ridge on the back.
Propagation Vegetative.
Environment Clean water. *Temperature:* 50–59 °F (10–15 °C). *pH:* neutral. *Water hardness:* medium. *Illumination:* good, but not excessive. Too much light leads to excessive growth of algae, which enshroud the moss. *Soil:* mixture of sand and peat.
Note *Fontinalis antipyretica* is suited only to cold aquaria. High temperatures cause rapid wilting.

---

21 HYGROPHILA spp.
Hygrophila spp.

Family Acanthaceae. The generic name is derived from Greek words meaning "humidity-loving."
Distribution Tropical America, Asia.
Description This genus includes perennial plants both surface-living and submerged, with herbaceous or semiwoody stems. The leaves are arranged on opposite sides of the stem, oblong or lanceolate, often pointed, light green, slightly darker when growing in air. The genus contains some twenty species, a quarter of which are suitable for aquarium use.
Propagation By cuttings.
Environment *Temperature:* 59–77 °F (15–25 °C), but the extremes may vary by a few degrees. *pH:* neutral. *Water hardness:* medium. *Illumination:* normal to intense. *Soil:* sandy.

22 HYGROPHILA POLYSPERMA
Hygrophila polysperma

Family Acanthaceae.
Distribution East Indies, Malaysia. This plant was first brought to Europe more than thirty years ago and is among the most popular of aquarium plants.
Description Perennial plant, with oblong, stalkless leaves arranged on opposite sides of the stem, borne by thin woody stalks. Leaf-blade color varies from light green to dark green when all or part of the plant is out of water.
Propagation By cuttings.
Environment *Temperature: Hygrophila polysperma* is a plant for warm aquaria, preferring temperatures around 68–77 °F (20–25 °C). However, it can adapt itself to higher or lower temperatures, from 50 °F (10 °C) to 82–86 °F (28–30 °C). *pH:* neutral. *Water hardness:* soft. *Illumination:* rather intense, if completely submerged. The aerial parts of the plant should not be exposed to intense light. *Soil:* sand and mud.
Note Because of its modest requirements, *Hygrophila polysperma* is widespread in thick growths in aquaria.

23 DUCKWEED
Lemna minor

Family Lemnaceae. The name *Lemna* derives from the Greek *lemma* (scale or blade), referring to the form of the plants.
Distribution Worldwide.
Description Annual floating, short-stemmed plant, composed of a single blade and its root, egg-shaped or round, $\frac{1}{3}$ in (7–8 mm) or so in diameter, bright green, smooth, without veins on either side. It usually forms colonies of two to four individuals. *Lemna, Wolffia* and *Spirodela* are all genera of Lemnaceae and are among the smallest flowering plants known.
Propagation Rapid, vegetative.
Environment *Temperature:* 41–77 °F (5–25 °C), best around 59–65 °F (15–18 °C). *pH:* neutral. *Water hardness:* medium. *Illumination:* intense.
Note Like all other species of the genus *Lemna, Lemna minor* is not recommended for aquarium use because it reproduces rapidly and would soon cover all the available surface, thereby depriving other plants of light and nutrients.

24 LOBELIA VARIEGATA
Lobelia variegata

Family Campanulaceae. The generic name is dedicated to the Flemish botanist and physician M. de l'Obel.
Distribution North America.
Description Although it is a perennial plant typical of humid environments, it adapts itself to life in both cold and temperate to warm aquaria. For growth underwater, it is best if the plant does not grow a principal stem; the tips should therefore be frequently trimmed to encourage lateral growth and maintain height more suited to an aquarium environment. The plant has magnificent scarlet flowers and oblong, lanceolate leaves on longish stalks, and the blades are 1½–2 in (4–5 cm) long and approximately ¾ in (2 cm) wide.
Propagation By division of the tufts.
Environment *Temperature:* 59–72 °F (15–22 °C), best around 64–68 °F (18–20 °C). It is able to stand temperatures as low as 50 °F (10 °C). *pH:* neutral. *Water hardness:* medium. *Illumination:* low to normal. *Soil:* sandy.
Note *Lobelia variegata* tends to grow out of the water very rapidly if too strongly illuminated.

25 LUDWIGIA spp.
Ludwigia spp.

Family Onagraceae. The genus is dedicated to C. G. Ludwig, a contemporary of Linnaeus.
Distribution The genus includes some twenty species, distributed in Europe, Asia, Africa and the Americas.
Description Members of this genus are perennial and annual plants, aquatic as well as semiaquatic and marshy. The leaves are smooth, arranged on opposite or alternate sides of the stem, with weak stalks, and the flowers are small and yellow or greenish.
Propagation Vegetative.
Environment *Temperature:* 59–77 °F (15–25 °C), best around 68 °F (20 °C). *pH:* neutral. *Water hardness:* medium. *Illumination:* intense. *Soil:* sand may be sufficient, but a mixture of equal parts of earth, loam and sand is recommended to produce robust plants.
Note When the plant is grown in an aquarium, the water should be kept cold or temperate. The plant, however, is not recommended because it deteriorates rapidly when completely submerged.

26 WATER MILFOIL
Myriophyllum spp.

Family Haloragaceae. The term *Myriophyllum* is derived from the Greek words *myrios* (myriad) and *phyllon* (leaf).
Distribution Practically worldwide.
Description Submerged or partly aerial plant with feathery leaves arranged on the stem in whorls of three or four and with a rhizome that roots at the nodes. Among the most important species are *M. alterniflorum* for cold aquaria, *M. brasiliense* for tropical aquaria and *M. verticillatum,* with leaves in whorls of four or five.
Propagation By cuttings.
Environment *Temperature:* 50–72 °F (10–22 °C), best around 60–65 °F (16–18 °C) for exotic species. *pH:* generally alkaline, but *M. alterniflorum* needs an acid pH. *Water hardness:* *M. alterniflorum* needs soft water, *M. brasiliense* hard water and *M. verticillatum* medium-hard water. *Illumination:* rather intense. *Soil:* sand or a mixture of equal parts of field earth, loam and sand.
Note The *Myriophyllum* species are excellent for increasing oxygen content in ponds as well as aquaria.

27 NOMAPHILA STRICTA
Nomaphila stricta

Family Acanthaceae.
Distribution Thailand, Malayan peninsula, Indonesia.
Description Robust plant with woody stems bearing rather large leaves, light green when submerged or darker when aerial. These are lanceolate with a pointed tip, fairly wide and running down the longish stalk. The leaf blade is divided by a conspicuous median rib as well as visible lateral veins.
Propagation By cuttings.
Environment *Temperature:* 59–77 °F (15–25 °C), best around 72 °F (22 °C). *pH:* neutral. *Water hardness:* hard. *Illumination:* sufficient light to facilitate the growth of ample leaves. *Soil:* sand, or sand and mud.
Note *Nomaphila stricta* is one of the most attractive aquarium species, but is subject to attack by mollusks.

28 BANANA PLANT
Nymphoides aquatica

Family Gentianaceae. *Nymphoides* means water lily-like, referring to the resemblance between these two plants.

Distribution Atlantic coast of North America, particularly Florida.

Description Adult leaves varying from rounded to kidney-shaped, 3–4 in (8–10 cm) in diameter. Submerged leaves, light green with dark red netlike patterns; aerial leaves more intensely green, dark red on the reverse and heavily spotted. This plant is called the "banana plant" because the top part of the root is swollen and resembles a bunch of bananas. The plant will flower only if it is partly submerged. Its flowers are white and rather small.

Propagation By division of the shoots that grow on the leaf stalks. The shoots grow tufts of swollen young roots.

Environment *Temperature:* 50–77 °F (10–25 °C), best around 64–68 °F (18–20 °C). *pH:* neutral. *Water hardness:* medium. *Illumination:* bright, but not excessive. *Soil:* sandy.

Note This plant is suitable for temperate and warm aquaria.

29 POTAMOGETON DENSUS
Potamogeton densus

Family Potamogetonaceae. The term is derived from two Greek words meaning "living near the river."

Distribution Europe, Asia, North Africa.

Description Perennial submerged plant with creeping rhizome; cylindrical stem; oval, lanceolate or nearly linear light green leaves, joined to the stem by a dilated base.

Propagation By cuttings. The tips are cut and embedded in the soil.

Environment *Temperature:* 50–59 °F (10–15 °C), but able to survive at lower temperatures; it has been a popular plant for cold aquaria. *pH:* neutral or slightly alkaline. *Water hardness:* medium. *Illumination:* intense. *Soil:* sand and mud.

Note *Potamogeton densus* is often used to oxygenate and purify the water of cold aquaria, where it grows well as long as the light level is sufficent. In general, species of the genus *Potamogeton* are not considered best for warm-water aquarium use.

30 WATER CROWFOOT
Ranunculus aquatilis

Family Ranunculaceae.
Distribution Temperate regions of the northern hemisphere, America and North Africa.
Description Herbaceous perennial plant with leaves of two kinds. Submerged leaves are narrow, much branched and short-stalked; floating leaves are kidney-shaped, notched, with three to five lobes, and have long stalks. Strong stalks reaching higher than the leaves bear the flowers. These are white, with petals much larger than their sepals.
Propagation By division.
Environment *Temperature:* 53–65 °F (12–18 °C). *pH:* near neutrality. *Water hardness:* medium. *Illumination:* normal to good. *Soil:* sand and mud.
Note *R. aquatilis* could be used as a cold-aquarium plant, but is not recommended because it soon becomes covered with algae. Furthermore, these plants, when moved to an aquarium, do not adapt to the artificial environment and tend to wilt.

---

31 RICCIA FLUITANS
Riccia fluitans

Family Ricciaceae, belonging to the Bryophyta, or mosses. The generic name honors the Italian botanist Ricci.
Distribution Practically worldwide.
Description Small, floating plant with vegetative structures consisting of an almost undifferentiated branched thallus $1\frac{3}{16}$–$2\frac{3}{8}$ in (3–6 cm) long and at most $\frac{1}{16}$ in (1 mm) wide. It forms light green masses on water.
Propagation Very simple, by natural division of the thallus.
Environment *Temperature:* 59–77 °F (15–25 °C). *pH:* neutral. *Water hardness:* soft. *Illumination:* normal. *Soil:* the water must be rich in organic substances.
Note *Riccia fluitans* is one of the best species for oxygenating the water. A prolific microfauna lives in the midst of its rapidly growing bunches, including very young fishes.

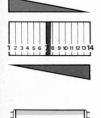

32 SAGITTARIA spp.
Sagittaria spp.

Family Alismataceae. The generic name is derived from the Latin *sagitta* (arrow), referring to the leaf shape of some species.

Distribution Temperate and warm regions.

Description Perennial aquatic or marsh plants, partly or completely submerged. The leaves are often polymorphic—radical, linear, lanceolate or arrow-shaped, sometimes oval when floating—and the plants bear whorled flowers with three white petals. *Sagittaria sagittaefolia* grows wild in Europe and is partly aerial, but *S. subulata* and *S. platyphylla*, from the southern U.S.A., are preferred for aquarium use and have long, rather wide leaves.

Propagation By offshoot and by seed; the latter method applies only to flowering, partly aerial plants.

Environment *Temperature:* 59–77 °F (15–25 °C), best around 68 °F (20 °C) for exotic species. *pH:* neutral or slightly alkaline. *Water hardness:* fairly hard. *Illumination:* weak to normal for totally submerged plants, normal to intense for aerial ones. *Soil:* sandy, or loam and sand.

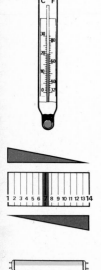

33 SYNGONIUM spp.
Syngonium spp.

Family Araceae.

Distribution The genus *Syngonium* includes twenty or so species, from central and tropical America.

Description Members of this genus are usually "crawling" plants with flexible stems and nodal aerial roots. The leaves, which are supported by sheathing stalks, are arrow-shaped in the young plant and subdivided into five to nine unequal lobes in the adult. The flowering stalks, seldom seen in our climates, are composed of a sheath covering a "spike" arrangement and a fleshy stem. The reason for the inclusion of *Syngonium* in this list of aquarium plants lies in the recent fashion for growing young plants of this genus underwater. They are graceful plants and their patterning and shape may be esthetically very pleasing. There are, however, disadvantages. In this environment, to which they are not suited, the plantlets are short-lived and should be used only in temporary aquaria (e.g., in an exhibition).

Environment *Temperature:* 59–77 °F (15–25 °C), or at any rate in temperate to warm aquaria. *pH:* neutral. *Water hardness:* medium. *Illumination:* weak to normal. *Soil:* sandy.

34 HYGROPHILA DIFFORMIS
Hygrophila difformis

Family Acanthaceae. This species grows wild in tropical and equatorial Asia and is considered a weed in rice cultivation.
Distribution India and Malayan Peninsula.
Description This species was imported for ornamental aquarium use about twenty years ago and was subsequently classified. Its elegance and great decorative effect have contributed to its wide popularity among aquarium owners. It is a fairly large plant of varying leaf structure, with blades ranging from oval, barely serrated to deeply indented, almost fringed. Submerged leaves are pale green, while partly aerial leaves are darker.
Propagation By cuttings.
Environment *Temperature:* 74–86 °F (23–30 °C). *pH:* neutral. *Water hardness:* hard or very hard. *Illumination:* normal to good; if light levels are too high the plant grows normally but becomes discolored. *Soil:* sandy to pebbly, with some fertilizer if possible.

35 UTRICULARIA spp.
Utricularia spp.

Family Lentibulariaceae. The term *Utricularia* is derived from the Latin *utriculum* (small bag), referring to the vesicles on the leaves.
Distribution The genus is widespread in temperate and warm areas of the world.
Description Herbaceous perennial plants, submerged, floating or sometimes terrestrial. Simple, alternate, more rarely whorled, limp, finely subdivided leaves. Many species carry small vesicles which serve to capture insects, crustaceans and young fishes. The flowers are usually yellow and appear on the water surface.
Propagation By division of the stems.
Environment *Temperature:* for *Utricularia vulgaris*, 59–77 °F (15–20 °C), best around 65 °F (18 °C). *pH:* acid. *Water hardness:* soft. *Illumination:* intense. *Soil:* sand or peat.
Note The best species for use in a tropical aquarium is *Utricularia gibba. U. minor* and *U. vulgaris* are not recommended for aquarium use.

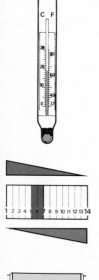

36 VALLISNERIA
Vallisneria spiralis

Family Hydrocharitaceae. The genus is named after A. Vallisnier, a 17th-century naturalist and physician.
Distribution Tropical and subtropical areas; introduced elsewhere.
Description Submerged plant with long, ribbonlike leaves low down on the stem, $\frac{1}{4}-\frac{3}{8}$ in (.5–1 cm) wide and with tiny notches at their extremities. Male and female plants separate. The male flowers are very small and appear near the roots; they then become detached and float to the surface before opening. The female flowers are on long, threadlike, twisted stalks.
Propagation By offshoots, which should carry a leaf rosette.
Environment *Temperature:* 59–72 °F (15–22 °C), best at 64–68 °F (18–20 °C). *pH:* neutral. *Water hardness:* medium. *Illumination:* intense. *Soil:* sandy, but a mixture of equal parts of sand, clay and loam is preferable.

37 VESICULARIA DUBYANA
Vesicularia dubyana

Family Hypnaceae, belonging to the mosses.
Distribution Tropical Asia, Java, Malaysia and the islands of the East Indian archipelago.
Description A good species for warm-water aquaria. Similar in appearance to *Fontinalis antipyretica*, but grows faster and better, in spite of its smaller size. It forms tufts which take root and grow partly buried in sand. They are composed of leafy stems with large numbers of small, oval or pointed, overlapping dark green leaves, arranged on opposite sides of the stem.
Propagation By division.
Environment This species requires clean water. *Temperature:* 64–77 °F (18–25 °C), never below 60 °F (16 °C). *pH:* neutral. *Water hardness:* medium. *Illumination:* barely sufficient; too much light leads to algal growth on the fragile tufts. *Soil:* sandy, rocky.

FRESHWATER
FISHES

38 COOLIE LOACH
Acanthophthalmus kuhlii

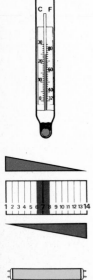

Family Cobitidae.
Distribution From the southern part of the Malayan peninsula to Sumatra, Java and Borneo.
Description *Shape:* eel-shaped, elongated, slightly compressed sides, very small fins. The dorsal fin starts behind the middle of the body, the anal fin well behind this. Eyes covered with transparent skin; a movable spine beneath them; four pairs of barbels; no lateral line. *Color:* fifteen to twenty dark brown to black vertical bars, the gaps between them salmon pink to yellowish. Underside light. *Size:* 3 in (8 cm). *Sexual differences:* unknown for nonbreeding fish; females often become monstrously fat before spawning.
Environment A bottom dweller which burrows into soft places. *Temperature:* 75–86 °F (24–30 °C). *pH:* slightly acid or neutral. *Water hardness:* soft water— below 10° general hardness. *Illumination:* subdued, at bottom of tank. *Substrate and furnishings:* a thick layer of soft sand, with additional cover in the form of stone cavities, flowerpots or coconut shells. Thick vegetation; some humus on the bottom.
Feeding Omnivorous.
Biology *Behavior:* very active at twilight and night-time; often buried in the sand by day. *Reproduction:* in the wild, the fish spawn communally in very shallow water. *Social life:* little known. *Compatibility:* easily kept with other nonaggressive fishes.

---

39 BLUE ACARA
Aequidens pulcher

Family Cichlidae.
Distribution Trinidad, Panama, northern Venezuela, Colombia.
Description *Shape:* relatively deep body; compressed, particularly at the caudal peduncle. *Color:* at spawning time, takes on a magnificent iridescence, and six to eight gleaming greenish-gold horizontal lines of spots appear on the sides. *Size:* up to 6¾ in (17 cm). Sexually mature from 3 in (7–8 cm). *Sexual differences:* difficult to distinguish: The males have elongated tips to dorsal and anal fins, which sometimes extend farther than the caudal fin itself.
Environment *Temperature:* 72–79 °F (22–26 °C); frequently replace about one-third of the water with fresh water. *pH and water hardness:* no special requirements. *Illumination, substrate, furnishings:* good lighting; deep bottom matter with thickly planted vegetation in places, stones and roots as hiding places, also plenty of free swimming space.
Feeding Many types of live food.
Biology *Behavior:* A very peaceful cichlid which causes no damage to plants. *Reproduction:* very easy. An open breeder which spawns many times a year; in other respects like other cichlids. *Social life:* territorial, but peaceable. *Compatibility:* good with other cichlids.

40 LONG-FINNED CHARACIN
Alestes longipinnis

Family Characidae.
Distribution Tropical West Africa, from Sierra Leone to Zaïre.
Description *Shape:* elongated body, very compressed sides, dorsal fin approximately in the middle of the body, adipose fin present; very large eyes. *Color:* back olive green to yellow, sides muddy yellow with a beautiful silver sheen. Underside silvery white. *Size:* up to 6¼ in (16 cm). *Sexual differences:* male high-backed, with dorsal-fin rays extending as far as the caudal fin. The female has a crooked line along the back and a similar one along the belly; the dorsal fin does not have extended rays.
Environment A schooling fish occupying the middle water levels. *Temperature:* 73–77 °F (23–25 °C). *pH:* value about 6.5. *Water hardness:* up to 10° general hardness. *Illumination:* strong lighting; some sun. *Substrate:* dark bottom, some floating plants. *Furnishings:* a large tank with about half its area planted.
Feeding Live food, plenty of insects and vegetation.
Biology *Behavior:* lively, peaceful schooling fish. *Reproduction:* prepare a tank 3 ft (1 m) deep with water of pH 6–7 and 6–7° general hardness and some nylon netting held down with stones as a support for the eggs. The young fish eat rotifers. *Social life and compatibility:* good to keep with other African characins.

---

41 BLIND CAVE-FISH
Astyanax mexicanus

Family Characidae. Cave-dwelling variety once considered to be a separate species, *Anoptichthys jordani*.
Distribution Cave form in underground waters of Mexico; surface form widespread from Texas to Panama.
Description *Shape:* small, elongated, fairly flat-sided, with a profile curved equally above and below. Adipose fin present; anal fin with long base. *Color:* surface form: a silvery to light brassy sheen on sides, back olive. Cave form: monotone pink tint with a silver sheen; eyes minute, completely buried beneath skin. *Size:* up to 3½ in (9 cm). *Sexual differences:* females become thickset.
Environment *Temperature:* preferred temperature 64–75 °F (18–24 °C). The subterranean form is said to tolerate temperature range of 63–89 °F (17–29 °C). *pH:* 7.5. *Water hardness:* hard water is preferable. *Illumination:* full lighting for the surface form, subdued lighting for the cave one. *Substrate:* deep sandy bottom; the cave form can be given large caves made from stones. *Furnishings:* not too thick; shadow-loving plants.
Feeding Omnivorous; a voracious eater.
Biology *Behavior:* lively, peaceable schooling fish. *Reproduction:* the surface and cave forms can be crossed with each other. *Social life and compatibility:* specimens of the surface form are good for a communal tank; the cave form are best kept in a species tank.

42 STRIPED ANOSTOMUS
Anostomus anostomus

Family Anostomidae.
Distribution Amazon and Orinoco river systems; rivers of the Guyanas.
Description *Shape:* a long, slightly flat-sided fish with a high-set mouth. *Color:* mature fish have three horizontal stripes (brown to brownish black), with a dark green sheen. *Size:* up to 7 in (18 cm). *Sexual differences:* minimal.
Environment *Temperature:* 75–80 °F (24–27 °C). *pH and water hardness:* medium soft, neutral to slightly acid water. *Illumination, substrate, furnishings:* a large tank with large, sparsely planted vegetation and hiding places provided by stones, pieces of bog wood and flowerpots; dark bottom and medium lighting.
Feeding Omnivorous, feeding on both animal and vegetable matter (bryozoans and algae); they will take soft and decaying leaves, also swimming and crawling aquatic invertebrates.
Biology *Behavior:* a schooling fish, which spends most of its time "on its head" but streaks away horizontally when disturbed. *Reproduction:* breeding has been carried out successfully a number of times, but little reliable information is available. *Social life and compatibility:* best mixed only with members of its own species; generally peaceable, but often given to chasing other fishes.

43 LYRETAILS; APHYOSEMIONS
Aphyosemion spp.

Family Cyprinodontidae.
Distribution Tropical West Africa from Nigeria to Zaïre, chiefly in slowly flowing or still waters.
Description *Color:* very varied. Species in photograph is possibly *A. christyi. Size:* from 1¼ to 5 in (3 to 13 cm). *Sexual differences:* the females of most species are far less striking and colorful than the males.
Environment Most were originally inhabitants of the tropical forest; only *A. bualanum* is found exclusively in the savanna. *Temperature:* 64–72 °F (18–22 °C). *pH:* 6.5 is usually sufficient, but some species require pH down to 4.5. *Water hardness:* soft to medium-hard water; many species must have soft water. *Illumination:* subdued lighting. *Substrate:* peat, preferably sterilized. *Furnishings:* preferably feathery-leaved plants.
Feeding Generally eat insects in the wild, and these will be needed for their well-being in the tank; the female's capacity to produce eggs often depends on this.
Biology *Behavior:* a surface fish swimming about in schools just under the surface of their native shallow pools in search of food. *Reproduction:* according to species, they lay eggs on the bottom or on plants (the perennial varieties only). *Social life:* in large groups or two females to one male, according to species. *Compatibility:* unsuitable for a community tank.

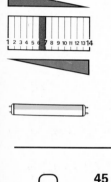

44 AGASSIZ'S DWARF CICHLID
Apistogramma agassizi

Family Cichlidae.
Distribution Amazon basin.
Description *Shape:* typical South American dwarf cichlid: elongated body, compressed sides. Very long dorsal fin. *Color:* back brownish yellow to greenish blue; orange sides, shading to greenish blue at the rear. Gill covers have brilliant blue lines and vermiculations. Numerous sparkling greenish-blue spots on back and sides. A brownish-black line extends from the mouth to the base of the caudal fin, without touching the eye. A similar line extends from the mouth steeply downward to the lower edge of the gill cover. The caudal fin is heart-shaped with color graduations similar to those of a gas flame—grayish green on the outside, then smoky gray, then a luminous ivory-colored or blue-green zone with a luminous orange-red center. *Size:* 3 in (7.5–8 cm); males often larger. *Sexual differences:* males larger, with pointed, elongated dorsal, caudal and anal fins.
Environment Similar to *A. ramirezi,* but less particular. *Temperature:* 66–77 °F (19–20 °C). *pH:* slightly acid. *Water hardness:* soft water. *Substrate and furnishings:* as for *A. ramirezi.*
Feeding Omnivorous, but prefers live food.
Biology *Behavior:* peaceable, territorial dwarf cichlid, similar to *A. ramirezi. Reproduction:* breeds in cavities; see *A. ramirezi. Social life:* similar to *A. ramirezi.*

45 RAMIREZ' DWARF CICHLID
Apistogramma ramirezi

Family Cichlidae.
Distribution Venezuela and Bolivia.
Description *Shape:* typical dwarf cichlid. Characteristic deep, flat body and great compression. The dorsal fin is high, the first three spines black and the second, in males, elongated. *Color:* base color in fine specimens pale purplish red. A vertical bar through the eye; a black spot under the spiny part of the dorsal fin, surrounded by spots of blue (or some other metallic color). *Size:* $2\frac{3}{4}$ in (7 cm). *Sexual differences:* male more brightly colored, with elongated second ray on dorsal fin.
Environment *Temperature:* 73–77 °F (23–25 °C); 81–82 °F (27–28 °C) for breeding. *pH:* slightly acid; filter through peat. *Water hardness:* soft water. *Illumination, substrate, furnishings:* ample vegetation (three-fourths of tank area), medium lighting, numerous hiding places.
Feeding Preferably not too coarse or large live food.
Biology *Behavior:* territorial and living in pairs. *Reproduction:* not very easy. Breeds in cavities. A good spawning produces 150–200 eggs, which are laid on stones or in hollows in the bottom. Both partners look after the eggs; the young hatch out after 48 hours and swim free after 5–6 days. The shoal is cared for largely by the male. *Social life:* as with nearly all cichlids, the shoal of young fish is broken up by the formation of pairs.

46 BLUE PANCHAX
Aplocheilus panchax

Family Cyprinodontidae.
Distribution India, Indochina, Sri Lanka, Malaysia and Indonesia; several geographical forms.
Description *Shape:* flattened head and back, dorsal fin placed well along the back; smoothly rounded ventrally. Anal fin long-based and large; very long, large pectoral fins; pelvic fins small and somewhat elongated. The caudal fin is shaped like a spade. *Color:* generally a grayish yellow, with the back darker. Each scale has a bluish center with a dark border around the edge. *Size:* up to 3 in (8 cm). *Sexual differences:* females much paler, fins more orange.

Environment Above all a surface creature. *Temperature:* 68–77 °F (20–25 °C). *pH:* neutral. *Water hardness:* soft water. *Illumination:* intense lighting, shaded by floating plants. *Substrate:* dark. *Furnishings:* Lots of plants. Cover the top of the tank, as the fish are excellent jumpers.
Feeding All sorts of live food, also a little dried food.
Biology *Behavior:* a relatively peaceable schooling fish which lives in the uppermost water levels. *Reproduction:* very easy. Large eggs, $\frac{3}{32}$ in (1.6–1.8 mm) in diameter; the young fish quite large. *Social life and compatibility:* keeps in schools; good to keep with fishes of the middle and lower water levels, as long as these are as big or bigger.

47 OSCAR or VELVET CICHLID
Astronotus ocellatus

Family Cichlidae.
Distribution Amazon, Paraná, Rio Paraguay, Rio Negro.
Description *Shape:* fairly deep body, an elongated oval shape, moderately compressed. Upper and lower profiles similarly curved. *Color:* highly variable according to size, age, sex and above all mood. Most have brilliant, irregular black-edged stripes on an olive-green to chocolate-brown ground. There is a round, red-rimmed eyelike patch on the upper part of the caudal-fin base. *Size:* up to 1 ft 1 in (33 cm). *Sexual differences:* not apparent, examine sexual genital organs of spawning fish.
Environment *Temperature:* 68–77 °F (20–25 °C). *pH and water hardness:* no special requirements; dechlorinated water, a proportion of it changed regularly but not too suddenly. *Substrate and furnishings:* a large cichlid tank with stones and roots but without rooted plants. Good aeration and filtration. Deep gravel bottom.
Feeding Omnivorous.
Biology *Behavior:* typical large cichlid, but fairly peaceable. *Reproduction:* already sexually mature when 4 to 4¾ in (10–12 cm) long. Eggs are whitish at first, becoming transparent after 24 hours. Forms long-lasting pairs. *Social life and compatibility:* they can be kept together with *Cichlasoma meeki*.

48 BLACK RUBY BARB
Barbus nigrofasciatus

Family Cyprinidae.
Distribution Southern Sri Lanka.
Description *Shape:* deep-bodied species with a pointed head; no barbels. *Color:* normally yellowish gray. In both sexes the head is a fine purple red. *Size:* up to 2¼ in (6 cm). *Sexual differences:* in the female, the basal part of all the vertical fins is black; in the male, the whole dorsal fin is a deep black, the anal fin blackish red, the pelvic fins reddish. At spawning time the male changes color as represented in the photograph.
Environment Quietly flowing, flat stretches of water; plenty of room needed in an aquarium. *Temperature:* 68–82 °F (20–28 °C); for breeding 77–82 °F (25–28 °C). *pH:* around 7. *Water hardness:* soft water; at best use old water, replacing part of it with fresh water regularly. *Illumination and substrate:* plenty of light; a shallow covering of floating plants and ample vegetation (half to two-thirds of tank area); a layer of humus should be left on the bottom.
Feeding Omnivorous, with a healthy appetite.
Biology *Behavior:* a lively fish, constantly active, found at any depth. *Reproduction:* breeding is very simple and productive; but the fish are egg-eaters. *Compatibility:* good for keeping with other barbs and similar fishes.

---

49 TIGER BARB
Barbus pentazona hexazona

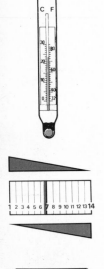

Family Cyprinidae.
Distribution Central Sumatra.
Description *Shape:* typical barb shape but somewhat longer. *Color:* silvery-golden body. The wide vertical black bands recall the related *Barbus tetrazona* (see No. 51). *Size:* 2¼ in (5.5 cm). *Sexual differences:* the female is much fuller in the belly and paler in color. The male is slimmer; its splendid coloring makes it one of the most beautiful barbs. *Temperature:* 68–77 °F (20–25 °C); for breeding 81–86 °F (27–30 °C). *pH:* 6.5–7. *Illumination, substrate, furnishings:* good lighting; a deep layer of sand on the bottom with a little humus and ample vegetation (two-thirds of tank space), the rest free swimming space.
Feeding Omnivorous; needs large quantities of food.
Biology *Behavior:* a lively, peaceable schooling fish. *Reproduction:* not simple; needs high temperatures. *Social life:* forms loose schools. *Compatibility:* easily kept with other nonaggressive fishes of similar size.

50 CHINESE BARB
Barbus semifasciolatus

Family Cyprinidae.
Distribution Southeast China.
Description *Shape:* medium-long barb. Adult specimens have highly arched backs. A short pair of barbels on the upper jaw at the corners of the mouth. *Color:* back light to reddish brown. Sides metallic green or yellow-green, with brassy or golden sheen below. Whitish belly, turning orange-red in males at mating time. Numerous color variations. *Size:* 2¾–3 in (7–8 cm). *Sexual differences:* females dully colored; become very bulky.
Environment Inhabit running water. *Temperature:* 68–75 °F (20–24 °C); 79 °F (26 °C) for breeding. *pH and water hardness:* of little importance; tap water will usually do. *Illumination and furnishings:* good lighting and oxygenation. Half to two-thirds thick vegetation; the rest for swimming.
Feeding Omnivorous.
Biology *Behavior:* a lively schooling fish, tending to frequent the upper water levels. *Reproduction:* mating is fairly violent. Eggs are medium-sized, yellowish; they hatch out after 25 hours. Very prolific. *Compatibility:* good to keep with other peaceable fishes.

51 SUMATRA BARB
Barbus tetrazona

Family Cyprinidae.
Distribution Sumatra, Borneo, Thailand, Cambodia.
Description *Shape:* deep-bodied "banded barb." Blunt snout. *Color:* brownish to olive on top; sides have a pale reddish sheen, edges of scales a rich gleaming gold. Four black vertical bars, the first passing through the eye. *Size:* up to 2¾ in (7 cm). Largest of the "banded barbs." *Sexual differences:* female recognizable only by its larger belly.
Environment *Temperature:* 68–77 °F (20–25 °C). *pH and water hardness:* old water with occasional replacement of part by fresh water; soft, slightly acid to neutral. *Illumination:* ample but not excessively strong lighting. *Substrate:* soft, deep bottom layer with some humus. *Furnishings:* plant edges and background of aquarium. Do not use feathery-leaved plants; the fish will gnaw them to pieces.
Feeding Omnivorous: live and dried food and additional plant food.
Biology *Behavior:* a lively, peaceable and active schooling fish; an active swimmer. *Reproduction:* not too difficult. *Social life:* single fish become very aggressive. *Compatibility:* good to mix with other fishes, but not with peaceable long-finned fishes, since this barb will snap at their fins.

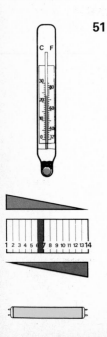

52 CHERRY BARB
Barbus titteya

Family Cyprinidae.
Distribution Sri Lanka.
Description *Shape:* elongated, rather compressed body. One pair of barbels. *Color:* fawn-colored on top with a greenish sheen; sides and belly a gleaming silver, often reddish. A horizontal stripe (brownish black to deep bluish black) extends from the tip of the snout through the eye to the base of the caudal fin. Above it is an iridescent, metallic line, gold at the front turning to blue or sea green toward the tail. *Size:* up to 2 in (5 cm). *Sexual differences:* males a sumptuous red at breeding time. Females darker, with yellowish fins.
Environment *Temperature:* 75–79 °F (24–26 °C). *pH:* around 7. *Water hardness:* soft, old water. *Illumination:* subdued lighting. *Substrate:* dark bottom material, medium layer of sand. *Furnishings:* abundant vegetation, about two-thirds to three-quarters of the tank.
Feeding Omnivorous.
Biology *Behavior:* likes shade and will withdraw under cover of plants. *Reproduction:* breeding not too difficult. At 77–79 °F (25–26 °C) the eggs hatch after 24 hours. 150–250 young would be an excellent spawning. *Social life:* the younger males are often aggressive. *Compatibility:* good for keeping with *Rasbora* and similar peaceable fishes.

53 FIGHTING FISH
Betta splendens

Family Anabantidae.
Distribution Malayan peninsula and Thailand.
Description *Shape:* slender-bodied with compressed sides. Long, broad anal fin; dorsal fin long and high. Rounded caudal fin. Pelvic fins narrow, pointed and elongated. *Color:* many beautiful color variations. *Size:* up to 2½ in (6 cm). *Sexual differences:* female much plainer than the male.
Environment *Temperature:* 77–86 °F (25–30 °C), the higher temperature only for breeding. *pH and water hardness:* not significant; it is best to use not-too-hard water. *Illumination, substrate, furnishings:* moderate or good lighting. Medium to thick vegetation, not too high a water level; soft bottom matter with a thin layer of humus; a sparse layer of floating plants and a well-covered tank to prevent the fish from jumping out.
Feeding Chiefly live, but also dried food.
Biology *Behavior:* the males are extraordinarily aggressive and indulge in vicious battles. *Reproduction:* builds bubble nests among water plants, the large air bubbles supporting the eggs. Remove the female after spawning, as the brood is looked after by the male. The eggs hatch after 24–30 hours; remove the male as well after about three days. *Compatibility:* do not keep males of the same species together. Best in a species tank.

54 CLOWN LOACH
Botia macracantha

Family Cobitidae.
Distribution Sumatra and Borneo.
Description *Shape:* the body is thickset. The sides are somewhat compressed, the belly profile almost straight. The dorsal fin arises in front of the ventral fin; four pairs of barbels. *Color:* basic color a bright orange-red, marked with three wedge-shaped velvety-black vertical bars. Typically, all fins at least partly blood red. *Size:* up to 11¾ in (30 cm). *Sexual differences:* unknown.
Environment In flowing and still waters; a bottom fish. *Temperature:* 75–86 °F (24–30 °C). *pH and water hardness:* no special requirements. *Illumination, substrate, furnishings:* subdued lighting. Deep, soft sandy bottom, with two-thirds to three-quarters of tank planted, the rest as swimming space. Provide plenty of cover. Regular addition of fresh water necessary.
Feeding Omnivorous.
Biology *Behavior:* a lively schooling fish, although older specimens in particular are often solitary; clicking noises are made as a territorial signal. *Reproduction:* unknown. *Compatibility:* easily kept with peaceable schooling fishes.

55 ZEBRA DANIO
Brachydanio rerio

Family Cyprinidae.
Distribution Northeastern India.
Description *Shape:* very slim, small, very compressed sides. Two pairs of barbels. *Color:* back brownish olive, belly yellowish white, the sides a luminous blue and marked with four splendid, gleaming gold horizontal lines, reaching from the gill cover to the caudal fin. Blue-gold markings also on the anal fin; dorsal fin yellow at base, then blue with a white tip. Colorless pectoral and pelvic fins. *Size:* 2–2½ in (5–6 cm). *Sexual differences:* female more silvery and growing larger.
Environment Surface swimmer, in shallow running water. Needs large, shallow, long tank, preferably exposed to the sun. *Temperature:* 64–75 °F (18–24 °C); 75 °F (24 °C) for breeding. Keep replacing part of the water with fresh water. *pH and water hardness:* no special requirements. *Illumination, substrate, furnishings:* good lighting. Ample vegetation (half to two-thirds of tank area), plenty of free swimming space, good aeration. Gravelly bottom, especially for spawning tank.
Feeding Omnivorous and easily satisfied.
Biology *Behavior:* lively, nonaggressive. *Reproduction:* very easy and prolific. Use a breeding tank with a gravelly bottom. *Compatibility:* good for mixing with other members of the genus *Brachydanio*.

56 BUMBLEBEE GOBY
Brachygobius xanthozona

Family Gobiidae.
Distribution Rivers and estuaries in Sumatra, Java and Borneo.
Description *Shape:* thickset, torpedo-shaped; rounded in cross section at the front, slightly compressed toward the tail. *Color:* distinguished by three vertical dark-brown bars. *Size:* up to $1\frac{3}{4}$ in (4.5 cm). *Sexual differences:* mature females are bulkier.
Environment *Temperature:* 75–86 °F (24–30 °C). *pH:* high; acid and normal fresh water lead to illness. *Water hardness:* the addition of 1 to 2 spoonfuls of sea salt or cooking salt to every 2 gallons (10 liters) of water is highly recommended. (Remember the plants.) *Illumination and substrate:* lighting should be softened by floating plants or large single plants attached to the bottom. Provide a dark bottom.
Feeding Small live foods only.
Biology *Behavior:* generally a bottom fish, it is also given to clinging to plants by means of its pelvic fins, either in the normal position or upside down. *Reproduction:* lays 100–150 large eggs in protected positions. The male guards the eggs, which hatch in $2\frac{1}{2}$ to 5 days. The young feed on rotifers, and later on brine shrimp nauplii. *Social life and compatibility:* strong territorial sense; fishes often live in one place, which they leave only to feed or when disturbed. Difficult to keep with other fishes.

1 2 3 4 5 6 7 8 9 10 11 12 13 14

57 BANJO CATFISH
Bunocephalus spp.

Family Aspredinidae.
Distribution Tropical South America east of the Andes from Venezuela to Argentina.
Description *Shape:* low, very flat, something like a dragon kite in shape. Very long, compressed caudal peduncle. Caudal fin square-cut. Spine of pectoral fins thickened and barbed. A pair of barbels on the upper jaw, very long and reaching the pectoral fins. Two pairs of short barbels on the lower jaw. Rows of outgrowths of the skin along the sides of the body. *Color:* relatively uniform; according to mood, ranges from dark to light brown with dark spots and bands, also small light spots. Lighter underside, often with spots. *Size:* $4\frac{3}{4}$–6 in (12–15 cm), sometimes more. *Sexual differences:* unknown.
Environment *Temperature:* 68–77 °F (20–25 °C). *pH and water hardness:* no special requirements. *Substrate:* open surfaces of medium-grade sand.
Feeding Omnivorous.
Biology *Behavior:* during the day burrows in the sand. Becomes active at dusk. Swims mostly on the water-jet principle, ejecting water with great force through the gill openings. *Reproduction:* digs hollows for spawning and lays very large numbers of eggs. *Social life:* unknown. *Compatibility:* can be kept with all schooling fishes.

1 2 3 4 5 6 7 8 9 10 11 12 13 14

58 REEDFISH
Calamoichthys calabaricus

Family Polypteridae.
Distribution West Africa.
Description *Shape:* cylindrical, eel-shaped body. Nine to fourteen separate small dorsal finlets, usually folded against the back. No pelvic fins. The body ends in a fringed, tadpolelike tail fin. *Color:* upper part mud green, growing gradually lighter down the sides and becoming yellowish white on the belly. A dark spot at the base of each pectoral fin. *Size:* up to 3 ft (90 cm) long. *Sexual differences:* rays of anal fin said to differ: 9–12 in females, 12–14 in males.
Environment *Temperature:* 73–79 °F (23–26 °C). *pH:* around 7 or below. *Illumination and substrate:* these require a well-planted tank with dark bottom and subdued lighting.
Feeding A predatory fish living chiefly on crustaceans and insects. Will not take dry food.
Biology *Behavior:* exclusively crepuscular, becoming active only at twilight with sinuous, snakelike movements. Should also be allowed to move onto dry land. Caution: can escape through the smallest hole in an aquarium. *Reproduction:* has very seldom been bred; very large eggs with substantial yolks, producing larvae having external gills and gradually turning into the lung-breathing adult fish. *Social life and compatibility:* best kept in species tanks.

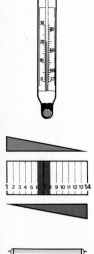

59 GOLDFISH
Carassius auratus

Family Cyprinidae.
Distribution Originally from East Asia, Siberia to China; now also widely dispersed throughout Europe.
Description *Shape:* very similar in form to the carp, rather less deep in profile and less compressed; there are innumerable ornamental forms of goldfish with various exotic features. *Color:* grayish yellow or grayish silver. All strains of goldfish have been developed through deliberate breeding from this natural coloring. *Size:* natural form up to 1 ft 6 in (45 cm). *Sexual differences:* males have characteristic pearly formations (breeding tubercles) at spawning time.
Environment Still or slowly flowing water with plenty of vegetation. *Temperature:* adapts to room temperature, but best suited to open pools. *pH and water hardness:* not important. *Illumination and furnishings:* as similar as possible to natural conditions.
Feeding Omnivorous: live and dried food, animal and vegetable material.
Biology *Behavior:* an undemanding schooling fish, very peaceable. *Reproduction:* best achieved in open ponds with plenty of water plants. Very prolific. Eggs laid on plants. *Compatibility:* can be kept with other cold-water fishes.

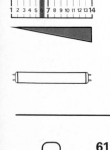

60 MARBLED HATCHETFISH
Carnegiella strigata

Family Gasteropelecidae.
Distribution Amazon basin, the Guyanas.
Description *Shape:* unmistakable shape; straight, horizontal back. From under the slightly high-set mouth, the "keel" runs in a semicircular curve. From the anal fin the underside continues almost in a straight line up to the caudal peduncle. Most notable are the very long, winglike pectoral fins. *Color:* basic color yellowish or greenish, often pale purple with a marked silvery sheen in places. *Size:* up to 1¾ in (4.5 cm). *Sexual differences:* unrecognizable, except that the eggs are visible in the female.
Environment Said to originate in woodland streams. *Temperature:* 77–86 °F (25–30 °C). *pH:* 5.5–6.5. *Water hardness:* soft water. *Illumination, substrate, furnishings:* subdued lighting; surface should be covered with floating plants; dark bottom matter and fairly thick vegetation (up to half of bottom area of tank).
Feeding Live food, small flies; occasionally a little dried food.
Biology *Behavior:* schooling fish, always resting near the surface of the water, also able to leap distances of 3–5 yds (3–5 m). *Reproduction:* no reliable reports are available. *Social life:* a peaceable schooling fish. *Compatibility:* keep with fishes that occupy the lower levels of the water.

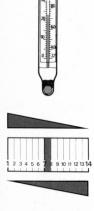

61 INDIAN GLASSFISH; GLASS PERCH
Chanda ranga

Family Centropomidae.
Distribution India, Burma, Thailand.
Description *Shape:* rhomboid body shape, deep profile, flattish sides; large eyes; two separate dorsal fins set very close together, the second rounded. The spine and swim bladder can be recognized through the muscles, together with the gut, pigmented with particles of guanine. *Sexual differences:* the mature male is much more brightly colored, and the fins bigger. The male's swim bladder is pointed at the rear; the female's is rounded.
Environment All types of water, even brackish. *Temperature:* 64–77 °F (18–25 °C). *pH:* 7–8. *Water hardness and density:* medium to extremely hard water. The fish's condition will be enhanced by a small addition of salt (preferably sea salt), 3–6 teaspoons to 2 gallons (10 liters) of water. *Substrate and furnishings:* ample vegetation, dark bottom material.
Feeding Only small, well-chopped-up live food will be taken. Plenty of small crabs and enchytraeids.
Biology *Behavior:* strictly territorial. *Reproduction:* breeding is relatively simple. One pair of fish can produce about 200 young. They should be fed on rotifers and *Artemia* nauplii three times a day. *Compatibility:* unsuitable company for lively schooling fishes.

62 SNAKEHEADS
Channa spp.

Family Channidae.
Distribution Many Asiatic species from eastern Afghanistan to Southeast Asia; others from the White Nile to West Africa.
Description *Shape:* large, broad head with wide extendable mouth, anterior nostrils elongated into tubes. The caudal peduncle slightly flattened. The pelvic fins are absent in certain species. Lateral line present. *Size:* from 8 in (20 cm) to over 3 ft. 3½ in (1 m), according to species. *Sexual differences:* in certain species the females become very swollen when ripe.
Environment mostly warm waters, rich in vegetation. *Temperature:* 75–82 °F (24–28 °C). *pH and water hardness:* no special requirements. *Illumination and furnishings:* subdued lighting; thick vegetation with fairly robust plants. Plenty of cavities and plant cover.

Feeding Eat only fish.

Biology *Behavior:* young fish are in almost constant motion, always on the look-out for prey. They possess a supplementary breathing organ, which is capable of absorbing atmospheric air. Excellent jumpers, so cover the tank carefully. *Reproduction:* the eggs are cared for by the male. *Social life:* the young fish form loose schools, then tend toward cannibalism. Finally they are strictly territorial. *Compatibility:* to be kept only with fishes larger than they are.

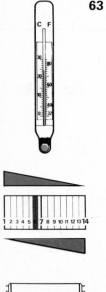

63 CARDINAL TETRA
Cheirodon axelrodi

Family Characidae.
Distribution Tributaries of the Rio Negro and the Orinoco.
Description *Shape:* long and thin. *Color:* brilliant red lateral stripe begins at the tip of the snout and reaches to the base of the tail fin, extending over the belly and throat. Luminous green lateral stripe. Back reddish brown, belly silvery. *Size:* 1½ in (4 cm). *Sexual differences:* the female is a heavier fish, with a fuller belly.
Environment *Temperature:* 73–75 °F (23–24 °C); 79–82 °F (26–28 °C) for breeding. *pH:* 5.5–6.5. *Illumination, substrate, furnishings:* medium lighting with plenty of space for free swimming; background of alternate light and dark water plants; black tank bottom.
Feeding Omnivorous; small live food, especially fruit flies (*Drosophila*), necessary when conditioning for breeding.
Biology *Behavior:* a lively, active, sociable fish from the "black-water region." *Reproduction:* difficult in captivity. The adult fish should be removed after the eggs have been laid. Soft, slightly acid water is best for breeding. *Social life and compatibility:* lives peaceably in schools and can be readily mixed with other species of similar habits.

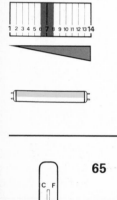

64 PEACOCK CICHLID
Cichla ocellaris

Family Cichlidae.
Distribution Widely distributed over the entire tropical region of South America, chiefly in still waters.
Description *Shape:* relatively elongated for a cichlid. Very compressed; typical shape for a predator. Dorsal fin notched between spiny and rayed portions. *Color:* juveniles gray-green; mature fish silvery on the sides, leaf green on the back. Young specimens usually have a lengthwise stripe; after a middle phase marked by vertical bars, mature fish show none of these markings. On the upper part of the caudal-fin base is a solid black patch edged with gold. *Size:* up to 2 ft (60 cm). *Sexual differences:* unknown.
Environment *Temperature:* over 68 °F (20 °C). *pH and water hardness:* no special requirements. *Illumination and furnishings:* can be kept in well-planted tank for some time, but needs a great deal of oxygen. Does not dig in the substrate. Medium lighting.
Feeding Exclusively a predator.
Biology *Behavior:* only young fish can adapt to small private aquaria; mature specimens are only for large public aquaria. *Reproduction:* Unknown. *Compatibility:* should be kept only with fishes of the same size.

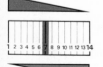

65 JACK DEMPSEY
Cichlasoma octofasciatum

Family Cichlidae.
Distribution Central Amazon basin, Rio Negro.
Description *Shape:* typical cichlid shape, perchlike with relatively straight belly profile, large dorsal and anal fins. *Color:* basic color gray-brown to brilliant red-brown, clearest on the back. Seven or eight clearly marked vertical bars, disappearing completely in old age. A black lateral stripe begins on the gill cover, ending in a black patch edged with yellow in the middle of the body. *Size:* up to 7 in (18 cm); sexually mature at 3–4 in (8–10 cm). *Sexual differences:* female paler, the male a brilliant deep blue at spawning time. Female's dorsal fin is rounded at the tip, male's extended into a point.
Environment *Temperature:* 72–75 °F (22–24 °C) for normal upkeep; 77–82 °F (25–28 °C) for breeding. *pH and water hardness:* medium values. *Illumination, substrate, furnishings:* medium lighting. Large, unplanted tank; coarse sand or fine gravel with stones and coconut shells, etc., on the bottom.
Feeding Plenty of coarse live food, little dried food.
Biology *Behavior:* territorial, forming schools only when young. *Reproduction:* open spawners; form strongly united pairs. *Social life and compatibility:* highly aggressive and excitable, especially during the spawning period. Must be kept in a species tank.

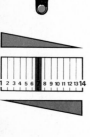

66 FIRE-MOUTH CICHLID
Cichlasoma meeki

Family Cichlidae.
Distribution Guatemala and Yucatán (Mexico).
Description *Shape:* typical cichlid shape with large head. Upper profile much more arched than the lower one. *Color:* basic color a bluish gray with purple sheen. The back is darker, the belly a yellowish olive, the throat and lower jaw a magnificent brick red. All scales, especially on the sides of the body, have a red stripe, so that the body has a netlike appearance. A black line extends from the top edge of the gill cover to the tail base, often divided into individual spots. There is a large, round gray-edged patch in the middle of the body. *Size:* up to 6 in (15 cm); sexually mature from approximately 3 in (8 cm). *Sexual differences:* female has duller coloring, and the spines of the anal and dorsal fins are less pronounced.
Environment Even in springs and underground waters. *Temperature:* 68–73 °F (20–23 °C); 75–79 °F (24–26 °C) for breeding. *pH and water hardness:* not important; middle values the best. *Furnishings:* can be kept easily in well-planted tanks.
Feeding Live food, plus a small amount of plant food.
Biology *Behavior:* for the most part relatively peaceable. *Reproduction:* forms stable pairs. *Social life and compatibility:* territorial; should be kept only with other cichlids.

67 BANDED CICHLID
Cichlasoma severum

Family Cichlidae.
Distribution Northern Amazon basin and the Guyanas. Naturalized in southern Nevada (U.S.A.).
Description *Shape:* very deep body, almost oval; compressed profile. *Color:* very variable according to provenance, age and mood. Ground color ranges from brassy yellow to dark brown, the belly always lighter; head and nape often greenish, with reddish-brown or greenish spots and small stripes. *Size:* up to 8 in (20 cm). *Sexual differences:* males already recognizable at 2 in (5 cm) by bright red-brown flecks on the head.
Environment *Temperature:* 72–81 °F (22–27 °C). *pH and water hardness:* no special requirements. *Furnishings:* during mating period keep in species tank, without vegetation.
Feeding Omnivorous; give plenty of large live food (earthworms, fish), but dried food also.
Biology *Behavior:* territorial and aggressive when mating. *Reproduction:* suitable partners can produce 1,000 or more eggs. *Social life:* young fish are peaceable and form schools, as do adults outside the mating period; very territorial in summer. *Compatibility:* may be kept with other nonaggressive species.

68 GIANT GOURAMI
Colisa fasciata

Family Belontiidae.
Distribution Bengal, Burma, Thailand, Malayan peninsula.
Description *Shape:* elongated body, very compressed; long dorsal and anal fins. Pelvic fins elongated like threads. Thickened upper lip, especially on the male. *Color:* highly variable according to provenance and breeding strain. Brown with a greenish sheen, and with several narrow orange-red to red stripes slanting diagonally backward. Back fairly dark brown, chest and belly blue-green, often with a purple sheen. A brilliant blue-green spot on the gill cover. *Size:* up to 4¾ in (12 cm). *Sexual differences:* female less strongly colored, with the dorsal and anal fins rounded; these are elongated into a point in the male.
Environment *Temperature:* 75–82 °F (24–28 °C). *pH and water hardness:* no special requirements. *Substrate and furnishings:* well-planted tank including feathery-leaved plants (two-thirds to three-quarters of tank area); plenty of floating plants to provide cover; the remainder free swimming space. Some humus to be left on the bottom.
Feeding Omnivorous.
Biology *Behavior:* a lively fish, somewhat timid before becoming acclimatized to the tank. *Reproduction:* bubble-nest builder, very productive. *Compatibility:* peaceable, easily kept with other fishes.

69 DWARF GOURAMI
Colisa lalia

Family Belontiidae.
Distribution Indian subcontinent.
Description *Shape:* body an elongated ovoid, very compressed. Dorsal and anal fins reach almost to caudal fin; pelvic fins extend into long threads. *Color:* bright red basic color; males have a slanting double row of luminous light blue-green to emerald spots which also extend onto the fins. Head-and-shoulder region and belly brilliant blue-green. Caudal fin and rear end of anal fin red; pelvic fins orange. *Size:* 2 in (5 cm). *Sexual differences:* body color of females is much paler. The anal and dorsal fins are rounded.
Environment *Temperature:* needs warmth— 75–82 °F (24–28 °C). *pH and water hardness:* no special requirements. *Illumination and furnishings:* thickly planted tank with medium lighting and a covering of small floating plants.
Feeding Live and dry food.
Biology *Behavior:* territorial, but extremely peaceable and harmless. *Reproduction:* bubble-nest builder. Algae, floating leaves and plant stems, etc., are incorporated into the nest. Multiple acts of spawning. The eggs are looked after by the male. *Compatibility:* suitable for coexistence with other territorial species.
Caution A good jumper.

70 SPRAYING CHARACIN
Copella sp.

Family Lebiasinidae.
Distribution Amazon and Rio Pará.
Description *Shape:* small, very elongated, slightly flattened profile. Large, protruding horizontal mouth. Upper lobe of caudal fin particularly elongated in the male. *Color:* back a dark brownish yellow; sides and belly yellowish or greenish with a rust-brown sheen; large dark-edged scales, producing a netlike pattern. Gill cover has a greenish-gold spot. A narrow dark line runs from the mouth to the eye. *Size:* males up to $3\frac{3}{4}$ in (8 cm), females up to $2\frac{1}{4}$ in (6 cm). *Sexual differences:* fins on the male are all longer and more pointed.
Environment Primarily inhabit the upper water levels; floating plants desirable. *Temperature:* 72–82 °F (22–28 °C), the higher value only for breeding. *pH:* 6.5–7. *Illumination:* good lighting, some sunlight. *Furnishings:* broad-leaved plants, not too thick. Cover tank, as the fish are excellent jumpers.
Feeding Plenty of live food, especially insects of all kinds when breeding.
Biology *Behavior:* lively, peaceable fish. *Reproduction:* from 50 to 200 eggs are laid above the surface of the water. The young fish are fed with very fine food. *Social life:* schooling fish. *Compatibility:* best kept in species tanks, or with quiet, nonaggressive fishes of about the same size.

---

71 MAILED CATFISHES
Corydoras spp.

Family Callichthyidae.
Distribution Tropical South America; about 70 species occurring from Colombia to the Rio de la Plata.
Description *Shape:* short and thickset with an arched back and flat belly, more or less compressed in cross section. The adipose fin lies in an unarmored area, and the snout is unarmored also. *Size:* $1\frac{1}{4}$–$4\frac{3}{4}$ in (3–12 cm). *Sexual differences:* female larger with rounder belly.
Environment Shallow spots in slowly moving, almost still waters. They find a stretch of sandy bottom and remain there chewing plant matter. *Temperature:* 59–86 °F (15–30 °C); many species can withstand this wide variation, others not. 75–77 °F (24–25 °C) is usually adequate for good maintenance and breeding. *pH:* around 7. *Water hardness:* 5–10° general hardness. *Substrate and furnishings:* a large tank with an extensive floor area and not too high a water level is recommended. Also water plants or some other form of cover.
Feeding Omnivorous.
Biology *Behavior:* schooling fish. *Reproduction:* the fertilized eggs are caught up by the female in a kind of pocket formed by her pelvic fins folded together. The young are best kept in a glass tank with no bottom covering and should be liberally fed. *Compatibility:* very peaceable; can be kept with other aquarium creatures.

72 GIANT DANIO
Danio malabaricus

Family Cyprinidae.
Distribution West coast of India, Sri Lanka.
Description *Shape:* elongated, laterally very compressed, deep-bodied for a danio. Profile of underside more strongly convex than the back; pointed head, high-set mouth, one pair of barbels on lower jaw. *Size:* 4¾ in (12 cm); sexually mature at 2½–2¾ in (6–7 cm). *Sexual differences:* the male brilliantly colored, the central blue line on the caudal peduncle is straight.
Environment Running waters. *Temperature:* 68–70 °F (20–21 °C) in winter, 72–75 °F (22–24 °C) in summer; 77–82 °F (25–28 °C) for breeding. *pH:* around 7. *Water hardness:* medium-soft to medium-hard water. *Illumination and furnishings:* large and above all elongated tank with plenty of swimming space (at least two-thirds of tank) and thick background vegetation. Good lighting; for breeding, morning sun and fine-leaved feathery plants.
Feeding Eats dried and live food. Give lots of insects during breeding.
Biology *Behavior:* lively, peaceable, undemanding schooling fish. Leaps energetically, so make sure the tank is properly covered. *Reproduction:* breed easily, but eat their own eggs. The young should be given very small live and dried food. *Compatibility:* good to keep with other schooling fishes.

73 TIGER FISH
Datnioides microlepis

Family Lobotidae.
Distribution Central Thailand, Cambodia, Sumatra, Borneo.
Description *Shape:* thickset, compressed and high-backed. Long, spiny and soft-rayed joined dorsal fins. Short anal fin and caudal peduncle; caudal fin rounded. Straight underside and back. *Color:* a number of black vertical bars (usually six) of varying distinctness. *Size:* in the wild up to 1 ft 3¾ in (40 cm); in aquaria up to 11¾ in (30 cm). *Sexual differences:* unknown.
Environment Chiefly brackish water, but also in clean fresh water, where they are said to breed. *Temperature:* 72–82 °F (22–28 °C). *pH and water hardness:* relatively unimportant. Avoid rapid changes of conditions. Neutral to slightly alkaline water of medium hardness makes the best combination. *Furnishings:* build hiding places of wood or flowerpots in the corners of a roomy tank; at least two-thirds should be planted with vegetation.
Feeding Exclusively a predator. Quite large fishes are consumed headfirst.
Biology *Behavior:* territorial; intolerant of intruders in its territory. Often swims holding itself at an angle. *Reproduction:* not yet achieved in an aquarium. *Compatibility:* in tanks can be kept only with members of the same species.

74 FRESHWATER HALFBEAK
Dermogenys pusillus

Family Hemiramphidae.
Distribution Malaysia, Indonesia, Thailand.
Description *Shape:* elongated body with narrow caudal peduncle; dorsal and anal fins opposite each other and set very close to the tail. The elongated, immovable lower jaw is typical, forming a kind of "flytrap" with the movable upper jaw. *Color:* upper surface dark; sides of body gleaming silver with a mother-of-pearl sheen; sides of belly creamy-white to yellow. Some populations have a black and a red lateral stripe on the lower jaw. *Size:* males up to $2\frac{1}{4}$ in (6 cm), females up to $2\frac{3}{4}$ in (7 cm). *Sexual differences:* in the male the foremost ray of the anal fin is shortened and formed into a sexual organ.
Environment Fresh or brackish waters (river estuaries), always near the surface. *Temperature:* 64–72 °F (18–22 °C); avoid high temperatures. *Water hardness and density:* neutral, hard water; additional salt recommended—2–3 teaspoons per 2 gallons (10 liters) water. *Furnishings:* wide, shallow tank with spongy plants floating on the surface.
Feeding Live food only. The diet should be varied.
Biology *Behavior:* schooling fish, living near the surface. The males are very aggressive. *Reproduction:* live-bearers. *Compatibility:* can be kept with schooling fishes occupying the middle and lower strata of the tank.

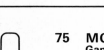

---

75 MOSQUITO FISH
Gambusia affinis

Family Poeciliidae.
Distribution From New Jersey to Florida, from Alabama to East Texas (U.S.A.).
Description *Shape:* females resemble the guppy *(Poecilia reticulata)*; males somewhat more robust. *Color:* male is transparent gray with a bluish shimmer on the sides, olive-brownish back, silvery belly. A black vertical bar through the eye. The original form has numerous loosely distributed black spots. *Size:* male up to $1\frac{3}{8}$ in (3.5 cm), female up to $2\frac{3}{8}$ in (6 cm). *Sexual differences:* size, shape and male gonopodium.
Environment Medium-fast-flowing and still waters; brackish water also tolerated. *Temperature:* room temperature. In the wild, survives temperatures from 37 °F (3 °C) to 86 °F (30 °C). *pH and water hardness:* not important. *Furnishings:* ample vegetation and a certain amount of swimming space.
Feeding A hearty eater, consuming up to its own body weight of foodstuff per day. Mosquito larvae are particularly popular.
Biology *Behavior:* lively, somewhat quarrelsome schooling fish. *Reproduction:* very simple, as long as they are well fed. Will eat their own young. *Social life:* best kept in single-species schools, in a large, shallow tank. *Compatibility:* unsuitable for community aquaria.

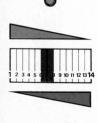

76 GYMNOCHANDA FILAMENTOSA
Gymnochanda filamentosa

Family Centropomidae.
Distribution Malayan peninsula.
Description *Shape:* similar to the ordinary glass perch (cf. *Chanda ranga*). Moderately long, very compressed in profile. Large eyes (one-third of head length). No scales. *Color:* transparent. Male, when in good color, honey yellow to delicate yellowish brown. Body cavity covered with a silvery membrane. Six to ten delicate vertical bars. Reddish mouth. Yellowish, transparent fins. Dark rays to dorsal and anal fins. Female much less brightly colored. *Size:* up to 2 in (5 cm). *Sexual differences:* males have blackish membrane between the extremely elongated rays of the second dorsal and anal fins.
Environment In shallow, brackish waters. The fish is very similar to *Chanda ranga*, but even more sensitive to conditions.
Feeding Only small living food.
Biology Comparable to the ordinary glass perch, and has even been bred in the same way, though the young fish never grow the splendidly elongated fin rays.

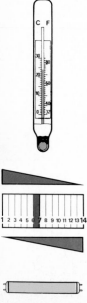

77 STRIPED SUCKERMOUTH CATFISH
Hemiancistrus vittatus

Family Loricariidae.
Distribution Tropical South America.
Description *Shape:* characteristic for a bottom-living fish: low-set sucking mouth, surrounded by fleshy lips; pectoral and pelvic fins broad and flat. Dorsal fin long, high and bannerlike. The adipose fin and caudal fin have an elongated lower lobe. Nasal openings have pipelike extensions; mouth has barbels. *Color:* see illustration; variable as with all Loricariidae. *Size:* about 4 in (10 cm). *Sexual differences:* the males probably have whiskerlike appendages on the head.
Environment *Temperature:* 70–77 °F (21–25 °C). *pH:* neutral to slightly acid. *Water hardness:* soft to medium-hard water. *Illumination:* medium to strong lighting. *Substrate:* sandy bottom with hiding places made from roots, etc. *Furnishings:* thick vegetation, but plants not too feathery.
Feeding Eats algae and other vegetable matter in its native habitat. Easily accustomed to commercial foodstuffs, but must have plenty of plant matter and food with bulk.
Biology *Behavior:* lives on the bottom, in running water; territorial. *Reproduction:* unknown. *Social life:* aggressive toward members of its own species. *Compatibility:* very peaceable and harmless toward other species, even the smallest fishes.

78 RED CICHLID; JEWEL FISH
Hemichromis bimaculatus

Family Cichlidae.
Distribution The river systems of the Nile, Niger and Zaïre.
Description *Shape:* elongated, compressed silhouette. *Color:* brown back with a greenish sheen; sides of body greenish yellow; yellowish underside. A dark horizontal band extending along side may break up into five or six large patches. At spawning time almost the whole body is red (brighter in the female), the forehead and back being olive green with a reddish sheen; bluish-black patches, accompanied by six or seven rows of sky-blue spots. *Size:* up to 6 in (15 cm). *Sexual differences:* apart from the color changes at the time of sexual activity, the spawning tube is pointed in the male, rounded in the female.
Environment *Temperature:* 72–82 °F (22–28 °C) (the higher value for breeding). *pH:* around 7. *Water hardness:* medium to medium hard. *Substrate and furnishings:* large tank with coarse sand or gravel. Single large plants.
Feeding Abundant, not-too-small live food.
Biology *Behavior:* only young fish can be kept in schools. Mature fish can be kept only in pairs. *Reproduction:* pairs must form from the same group. Excellent parents. *Social life and compatibility:* fairly aggressive. Can be kept only with equally powerful species—e.g., two or three different species of cichlids.

79 BLEEDING-HEART TETRA
Hyphessobrycon rubrostigma

Family Characidae.
Distribution Colombia.
Description *Shape:* deep-bodied. *Color:* upper part of body grayish green to brown, with light-red sheen; the lower part of the body shows a reddish silver color. Throat and belly orange, with mother-of-pearl highlights. Red dorsal fin with broad, white-edged black stripes. A vertical black bar through the eye. *Size:* $2\frac{1}{4}$ in (6 cm). *Sexual differences:* female bulkier; male has pointed, elongated and enlarged dorsal fin.
Environment *Temperature:* around 77 °F (25 °C). *pH and water hardness:* no reliable information. *Illumination and furnishings:* plenty of free swimming space, ample vegetation and good lighting.
Feeding Varied live food, occasional dried food.
Biology *Behavior:* lively, peaceable schooling fish; a good swimmer. *Reproduction:* seldom bred. *Compatibility:* easily maintained in mixed schools.

80 LEMON TETRA
Hyphessobrycon pulchripinnis

Family Characidae.
Distribution South America.
Description *Shape:* fairly elongated body with narrowish cross section; has an adipose fin. *Color:* glassily transparent; light lemon yellow in tone; sides of body silvery with an ill-defined shiny horizontal stripe on a level with the spine. The first rays of the anal fin are brilliant yellow and sharply divided from the succeeding rays, which are black. The dorsal fin is similarly colored. Large eyes, the upper half of the iris a brilliant red. *Size:* up to 2 in (5 cm). *Sexual differences:* the anal fin of males has a broad black fringe which is relatively narrow or missing completely in females.
Environment *Temperature:* 72–79 °F (22–26 °C). *pH and water hardness:* soft, slightly acid water. *Illumination and furnishings:* strong lighting; plenty of background vegetation and ample free swimming space.
Feeding Both live and dried food.
Biology *Behavior:* schooling fish which should not be kept isolated. Exhibits characteristic mating display. *Reproduction:* difficult to breed, since the female reputedly often has difficulty in starting to spawn. *Compatibility:* peaceable and good to keep with other schooling fishes of similar size.

81 BLACK-LINE TETRA
Hyphessobrycon scholzei

Family Characidae.
Distribution Pará region, Brazil.
Description *Shape:* very elongated. *Color:* back greenish or brownish; sides silver, with a bluish or brassy sheen; belly silvery. A broad black band runs from the gill cover to the base of the caudal fin, forming a large diamond-shaped patch at the end. The black band is topped by a thin gleaming metallic line. Colorless pelvic fins; all others pale reddish; anal fin edged with black at the front. *Size:* up to 2 in (5 cm). *Sexual differences:* male slimmer, with more deeply cleft caudal fin.
Environment *Temperature:* 72–77 °F (22–25 °C). *pH and water hardness:* use old water, not too hard and neutral to slightly acid. The species is generally undemanding. *Illumination and furnishings:* as for other *Hyphessobrycon* species (cf. *H. pulchripinnis*).
Feeding Live and dried food; also some additional vegetable food (e.g. lettuce).
Biology *Behavior:* a lively, peaceable schooling fish. *Compatibility:* good for community tanks.

82 SERPA TETRA
Hyphessobrycon serpae

Family Characidae.
Distribution Amazon basin and Rio Guaporé.
Description *Shape:* elongated. *Color:* very variable. Back dark olive; sides gray-green; belly yellowish with an iridescent sheen. When the fish is excited or in a state of well-being, the whole of the rear part of the body is blood red. Clearly marked dark patch on the shoulder. An indistinct lateral stripe, broadening toward the tail. *Size:* up to 1¾ in (4.5 cm). *Sexual differences:* males mostly a brighter red.
Environment No special needs. *Temperature:* 73–77 °F (23–25 °C). *pH:* slightly acid. *Water hardness:* medium soft. *Illumination, substrate, furnishings:* good but not-too-glaring lighting; not-too-light bottom material; about two-thirds of tank space thickly planted.
Feeding Omnivorous.
Biology *Behavior:* lively, peaceable, lives in schools. *Reproduction:* fairly easy. *Compatibility:* good to keep with other, not too closely related fishes.

83 JULIE
Julidochromis ornatus

Family Cichlidae.
Distribution Lake Tanganyika, in rocky areas.
Description *Shape:* slender body, almost completely cylindrical, with prominent pointed snout. Small mouth set low. *Color:* basic color white to gold. Three clearly marked brownish-black lines along the back, the uppermost passing through the base of the dorsal fin, the lowest extending from the snout through the eye and the middle of the side to middle of the tail-fin base. *Size:* male 2½–2¾ in (6–7 cm); female somewhat smaller. *Sexual differences:* only in size.
Environment *Temperature:* 72–77 °F (22–25 °C). *pH:* around 8. *Water hardness:* hard water. *Furnishings:* reasonably large tanks with hiding places (stone prominences with recesses, flowerpots, pipe sections, etc.).
Feeding Both live and a little dried food.
Biology *Behavior:* territorial, but easy to keep with other Tanganyikan cichlids. *Reproduction:* propagate freely. The young are tended by the male or by both parents.

84 GLASS CATFISH
Kryptopterus bicirrhis

Family Siluridae.
Distribution Indochina and Indonesia.
Description *Shape:* very compressed sides, short body cavity, long caudal peduncle. Dorsal fin consists of a single ray; anal fin very long, but separated from the deeply cleft caudal fin, whose lower lobe is longer than the upper. One pair of very long barbels on the upper jaw. *Color:* transparent, even when mature, sometimes with a rainbow-colored metallic sheen. *Size:* up to 4 in (10cm). *Sexual differences:* unknown.
Environment *Temperature:* 68–77 °F (20–25 °C). *pH:* 6.5–7.5. *Water hardness:* medium hard for preference, but not important. *Furnishings:* roomy, not-too-deep tank, about half planted.
Feeding Live food should not be too large. Cereals are taken only occasionally.
Biology *Behavior:* schooling fish which swims constantly but rather slowly and needs water plants for rest. *Reproduction:* unknown. *Social life:* single specimens do not live long. *Compatibility:* do not keep with fast swimmers.

85 RED-TAILED BLACK SHARK
Labeo bicolor

Family Cyprinidae.
Distribution Thailand, mainly in streams.
Description *Shape:* elongated body, laterally compressed; somewhat deeper body than *L. erythrurus*. *Color:* sharply divided into two colors: body black with caudal fin in strongly contrasting orange to blood red. *Size:* up to 4¾ in (12 cm). *Sexual differences:* female is significantly bulkier.
Environment Turbid streams. *Temperature:* 73–81 °F (23–27 °C). *pH:* 5.5–7; light peat content. *Water hardness:* soft water. *Illumination and furnishings:* large tank, with moderate lighting and plenty of cover.
Feeding As for *L. erythrurus*.
Biology *Behavior:* as for *L. erythrurus*; territorial adults even more aggressive. *Reproduction:* optimum temperature 79 °F (26 °C). Spawning tube appears some two weeks beforehand; 30–40 eggs are laid at a time. The young hatch in 48–72 hours and can immediately take nauplii; upkeep is simple. Males make violent thrusting motions during mating. *Social life and compatibility:* can be kept with other fishes in general aquarium. Antagonistic toward members of its own species.

86 REDFIN SHARK
Labeo erythrurus

Family Cyprinidae.
Distribution Thailand: the Mekong River at Komarat.
Description *Shape:* an elongated carp, torpedo-shaped, with an almost straight belly line and slightly arched back. Slimmer than many species of the same genus, with well-developed organs for sucking and chewing and grinding up vegetation in the low-set mouth. Two pairs of barbels. *Color:* back ranging from light brown to blue-black, lighter toward the underside, and spotted. A dark spot or vertical bar on the caudal peduncle. All the fins are red. *Size:* 4¾ in (12 cm). *Sexual differences:* unknown.
Environment *Temperature:* 70–75 (max. 81) °F (21–24, max. 27 °C). *pH and water hardness:* undemanding; best to provide soft, neutral to slightly acid water. *Furnishings:* large tank with ample vegetation (two-thirds to three-quarters of area) and many hiding places.
Feeding Live food of all kinds, algae, lettuce. Keep the diet varied.
Biology *Behavior:* the young live in schools; adults territorial. *Reproduction:* not yet achieved in the aquarium. *Compatibility:* easily maintained in a community tank.

---

87 BANDED LEPORINUS
Leporinus fasciatus

Family Anostomidae.
Distribution South America.
Description *Shape:* elongated, torpedo-shaped body, flattened very slightly along the sides. The head is conical with a small snout. A few, powerful teeth. *Color:* ten yellow bars on a yellow background, darker on adults. Size: up to 12 in (30 cm).
Environment Native habitat is slow-flowing, gravelly brooks. *Temperature:* 72–77 °F (22–25 °C). *pH and water hardness:* not important. *Substrate and furnishings:* as the fish are plant-eaters, do not plant feathery vegetation. Sand or gravel bottom with frequent replacement of part of the water with fresh.
Feeding Vegetable foods (lettuce, etc.) and worms.
Biology *Behavior:* a schooling fish which swims and leaps very quickly. Keep top firmly closed. *Reproduction:* not yet successful in the aquarium. *Social life:* a companionable fish. Very long-lived, if well fed and kept well supplied with fresh water. *Compatibility:* keep with other head-standers.

88 SPINY EEL
Macrognathus aculeatus

Family Mastacembelidae.
Distribution Southeast Asia to the Moluccas.
Description *Shape:* characteristic eel shape, with an extended snout which contains the nostrils. The head is also long and pointed. The dorsal, caudal and anal fins adjoin one another, but are not linked by a fin membrane. The soft-rayed dorsal fin is preceded by fourteen or fifteen isolated spines. No pelvic fins. *Color:* chocolate to tan, often with stripes on the back. The three to ten peacock's-tail spots on the dorsal fin are sometimes absent. *Size:* up to 6 in (15 cm). *Sexual differences:* females essentially stronger, becoming very stout at spawning time.
Environment Fresh and brackish waters. *Temperature:* 72–82 °F (22–28 °C). Fish kept permanently at too high a temperature are more susceptible to infections and are shorter-lived. *pH and water hardness:* not important. *Substrate and furnishings:* the chief requirement is for cover. The tank should be thickly planted. A particularly deep layer of sand should be provided.
Feeding All types of live food. The fish can suck up their prey.
Biology *Behavior:* peaceable; active at twilight and in darkness. *Reproduction:* not yet achieved in an aquarium. *Compatibility:* best suited to a species tank.

89 ELECTRIC CATFISH
Malapterurus electricus

Family Malapteruridae.
Distribution Africa.
Description *Shape:* long but thickset; thick head with small eyes that glow in the dark. No dorsal fin; adipose fin far back near the tail; no spines in pectoral fin. Three pairs of barbels; fleshy lips. *Color:* back grayish brown; sides flesh-colored to gray; belly reddish or yellowish white, with numerous irregularly arranged dark spots. *Size:* up to 3 ft 3½ in (1 m). *Sexual differences:* unknown.
Environment *Temperature:* 73–86 °F (23–30 °C). *pH and water hardness:* no particular requirements; neutral, fresh water is preferable. *Furnishings:* well-planted tank with plenty of cover.
Feeding A predator. Live food; first earthworms and lean meat in strips for young fish, later exclusively fish.
Biology *Behavior:* it possesses electric organs, arranged in pairs along its sides. Electrical discharges can be produced at will; they are used for self-defense and to stun the fish's prey. They also serve as a means of orientation in turbid waters. *Reproduction:* unknown. *Social life:* must be kept singly. *Compatibility:* only fishes intended as food should be put in the same tank.

90 BLACK-BANDED SUNFISH
Enneacanthus chaetodon

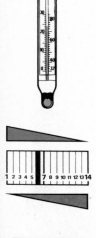

Family Centrarchidae.
Distribution U.S.A., New Jersey to Maryland.
Description *Shape:* thickset, short and deep body, flat-sided. *Color:* grayish yellow to greenish yellow with numerous but partly indistinct black vertical bars, often with irregular dark speckles in between. The first two spines of the dorsal fin are black; the following two, bright orange-red or red. The first two rays of the pelvic fins are orange; the next two, black. *Size:* up to 4 in (10 cm); sexually mature at 2 in (5 cm). *Sexual differences:* scarcely distinguishable; the females have brighter coloring during the spawning period.
Environment Still and gently flowing waters. *Temperature:* cold—39–72 °F (4–22 °C). The fish keep well in outdoor pools. *pH and water hardness:* medium-hard to hard water with occasional replacement of a portion by fresh water. *Illumination, substrate and furnishings:* good lighting; deep, sandy bottom; ample vegetation.
Feeding Live food.
Biology *Behavior:* relatively nonaggressive and peaceable. *Reproduction:* the father tends the young. *Social life:* form loose schools. *Compatibility:* may be mixed with peaceable surface-inhabiting fishes that are not too large, but a species tank is even better.

91 GLASS TETRA
Moenkhausia sanctaefilomenae

Family Characidae.
Distribution Rio Paraguay and Rio Paranaiba.
Description *Shape:* deep-bodied, elongated and very compressed. No adipose fin, and an incomplete lateral line. *Color:* sides of the body bright silver, darker toward the back, slightly yellow toward the belly. A broad black vertical band on the tail preceded by a yellow field with a metallic sheen. Eyes bright and luminous, with the upper part of the iris red. Smoky, mud-colored fins, with white tips to the dorsal and first anal fin rays. *Size:* up to 2¾ in (7 cm). *Sexual differences:* in females the line of the belly is more curved in profile.
Environment *Temperature:* 72–77 °F (22–25 °C). *pH:* 5.5–6.5. *Illumination and furnishings:* one-third vegetation, two-thirds swimming space; also one or two floating plants. Lighting should not be too bright.
Feeding Omnivorous.
Biology *Behavior:* lively, undemanding schooling fish. *Reproduction:* see *H. pulchripinnis*. *Compatibility:* good to mix with other peaceable tetras.

92 LEAF FISH
Monocirrhus polyacanthus

Family Nandidae.
Distribution Amazon basin, Rio Negro and western Guyana.
Description *Shape:* egg-shaped, thickset, very pointed head, mouth forming an extensible tube. The lower lip has a strong barbel. *Color:* very strong marbled coloring which varies in relation to mood; streaked, and yellow or brown; can resemble a dead leaf. Three thin dark lines extend from the eye suggesting the veins of a leaf. *Size:* up to $3\frac{1}{4}$ in (8 cm). *Sexual differences:* unknown.
Environment *Temperature:* 72–77 °F (22–25 °C). *Water hardness:* very soft. *Furnishings:* large, well-stabilized tank with thick vegetation.
Feeding Exclusively a fish-eater, eating almost its own weight of food per day. Great care needed to avoid upsets.
Biology *Behavior:* extremely interesting. It imitates the movements of a dead leaf, sneaks up on its prey and at the last moment sucks it in and swallows it. *Reproduction:* very simple display. Eggs are laid on plants, glass or stone and are looked after by the male. The female should be removed. The young hatch after 3–4 days. *Compatibility:* keep only a few individuals in a species tank.

---

93 ONE-STRIPED AFRICAN CHARACIN
Nannaethiops unitaeniatus

Family Citharinidae.
Distribution The whole of tropical Africa from the White Nile to the west coast.
Description *Shape:* medium-long body. Small mouth. Large adipose fin. Complete lateral line. *Color:* brown to brownish-olive back; belly and throat yellowish or whitish with a silver sheen. A dark narrow band extends from the mouth over the eye to the end of the caudal fin. This is topped by an iridescent metallic band, colored a brilliant copper to gold. *Size:* up to $2\frac{1}{2}$ in (6.5 cm). *Sexual differences:* male slender, brilliantly colored. During the mating season the front part of the dorsal fin and the lobes of the tail fin become a brilliant blood red.
Environment *Temperature:* 73–79 °F (23–26 °C). *pH and water hardness:* neutral reaction and medium hardness will suffice. *Illumination, substrate, furnishings:* bright lighting, occasional sun. Fine sand on the bottom is essential. Vegetation not too thick.
Feeding Live and dry food; plenty of insects.
Biology *Behavior:* a lively fish living near the bottom. *Reproduction:* The fish is very productive. Large spawning tank needed—10–12 gal (40–50 l). After spawning the breeding fish should be removed. *Social life:* a schooling fish. *Compatibility:* Can be mixed with fishes living near the surface, such as *Epiplatys* species.

94 THREE-BANDED PENCILFISH
Nannostomus trifasciatus

Family Lebiasinidae.
Distribution Central Amazonian region, Rio Negro and western Guyana.
Description *Shape:* small, long and slim; slightly flattened sides. *Color:* olive-brown back, white belly; a black horizontal stripe extends from the tip of the snout to the underside of the tail-fin base, with a second, narrower one above it, starting from the eye. A third, faintly visible, runs from the pectorals to the anal fin. By night the coloring appears different—green to yellowish gray, with three broad, dark vertical bars. *Size:* up to 2½ in (6 cm). *Sexual differences:* females more rounded, with paler coloring.
Environment In their native habitat they inhabit small, gently flowing streams that are well shaded with thickly growing water plants. *Temperature:* 72–82 °F (25–28 °C). *pH and water hardness:* very soft, allowed to stand for some time; light to medium acidity (filter through peat). *Furnishings:* as in natural surroundings.
Feeding Chiefly live food; fruit flies should be given.
Biology *Behavior:* a schooling fish. The swimming motion is characteristic—scurrying alternating with sudden long pauses. *Reproduction:* not very prolific. *Social life:* must have company, preferably of the same species. Place a strong cover over the tank, as they are good jumpers.

95 EMPEROR TETRA
Nematobrycon palmeri

Family Characidae.
Distribution Rio San Juan and its tributaries, Colombia.
Description *Shape:* club-shaped body, laterally compressed. Caudal fin cleft in the middle. No adipose fin; very long anal fin. Lateral line incomplete. *Color:* in males: brownish, shot with green or blue particularly on the forepart of the body. A broad black horizontal stripe extends from the hind edge of the gill cover to the elongated central rays of the caudal fin. The coloring of the smaller female is less brilliant, the central rays of the caudal fin only slightly elongated. *Size:* up to 2¼ in (5.5 cm).
Environment *Temperature:* 72–75 °F (22–24 °C); for breeding 79–82 °F (26–28 °C). *pH and water hardness:* not important. *Illumination and furnishings:* medium, angled lighting and dark water plants.
Feeding Live and dried food. Also a little plant food.
Biology *Behavior:* peaceable, hardy and undemanding. *Reproduction:* not very productive. Eggs laid on water plants. *Social life and compatibility:* must live in schools; also with other peaceable fishes.

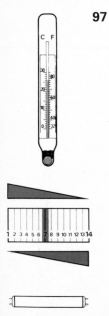

96 GUENTHER'S NOTHO
Nothobranchius guentheri

Family Cyprinodontidae.
Distribution Zanzibar, Mozambique, Mombasa (Kenya), Pangani River (Tanzania).
Description *Shape:* deep body, rounded fins. *Color:* males have a red tail fin, and each scale on their body is blue or greenish blue outlined in red, producing a network pattern. Females dull in appearance, with dark spots or rows of spots on body and fins. *Size:* up to $2\frac{3}{4}$ in (7 cm). *Sexual differences:* only in body color.
Environment Normal habitat consists of temporary pools and mudholes. *Temperature:* 64–72 °F (18–22 °C) is normally sufficient. *pH and water hardness:* soft to very soft and slightly acid water (pH 6.5) are sufficient. *Illumination:* strong lighting. *Substrate:* cover the bottom with a layer of sterilized peat. *Furnishings:* feathery water plants such as *Myriophyllum* are quite suitable.
Feeding Both live and dried foods. Insects (mosquito larvae) are essential for breeding.
Biology *Reproduction:* The eggs are laid in the bottom mud. The mature fish live for little more than a year. The eggs survive through the dry season buried in the mud. With the return of the rainy season, development is resumed, and the young hatch out and grow rapidly. *Social life and compatibility:* a schooling fish, but best kept with members of its own species.

97 FEATHERBACK
Notopterus chitala

Family Notopteridae.
Distribution *N. chitala* and three other species in Southeast Asia.
Description *Shape:* elongated, very compressed body. The anus is very far forward. The anal fin is very long and forms a continuous fringe with the very small caudal fin. Its great mobility makes the anal fin the main organ of propulsion. *Color:* varies according to species, especially among the younger fish. Photo shows a *Notopterus chitala*, which has a fine peacock marking. *Size:* differs according to species, from 8 in to 2 ft $7\frac{1}{2}$ in (20–80 cm) in length; *N. chitala* is one of the largest. *Sexual differences:* unknown.
Environment Quiet overgrown backwaters of large rivers with underwater roots and half-submerged undergrowth. *Temperature:* 73–81 °F (23–27 °C). *pH:* slightly acid to slightly alkaline. *Water hardness:* unimportant. *Illumination:* subdued. *Substrate:* sand with a little humus. *Furnishings:* richly planted.
Feeding Predatory; may catch quite large fishes.
Biology *Behavior:* At dusk the fish streak constantly around the tank in search of prey. Very large tank is needed. *Reproduction:* little information. *Social life:* loosely-grouped schools. Adults particularly aggressive and live alone. *Compatibility:* not with small, peaceable fishes.

98 GOURAMI
Osphronemus goramy

Family Osphronemidae.
Distribution The greater Sunda Islands.
Description *Shape:* oval, strongly compressed sides. Head very small; thick, protruding lower jaw. Pelvic fins have threadlike elongations. Young fish slimmer, with more pointed head. *Color:* adult specimens brownish, with dark back and lighter belly. *Size:* 1 ft 1½ in (60 cm), often up to 3 ft 3½ in (1 m) and 22 lb (10 kg). *Sexual differences:* females have rounded anal and dorsal fins.
Environment In quiet waters, preferably clean with plenty of vegetation, but also in slimy ponds and mudholes. *Temperature:* 63–81 °F (17–27 °C). *pH and water hardness:* no specific requirements. *Furnishings:* large tank with some floating plants for cover.
Feeding Omnivorous.
Biology *Behavior:* breathes atmospheric air using its respiratory organ called a labyrinth. *Reproduction:* bubble-nest builder. The male guards the young. *Social life:* very peaceable. Suitable for indoor aquaria only when young, as they grow very fast. *Compatibility:* very suitable for community tanks.

99 SCLEROPAGES
Scleropages formosus

Family Osteoglossidae.
Distribution Malay Archipelago and Thailand.
Description *Shape:* thin, straplike, very compressed body. Keel-shaped underside. Very large mouth, strongly oblique. Two downswept barbels on the chin. Very long dorsal and anal fins standing opposite each other and forming a fringe. Huge scales. *Color:* silvery yellow, iridescent; barbels can become blue or green; fins yellow-green with reddish shading. *Size:* up to 4 ft (120 cm) long. *Sexual differences:* sexually mature females larger in body circumference. Males have an elongated lower jaw and larger anal fins.
Environment In stagnant river backwaters and shallow pools with rich and overgrown vegetation. *Temperature:* circa 77 °F (25 °C). *pH:* 5.5–6. *Water hardness:* soft water. *Furnishings:* plenty of vegetation.
Feeding Live food only; dried food will be taken only in exceptional cases by young fish.
Biology *Behavior:* forms schools when young, tends to be territorial when older and at times is very aggressive. *Reproduction:* the male carries the eggs in his mouth until development is complete. *Compatibility:* to be kept only with larger but peaceable fishes. The tank should be well covered, as they are very good jumpers.

100 DWARF SUCKERMOUTH CATFISH
Otocinclus affinis

Family Loricariidae.
Distribution Southeast Brazil.
Description *Shape:* slender catfish with sucking mouth. Narrow-based but fairly high dorsal fin, no adipose fin. Twenty-three or twenty-four bony plates arranged in a row along each side of the body. *Color:* ground color a light greenish gray to muddy yellow; darker back; whitish or light yellow underside. Fins are colorless or slightly green. *Size:* up to 1½ in (4 cm). *Sexual differences:* mature females much bulkier.
Environment Inhabit running water. *Temperature:* 68–73 °F (20–23 °C). *pH and water hardness:* unimportant. *Furnishings:* ample vegetation with plenty of weeds and opportunities for cover.
Feeding Mainly vegetarian, but also small worms. Useful as a consumer of algae in community aquaria.
Biology *Behavior:* remains under cover during the day, feeding at dusk and at night. Mostly stays attached vertically to slabs of rock or plants. *Reproduction:* breeds like *Corydoras*. The small eggs hatch after 2–3 days. The young must be fed with small *Artemia* nauplii, microworms or egg yolk powdered as fine as possible. *Social life and compatibility:* territorial but harmless. Quite at home in a mixed aquarium, if there is enough room.

101 BUTTERFLY FISH
Pantodon buchholzi

Family Pantodontidae.
Distribution Tropical West Africa.
Description *Shape:* surface fish; flattened head and back, the belly smoothly curved. Wide mouth pointing upward. Protruding pipelike nostrils. Pectoral fins broad with long winglike rays. Small pelvic fins. *Color:* back and sides brownish or greenish with a silver sheen; a variable pattern of lines and spots. *Size:* up to 6 in (15 cm). *Sexual differences:* males: hind edge of the anal fin deeply cleft, with the middle rays forming a tube.
Environment Mainly in largish, well-grown still or slow-flowing water or backwaters; occasionally in pools and ditches. *Temperature:* 77–86 °F (25–30 °C); for breeding circa 86 °F (30 °C). *pH:* slightly acid; filter through peat. *Water hardness:* soft water. *Illumination:* medium lighting. *Furnishings:* shallow tank. Sparse, individually planted vegetation, some floating plants.
Feeding Live food.
Biology *Behavior:* is not a flying fish but is an excellent jumper. *Reproduction:* fairly difficult. The young fish float just under the surface, and feeding them is very difficult as they will take only food that floats past their noses. The best foods are springtails (Collembola), aphids and small flies, as well as *Artemia* nauplii. *Social life and compatibility:* aggressive; keep species alone.

102 COMMON KRIB
Pelvicachromis pulcher

Family Cichlidae.
Distribution Tropical West Africa, the Niger Delta.
Description *Shape:* general profile of a dwarf cichlid; elongated, the dorsal profile arched. *Color:* see photograph. Many different color forms known. *Size:* male up to 3½ in (9 cm), female up to 2¾ in (7 cm). *Sexual differences:* female smaller, fuller in the belly and more brightly colored than the male; photograph is of a female.
Environment Estuaries, lower courses of rivers and marshes, in flat-bottomed areas with plenty of vegetation. *Temperature:* 72–82 °F (25–28 °C). *pH:* not important; neutral or slightly alkaline water for preference. *Density:* add sea salt—1–2 dessert spoons per 2 gallons (10 liters) of water. *Illumination and furnishings:* muted lighting; dark bottom with plenty of cover (stones, flowerpots, ample vegetation).
Feeding Live food, but dry food will also be taken occasionally.
Biology *Behavior:* the young live in schools; mature fish are territorial in pairs. *Reproduction:* both partners look after the eggs (140–180). The young hatch after 2–3 days and swim free after 4–5 days, when they should be given the appropriate food. *Compatibility:* best with *Epiplatys* or similar species.

103 SUCKERMOUTH CATFISHES
Plecostomus spp.

Family Loricariidae.
Distribution From southern and southeastern Brazil to the La Plata basin.
Description *Shape:* by contrast with similar species, the belly is not armored with bony plates. Very large head with low-set sucking mouth. A long, high, bannerlike dorsal fin; pectoral and pelvic fins with thickened rays at the front. Adipose fin present; caudal fin slightly cleft, the lower lobe usually longer. Very small anal fin. About thirty bony plates in a lateral row. *Color:* an unassuming brown, but with elegant patterns. *Size:* according to species, 5½ in–1 ft 3¾ in (14–40 cm). *Sexual differences:* unknown.
Environment Probably all inhabitants of running water. *Temperature:* according to species, 64–79 °F (18–26 °C). *pH and water hardness:* no special requirements. *Furnishings:* hiding places must be provided among rich vegetation.
Feeding Licks detritus, algae and mosses. In an aquarium, ordinary dried foods are usually substituted.
Biology *Behavior:* peaceable and interesting. *Reproduction:* unknown. *Compatibility:* if in community tanks then only in very large ones.

104 MOLLIES and others
Poecilia spp.

Family Poeciliidae.
Distribution From southern U.S.A. to Colombia.
Description Somewhat similar to the swordtail (*Xiphophorus helleri*), but without the sword and with a generally larger dorsal fin. *Shape:* differs considerably according to species, sex and provenance. *Size:* female larger, 4–4¾ in (10–12 cm), male 3¼–4 in (8–10 cm). *Sexual differences:* size, coloring and gonopodium of male.
Environment Extremely varied; most inhabit running water, right down to estuaries. *Temperature:* 72–82 °F (22–28 °C). *pH:* 7–8. *Water hardness:* very hard water. Almost all types need additional salt. *Illumination and furnishings:* large, well-planted and well-lit tanks with a thin layer of humus on the bottom.
Feeding Omnivorous. Need plenty of vegetable foods: algae, cooked spinach, etc.
Biology *Behavior:* a lively schooling fish, usually found in flowing water and constantly on the move. *Reproduction:* live-bearers. Successful breeding requires a plentiful, rich and varied diet; otherwise will abort naturally. *Social life and compatibility:* best kept in large schools in a community tank or with other Poeciliidae.

105 GUPPY
Poecilia reticulata

Family Poeciliidae.
Distribution Venezuela, northern Brazil, Guyana, Barbados and Trinidad.
Description Numerous varieties of form and color through crossing and selection. *Shape:* upturned mouth, and large eyes. *Color:* males: extremely varied. The wild types are marked with irregular black spots or patches, while the sides of the body are shimmering red, blue and green. Females yellowish gray or a mixture of the two colors. *Size:* males up to 1¼ in (3 cm), females up to 2¼ in (6 cm). *Sexual differences:* considerable. Apart from differences of color and size, the mature females show the so-called "spawning patch." The anal fin of the males forms a sexual organ (gonopodium).
Environment In still and flowing waters. *Temperature:* 68–75 °F (20–24 °C). *pH:* 7–8. *Water hardness:* will live in hard or very hard water. *Illumination and furnishings:* brightly lit, medium-sized tank, richly planted with vegetation.
Feeding Needs abundant and varied foods.
Biology *Behavior:* living in loose schools, constantly on the move. *Reproduction:* breeding very easy but adults may eat young. If the young are stillborn, this is probably due to inadequate variety in food or the wrong temperature. *Compatibility:* easily kept with other live-bearing fishes.

106 SAILFIN MOLLY
Poecilia velifera

Family Poeciliidae.
Distribution Yucatán, coastal zone and river estuaries.
Description *Shape:* characterized by a long, high dorsal fin. *Color:* the male is beautiful, the dorsal fin being dark olive to blue. The sides are bluish green, covered all over with iridescent metallic spots. The back is bright orange; the caudal fin orange edged with black. The female is a bluish gray, with a similarly enlarged dorsal fin. *Size:* up to 6 in (15 cm). *Sexual differences:* color, and development of dorsal fin (smaller in the female).
Environment Brackish water. *Temperature:* 73–82 °F (23–28 °C). *pH and density:* old water with added sea salt—2–3 teaspoons per 2 gallons (10 liters) of water. Replace part of the water with fresh occasionally. *Illumination, substrate and furnishings:* good lighting; bottom with a little humus and detritus, well planted.
Feeding Omnivorous: plenty of live food and additional vegetable matter.
Biology *Behavior:* lively schooling fish; needs a large tank. *Reproduction:* possible; depends on proper feeding. *Social life and compatibility:* males tend to fight with one another. Should only be kept with fishes of similar requirements.

107 AFRICAN LUNGFISH
Protopterus dolloi

Family Protopteridae.
Distribution Zaïre river basin.
Description *Shape:* the slenderest type of lungfish. Caudal fin joins the dorsal and anal fins to form a fringe around the tail. Threadlike pectoral and pelvic fins. *Color:* dark brown, becoming somewhat lighter along the sides. *Size:* up to 2 ft 10 in (85 cm). *Sexual differences:* at spawning time, males have subsidiary breathing apparatus in the form of threadlike appendages to the pectoral fins.
Environment Quiet, completely overgrown creeks that have running water but are empty in the dry season, leaving the fish behind in the dried mud. *Temperature:* 72–over 84 °F (22–over 30 °C). *pH and water hardness:* can tolerate extreme conditions. *Substrate and furnishings:* in their natural habitat, lungfish live in very muddy waters, with low oxygen content. Keep them only in a large tank with abundant, relatively hardy plants (e.g., *Cryptocoryne affinis*).
Feeding In the wild, the fish prey particularly on snails, mussels, worms and slow-swimming fishes. Start with very lean meat (beef heart) and fish, cut into strips, and keep the water moving.
Biology Males take care of young, watching over the large-yoked eggs which females lay in holes in the mud.

108 GOLDEN MBUNA; AURATUS
Melanochromis auratus

Family Cichlidae.
Distribution Lake Malawi.
Description *Shape:* low, elongated body, not very compressed. *Color:* mature male has brownish-black ground color with two light horizontal stripes, each with a turquoise sheen; dark stripes across the forehead against a light ground. The female is golden yellow with two brownish-black horizontal stripes edged with a delicate gold. Two curved stripes on the forehead in front of the eyes. A yellowish-gold patch on the gill cover. Young fish are similar to the females. *Size:* males up to 4¾ in (12 cm); females 3½–4 in (9–10 cm).
Environment Lives on an open, rocky bottom. *Temperature:* 72–77 °F (22–25 °C). *pH:* around 8. *Water hardness:* medium hard. *Substrate and furnishings:* stone cavities and roots, high sandbanks and very robust plants in pots.
Feeding Plenty of live and dry food; additional vegetable food consisting of algae and green plants.
Biology *Behavior:* lively, aggressive and territorial. *Reproduction:* females are mouth-brooders. The young leave the mother's mouth after 22–26 days and can be fed immediately with young *Cyclops*. *Social life and compatibility:* kept with their own species, they may be too aggressive. Keep two or three species of cichlids together in a very large tank.

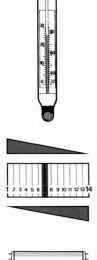

109 ELONGATE MBUNA
Pseudotropheus elongatus

Family Cichlidae.
Distribution Lake Malawi.
Description *Shape:* very slender, elongated cichlid. *Color:* head and chest black to beginning of dorsal fin, also pectoral and pelvic fins. Farther back, brilliant dark blue broken by three black vertical bars. Sometimes a light egg-shaped patch on the anal fin of the male. Occasionally further bands, such as one over the eye. Can be very pale. *Size:* 2¾–3½ in (7–9 cm). *Sexual differences:* females much lighter than males.
Environment Inhabits rocky shores. *Temperature:* 73–81 °F (23–27 °C). *pH:* around 8. *Water hardness:* medium-hard water. *Furnishings:* large, deep tank with rocky prominences built to enable several pairs to establish territories. Large single plants on the bottom.
Feeding Living foods of many different kinds.
Biology *Behavior:* territorial. *Reproduction:* the female takes the eggs in her mouth. Hatching takes place after 23 days at 73 °F (23 °C), after 17 days at 81 °F (27 °C). The young are carried in the mouth at least four days longer. *Social life and compatibility:* see *Melanochromis auratus*.

Pterophyllum spp.

Family Cichlidae.
Distribution Amazon basin, with Rio Tapajos for *P. scalare*, Orinoco for *P. altum*.
Description *Shape:* deep body. Body of *P. altum* has a depth-to-length ratio of 1.5:1 excluding fins. The head profile depends on age. Dorsal and anal fins very long and erect. *Color:* silver-gray ground with large scales bearing a number of dark vertical bars of different length and intensity (usually four, often up to seven), almost always arranged with the first curving through the eye, another (the third) through the center of the dorsal fin and the front part of the anal fin, and the last at the end of the caudal peduncle. Markings in general can vary in both intensity and extent with the mood of the fish. In addition to the bars *P. altum* has brown to black spots with a blue sheen, sometimes even red. *Size:* up to 6 in (15 cm) long and $10\frac{1}{4}$ in (26 cm) high including fins; usually smaller in captivity. *Sexual differences:* when the female is ready to lay, its belly appears to be inflated. The genital pore pointed in the male, rounded in the female.
Environment *Temperature:* at least 72 °F (22 °C); during breeding, 77–86 °F (25–30 °C). *pH:* 7 or slightly acid. *Water hardness:* not important. *Illumination:* subdued lighting. *Furnishings:* in the wild, members of this genus inhabit riverbanks with their vertically growing vegetation, such as reeds. They therefore require particularly deep tanks with thickly planted areas and also plenty of free space for swimming. Unless they are given cover, the fish will merely congregate in a corner. Broad-leaved water plants are also required for breeding.
Feeding All kinds of large live food.
Biology *Behavior:* provide plenty of cover or the fish will be nervous. They can be kept in pairs for several breeding periods. When breeding, they make a noise with bones in their throats. *Reproduction:* open breeders, laying their eggs on broad stems and leaves of water plants or the glass side of the tank. Both parents look after the eggs, fanning fresh water over them. After 24–36 hours, during which the temperature should be 79–86 °F (26–30 °C), the young hatch out and are first carried in the parents' mouths to water plants, where they are left hanging. Later they are removed to clean, shallow depressions dug in the sand. When a week old, the young fish will swim, helped by their parents. The young fish can be fed on powdered food (rotifers, etc.). First broods are best raised away from the parents. Many aquarium breeds have almost completely lost their rearing instincts through inbreeding. *Social life:* schools of young fish can easily be kept together, but breeding couples require well-defined territories. *Compatibility:* good fish to keep with all other peaceable species that are not too small.
Note In addition to the normal *P. scalare* (upper photo) there is also a black variety (lower photo).

111 HARLEQUIN FISH
Rasbora heteromorpha

Family Cyprinidae.
Distribution Malayan peninsula, Thailand, eastern Sumatra.
Description *Shape:* somewhat thickset and deep in profile. *Color:* silver gray with an opalescent sheen; lighter underside. The caudal peduncle has a wedge-shaped blue or purple-black patch. *Size:* up to 1¾ in (4.5 cm). *Sexual differences:* female thicker and longer; the lower front edge of the wedge over the beginning of the ventral fins somewhat blurred. In the male the lower edge of the wedge is well defined, reaching almost to the middle of the belly line.
Environment *Temperature:* 75–77 °F (24–25 °C) under normal conditions; up to 82 °F (28 °C) for breeding. *pH:* 5.3–5.7. *Water hardness:* 1.5–2.5° general hardness. *Illumination and furnishings:* plenty of free swimming space (two-thirds to three-quarters of tank); lightly peat-filtered water (water from woodland streams is excellent); subdued lighting.
Feeding Omnivorous. Insects can be given.
Biology *Behavior:* a very active schooling fish. *Reproduction:* very difficult with imported fish. The eggs are placed on the underside of broad-leaved plants. *Compatibility:* with *R. maculata, R. vaterifloris, R. pauciperforata.*

---

112 SCAT
Scatophagus argus

Family Scatophagidae.
Distribution Tropical East Indies.
Description *Shape:* roughly hexagonal body shape, with the upper part of the body more arched than the lower. Several spines in the dorsal fin. *Color:* very variable, according to age, provenance and population. *Size:* up to 11¾ in (30 cm). *Sexual differences:* unknown.
Environment Sea, brackish and fresh waters. *Temperature:* 68–82 °F (20–28 °C). *pH:* neutral to strongly alkaline. *Water hardness:* hard water, with 3–4 teaspoons of sea salt added to every 2 gallons (10 liters) of water. *Illumination, substrate, furnishings:* good lighting, some sand on the bottom. Even fairly tough plants are often completely eaten up.
Feeding Enormous quantities of live food, plus practically any kind of vegetable matter. A strong filter and regular changes of water are needed.
Biology *Behavior:* lively, peaceable. Wobbling swimming motion. *Reproduction:* impossible in an aquarium. The fish pass through a marine larval stage, swim up rivers, then return to the sea to spawn. *Compatibility:* it is best to get the mature fish accustomed to seawater, as they can then be kept with other fishes that have similar requirements.

113 PIRANHAS
Serrasalmus spp.

Family Characidae.
Distribution From the Orinoco and Amazon basins to the Paraná and La Plata rivers.
Description *Shape:* oval body, with a narrow cross section and an adipose fin. The jaws have one or more rows of large, pointed, razor-sharp teeth. *Color:* the coloring is quite variable. *Size:* $9\frac{1}{2}$ in–1 ft 4 in (24–40 cm) according to species and provenance. *Sexual differences:* generally unknown.
Environment Lives in flowing waters. *Temperature:* 73–82 °F (23–28 °C). *pH and water hardness:* cannot be generalized, since each of the sixteen species may have different requirements. *Furnishings:* free swimming space is essential; otherwise there is little definitive information.
Feeding Takes live food, including fish, exclusively, under some circumstances eating its own species. Stories abound of piranhas' being voracious man-eaters. All these species are potentially dangerous. Great care is necessary.
Biology *Behavior:* live in schools, but only of the same species. *Reproduction:* breeding has been successfully achieved several times in captivity. *Social life:* the aggressiveness of the school depends on its size. *Compatibility:* experiments in cohabitation with other fishes are reported to have been successful.

114 DISCUS CICHLIDS
Symphysodon spp.

Family Cichlidae.
Distribution Amazon basin.
Description *Shape:* the body is disk-shaped; with very compressed sides and a small mouth. *Color:* quite varied according to species and strain. *Size:* up to 8 in (20 cm).
Environment In the wild they live in the vegetation of riverbanks, where the half-submerged plants provide a well-protected habitat. *Temperature:* 75–86 °F (24–30 °C). *pH:* slightly acid water, pH 6.5. Add some peat. *Water hardness:* preferably very soft. *Illumination and furnishings:* not too bright a light. Some floating plants. Thick vegetation at edges and corners, and additional roots and other hiding places. Free swimming space should be left in the center. A deep, roomy tank is needed. Renew about one-fourth of the tank water every three weeks.
Feeding Good-quality live food; some plant matter.
Biology *Behavior:* very peaceable large cichlid. Remarkable territorial behavior. *Reproduction:* the large eggs hatch after 50 hours and are carried onto leaves by the parents. The larvae feed on a viscous secretion which is given off by the parents' skin. The young fish gain the disklike form when about three months old. *Social life:* the young form schools; the mature fish are territorial. *Compatibility:* suitable only for a species tank.

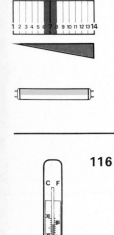

115 WHITE CLOUD MOUNTAIN MINNOW
Tanichthys albonubes

Family Cyprinidae.
Distribution Streams of the White Cloud Mountain near Canton and the region of Hong Kong.
Description *Shape:* elongated and slender, sides slightly compressed. Protractile, slanting mouth. A single nostril on each side. *Color:* many different color varieties in aquaria. They are mostly a darkish brown on top, often with a greenish sheen, which blends gradually into the white coloring of the belly. A dark line extends from the gill opening along the body, and above this a luminous stripe leads from the eye to the beginning of the caudal fin. Beneath the black stripe the body is a rich reddish brown. *Size:* up to $1\frac{1}{2}$ in (4 cm). *Sexual differences:* male narrower and more brilliantly colored.
Environment *Temperature:* 68–72 °F (20–22 °C) in summer and 61–64 °F (16–18 °C) in winter will be enough. Add fresh water frequently. *pH and water hardness:* not important. *Substrate and furnishings:* the bottom should not be too light. There should be feathery water plants and plenty of free swimming space.
Feeding Live and dry food. An insect-eater in its native habitat.
Biology *Behavior:* a lively schooling fish, swimming near the surface. *Reproduction:* the fish spawns readily. *Compatibility:* best kept with members of its own species.

116 CELEBES RAINBOWFISH
Telmatherina ladigesi

Family Atherinidae.
Distribution Interior of Makasar (Celebes Islands).
Description *Shape:* slender body, fairly compressed silhouette. Small first dorsal fin, the second markedly larger with a long base, opposite the anal fin of similar size and shape. *Color:* back, underside, and upper and lower edges of caudal peduncle lemon yellow; the remainder of the body in between duller, olive yellow, with a brilliant blue iridescent stripe along the middle of the body. *Size:* up to $2\frac{3}{4}$ in (7 cm). *Sexual differences:* males have threadlike extensions to the rays of the second dorsal and anal fins; more brightly colored.
Environment *Temperature:* 73–82 °F (23–28 °C). *pH:* 7–8. *Water hardness:* hard to very hard water. Regular replacement of part of the water with fresh recommended. *Illumination and furnishings:* largish tank with a few floating plants and plenty of free swimming space. Very fond of the morning sun.
Feeding Plenty of live food, also a little dried food.
Biology *Behavior:* a lively and elegant schooling fish. *Reproduction:* the eggs need 8–11 days to hatch, and the young hang just under the surface and require powdered food. Imported fish tend to be delicate and do not last long. *Compatibility:* can be kept with similar types from the same area.

117 ASIAN PUFFERFISH
Tetraodon fluviatilis

Family Tetraodontidae.
Distribution Southeast Asia.
Description *Shape:* wedge-shaped, with a large head, widely separated and independently movable eyes. No pelvic fins; the tail is very maneuverable and serves as a steering device. Both head and body are covered with small backward-pointing spines. *Color:* varies considerably according to provenance. Back and sides with large round brown or black patches, which can also merge into crossbands on the back. *Size:* up to 7 in (18 cm). *Sexual differences:* unknown.
Environment Clean, fresh or slightly brackish water. *Temperature:* 72–79 °F (22–26 °C). *pH and water hardness:* neutral or slightly alkaline; hard. Add a small amount of salt for breeding. *Furnishings:* a well-furnished tank with ample, not-too-delicate vegetation. Provide hiding places.
Feeding Omnivorous, but fondest of live food.
Biology *Behavior:* peaceable when young, aggressive when older. It can pump itself full of water and swell up into a ball bristling with spines. *Reproduction:* breeding is possible in captivity, and the fish exhibits a cichlidlike breeding pattern. When the young fish have resorbed their yolk sacs they must be fed with rotifers and other small live foods. *Compatibility:* can be kept with some other fishes as long as they are not too quiet and do not have overly long fins.

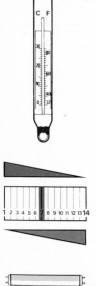

118 TILAPIAS
Tilapia spp.

Family Cichlidae.
Distribution Jordan, Syria, Israel, most of Africa.
Description *Shape:* large head; thickset, deep body. Very long dorsal fin, covering nearly the whole of the back; caudal fin straight-edged or slightly rounded. *Color:* highly varied according to species and physiological state. *Size:* 4¾ in–1 ft 8 in (12 to over 50 cm), according to species. *Sexual differences:* are more or less obvious; spawning females usually more robust.
Environment Occupies all types of fresh waters, both flowing and stagnant (even hot, shallow soda lakes with only a few inches of water). *Temperature:* some species can exist temporarily in temperatures of 59–63 °F (15–17 °C), while others can stand 86–90 °F (30–32 °C). *Furnishings:* large, deep tank is required, well furnished with rocky prominences, bogwood, etc. Only hardy individual plants in pots can be used.
Feeding All live foods. Additional plant food is generally required for breeding.
Biology *Behavior:* all *Tilapia* are schooling fishes. Many have the reputation of being highly combative; others are considered peaceful and sociable. *Reproduction:* generally easy, though one must have compatible pairs. In some species the eggs are incubated in the mouth of the male or the female; in this case, fertilization takes place in the mouth of the female.

119 TILAPIA MARIAE
Tilapia mariae

Family Cichlidae.
Distribution West Africa.
Description *Shape:* deep body, compressed sides. Typical *Tilapia*. *Color:* light-yellow ground color, five or six black spots along the sides of body. Behind the gill cover is an area with red-spotted scales. Red iris, divided by a diagonal black stripe. During spawning, the forward edge of the pelvic fins is a velvety black. Fish hunted by predators produce a pattern of gray-green, and those ejected from their territory, vertical bars. *Size:* up to 6 in (15 cm).
Environment *Temperature:* 77–81 °F (25–27 °C). *pH:* slightly acid or neutral. *Water hardness:* no special requirements. *Furnishings:* a large cichlid tank with stone constructions, roots and flowerpots. A few floating plants.
Feeding Chiefly vegetarians, which can be fed on oat flakes, soft green plants and similar foodstuffs; additional live and dried food.
Biology *Behavior:* territorial, very aggressive. *Reproduction:* eggs laid beneath stones in hollows dug by the female. On the second day after laying, the female brings the eggs to a depression where the young later hatch out. *Social life and compatibility:* should be kept in pairs, eventually each pair with a couple of other species.

120 ARCHERFISH
Toxotes jaculator

Family Toxotidae.
Distribution South and Southeast Asia, Philippines, Malaysia, Australia.
Description *Shape:* compressed, wedge-shaped body. Large, wide mouth tilted upward. Large eyes. *Color:* quite varied, depending on provenance and age. Younger specimens have four to six broad black vertical bars which grow shorter with age. *Size:* up to 9½ in (24 cm) long; sexually mature at 4 in (10 cm). *Sexual differences:* unknown.
Environment Brackish waters of river estuaries, mangrove swamps. *Temperature:* 79–82 °F (26–28 °C). *pH:* 7–8.5. *Water hardness and density:* hard water with additional salt—2–3 teaspoons of sea salt to 2 gallons (10 liters) of water. *Furnishings:* large, shallow tank with a few hardy plants, and plenty of free swimming space.
Feeding Live food, especially insects and small fish.
Biology *Behavior:* voracious eaters. They are capable of spitting a powerful jet of water at insects perched above the surface of the water. *Reproduction:* they are reputed to spawn in seawater; the young then find their way back to fresh water, returning to the brackish water once they are grown. *Social life:* the young specimens live in schools; mature ones are territorial. *Compatibility:* can be kept with other brackish-water fishes.

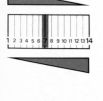

121 PEARL GOURAMI
Trichogaster leeri

Family Belontiidae.
Distribution Malayan peninsula, Thailand, Sumatra, Borneo.
Description *Shape:* very similar to *T. microlepis*, somewhat less compressed. *Color:* sides and fins light brownish marked with numerous round, pale spots with a fine mother-of-pearl sheen. Throat and chest bright orange or red. There is a dark horizontal stripe, partly broken by the mother-of-pearl spots. *Size:* up to 6 in (15 cm). *Sexual differences:* female more olive-colored; throat and chest silvery; dorsal fin rounded instead of long and bannerlike with elongated rays.
Environment See *T. trichopterus*. *Temperature:* 73–86 °F (23–30 °C). *pH and water hardness:* relatively undemanding; softish, neutral water is the best. *Furnishings:* plenty of vegetation including feathery-leaved plants, a partial cover of floating plants, some hiding places in plants and roots. The rest as free swimming space.
Feeding Omnivorous but often choosy.
Biology *Behavior:* lively, very peaceable. Occasionally somewhat anxious and shy. *Reproduction:* not quite so simple as with *T. trichopterus*. Builds large bubble nests. *Social life:* peaceful, nonaggressive, even in the territorial phase. *Compatibility:* do not keep with aggressive fishes.

122 MOONLIGHT GOURAMI
Trichogaster microlepis

Family Belontiidae.
Distribution Thailand and Cambodia.
Description *Shape:* long, rather deep body, very compressed, slender and graceful. Minute scales. *Color:* single-colored, silvery appearance, light gray or bluish with a silky sheen. Young fish have a suggestion of vertical bars. Large eyes. *Size:* up to 6 in (15 cm) long. *Sexual differences:* the flowing, threadlike pelvic fins are a brilliant red in the male.
Environment *Temperature:* 72–82 °F (22–28 °C); up to 86 °F (30 °C). *pH:* 6–8. *Water hardness:* they tolerate medium-hard water best. *Illumination and furnishings:* the lighting should be varied and full of contrast. Floating plants are essential, also thick clumps of vegetation.
Feeding Omnivorous. At breeding times, varied live food.
Biology *Behavior:* very quiet and peaceable fish; territorial only at breeding times. Very timid. *Reproduction:* constructs a large bubble nest with small branches and leaves. The young fish must be fed with very fine plankton. *Social life and compatibility:* a good mixer, but the tank must be large enough to hold several breeding territories. Keep only with peaceable species.

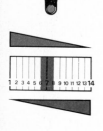

123 THREE-SPOT GOURAMI
Trichogaster trichopterus

Family Belontiidae.
Distribution Malayan peninsula, Thailand, South Vietnam, the Greater Sunda Islands.
Description *Shape:* similar to *T. microlepis* but essentially more powerful and much more thickset. Short dorsal fin. *Color:* extremely variable. Back bluish olive, sides silvery olive, belly white with a little silver. Usually two rather clearly marked round dark spots (one under the dorsal fin, the other on the caudal peduncle; and in addition up to twenty narrow and indistinct bars; a lateral stripe sometimes present. *Size:* up to 6 in (15 cm). *Sexual differences:* male has a long, pointed dorsal fin; on the female it is short and rounded.
Environment Found in a wide range of habitats. *Temperature:* 68–79 °F (20–26 °C). *pH and water hardness:* no special requirements. *Illumination, substrate, furnishings:* not-too-harsh lighting. Some humus on the bottom. Richly planted (two-thirds to three-quarters of tank area), also floating plants; the rest as free swimming space.
Feeding Omnivorous.
Biology *Behavior:* lively, peaceable, only males aggressive toward intruders into the territory. *Reproduction:* easily bred; very prolific. *Social life and compatibility:* gregarious and suitable for community tanks.

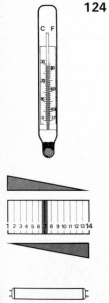

124 CHOCOLATE CICHLID
Uaru amphiacanthoides

Family Cichlidae.
Distribution Amazon basin, Guyanas.
Description *Shape:* oval body, very compressed sides, similar in appearance to some *Cichlasoma* species. *Color:* changeable. Young fish up to 2 in (5 cm) completely brownish-black except for the soft-rayed parts of the dorsal and anal fins. Medium-sized specimens are a yellow to yellow-brown with light irregular spots, stripes and flecks. Fully grown fish are yellowish to brownish with three large black patches on the sides. Fins are yellowish with a green sheen. Eyes bright red. *Size:* up to 10 in (25 cm). *Sexual differences:* distinguishable only by the genital pores of spawning fish.
Environment River regions affording ample plant cover. *Temperature:* needs plenty of warmth: 81–82 °F (27–28 °C); up to 86 °F (30 °C) for breeding. *pH:* 7 or slightly below. *Illumination:* weak lighting. *Substrate:* dark bottom with numerous roots, stone cavities and other hiding places. *Furnishings:* large single plants.
Feeding Copious vegetable food.
Biology *Behavior:* lively, peaceable schooling fish, the males territorial at spawning time only. *Reproduction:* spawns in hidden, dark places. Breeding may be difficult in the aquarium. *Compatibility:* can be kept with cichlids of the same region.

125 SWORDTAIL
Xiphophorus helleri

Family Poeciliidae.
Distribution Southern Mexico, Guatemala.
Description *Shape:* similar to the guppy (*Poecilia reticulata*), but bulkier. The lower rays of the caudal fin in the male are drawn out into a "sword" as long as the body. *Color:* original wild type with olive-green back, greenish-yellow sides, yellow belly; a red wavy or zigzag band. There are many color variations, such as the orange "high-fin" swordtail in the photograph. *Size:* male (without "sword") $3\frac{1}{4}$ in (8 cm); female up to $4\frac{3}{4}$ in (12 cm). *Sexual differences:* the "sword" on the male; difference in size; male gonopodium.
Environment *Temperature:* 72–73 °F (22–23 °C); young are born at the higher level. *pH:* 7–8. *Water hardness:* medium to very hard water. *Illumination, substrate, furnishings:* good lighting. Bottom not too light. Varied vegetation, plenty of free swimming space.
Feeding Takes both live and dried food.
Biology *Behavior:* lives in loosely grouped schools. *Reproduction:* the parents tend to eat their young. At least a day or so before birth takes place (there is an interval of 34 days between broods), the adults should be placed in a breeding trap through which the young can escape. The young can take fine powdered food immediately. *Compatibility:* easily kept with other live-bearing species.

126 VARIEGATED PLATY
Xiphophorus variatus

Family Poeciliidae.
Distribution Mexico.
Description *Shape:* quite variable; somewhat similar to *X. helleri*, but stockier. *Color:* variable in the numerous domesticated varieties. Males mostly brownish yellow. The "pregnancy" spot behind the anal fin also appears on the male in this species. Female olive brown to brownish gray with two reddish zigzag lines along the sides. *Size:* males up to $2\frac{1}{4}$ in (5.5 cm), females up to $2\frac{3}{4}$ in (7 cm). *Sexual differences:* male has a gonopodium.
Environment *Temperature:* 68–77 °F (20–25 °C). *pH:* around 8. *Water hardness:* medium-hard water; make partial changes of water regularly. *Illumination:* plenty of light. *Substrate and furnishings:* dark bottom matter, with a good layer of sand. Moderate vegetation (about half of tank area), with a light covering of floating plants.
Feeding All kinds of live and dried food; also some vegetable food. A hearty eater.
Biology *Behavior:* lively, peaceable, always swim in schools. The males are given to harmless scrapping among themselves. *Reproduction:* breeding is simple in the aquarium. *Social life and compatibility:* good for keeping with other live-bearers and the Mexican tetra, *Astyanax mexicanus*.

MARINE FISHES

127 POWDER-BLUE SURGEONFISH
Acanthurus leucosternon

Family Acanthuridae.
Distribution Tropical Indo-Pacific.
Description *Shape:* oval, compressed. Mouth small. Pectoral fins long; vertical fins long and rounded; shallow notch in caudal fin. *Color:* ground color of body sky blue, with black mask on face, white patch from throat to base of pectoral fin; jaws dark, separated from the dark mask by a narrow white zone. Dorsal fin yellow with light edge; yellow also on caudal peduncle and on "scalpel" spine. Caudal fin has two dark, oblique stripes and a sky-blue bar at the end. Size: up to $11\frac{3}{4}$ in (30 cm). *Sexual differences:* unknown.
Environment *Temperature:* 77–84 °F (25–29 °C). *pH:* 8.2–9.4. *Density:* 1.020–1.024. *Illumination:* good lighting. *Substrate:* large tank with sandy bottom.
Feeding Eats algae and small creatures. Enchytraea, mussel flesh and *Mysis* shrimps will acclimatize it to a variety of animal, vegetable and dried food.
Biology *Behavior:* active, always on the move. *Reproduction:* unknown. *Social life:* keep only single individual in a tank. *Compatibility:* take care in associating it with other fishes in the tank.

128 CLOWN SURGEONFISH
Acanthurus lineatus

Family Acanthuridae.
Distribution Widespread in the Indian and Pacific oceans.
Description *Shape:* oval, upper outline higher and rounded, high-set eyes. Vertical fins long; caudal fin has long lobes; pelvic fins long and pointed. *Color:* velvety orange-brown ground, with black-edged blue horizontal stripes which grow narrower and continue onto the caudal fin. Belly gray-blue or violet-blue. Young up to $1\frac{1}{2}$ in (4 cm) said to have red vertical fins. *Size:* up to 8 in (20 cm). *Sexual differences:* unknown.
Environment *Temperature:* 75–82 °F (24–28 °C). *pH:* over 8. *Density:* about 1.023. *Illumination:* good light. *Furnishings:* ample hiding places needed.
Feeding Does not adapt easily to an aquarium diet. Vary the food, also giving zooplankton.
Biology *Behavior:* not easy to acclimatize, rather nervous. *Reproduction:* unknown. *Social life:* very unsociable; keep only single specimens. *Compatibility:* take care when handling; they can inflict terrible wounds with their tail spines.

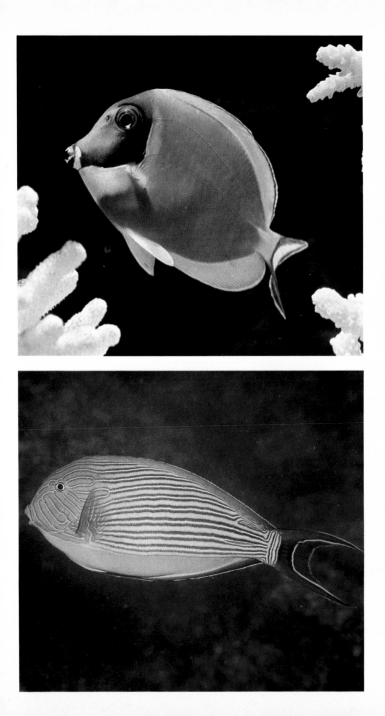

129 GOLD-RIMMED SURGEONFISH
Acanthurus glaucopareius

Family Acanthuridae.
Distribution Tropical Indo-Pacific.
Description *Shape:* very similar to *A. leucosternon.* *Color:* body brown with violet tints. Fins blue to orange with white edges. A broad white stripe on the "cheeks" between eye and mouth. *Size:* up to 13¾ in (35 cm). *Sexual differences:* unknown.
Environment *Temperature:* 75–77 °F (24–25 °C). *pH:* about 8. *Density:* about 1.027. *Illumination:* good lighting. *Substrate and furnishings:* soft sand with stone structures.
Feeding Omnivorous; often needs to be offered many kinds of food before it will begin feeding.
Biology *Behavior:* an active swimmer, needs plenty of room. *Reproduction:* unknown; presumably not possible in the aquarium. *Social life:* lives among its own kind; very unsociable. *Compatibility:* getting it to accept new companions presents some problems. The spines on the caudal peduncle can inflict very deep wounds.

130 LEOPARD FILEFISH
Amanses sandwichiensis

Family Balistidae.
Distribution Tropical regions of the Atlantic, Pacific and Indian oceans, including the Red Sea.
Description *Shape:* body deep and very compressed; snout profile slightly concave; mouth very small. First (visible) dorsal spine set above the eye, the second spine tiny. Skin has very small round scales, smooth in front but with fine teeth on the rear edge. A large erectile pelvic spine with a loose skin flap. *Color:* extremely variable, even in the life of a single individual; usually matches its surroundings. Generally dark olive, marbled, fins lighter. Young are bluish silver with yellow pectoral fins. *Size:* up to 15 in (38 cm). *Sexual differences:* unknown.
Environment *Temperature:* 75–82 °F (24–28 °C). *pH:* over 8. *Density:* about 1.023. *Illumination:* good lighting. *Substrate and furnishings:* sandy bottom; vertical structures for shelter.
Feeding Trouble-free; omnivorous, accepting any kind of food, even stinging sea anemones.
Biology *Behavior:* sociable in natural state and generally sociable in aquaria. *Reproduction:* unknown. *Compatibility:* can be kept successfully with other fishes.

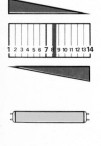

131 ORANGE-FINNED ANEMONE FISH
Amphiprion chrysopterus

Family Pomacentridae.
Distribution Tropical Indo-Pacific.
Description *Shape:* body short and deep. *Color:* brown-orange, underside lighter, with two or three narrow, pointed vertical whitish to bluish bars with dark edges. The first follows the same course as the similar bar on *A. ocellaris*, but is much broader. The third, on the caudal peduncle, is only found in young fish and disappears later. Snout, belly, fins and caudal peduncle a lighter orange-yellow. *Size:* up to 6 in (15 cm). *Sexual differences:* none.
Environment See *A. ocellaris. Temperature:* 75–82 °F (24–28 °C). *pH:* 8.2–8.6. *Density:* about 1.020–1.023. *Illumination:* well lighted. *Substrate:* a base for giant sea anemones is absolutely essential.
Feeding In natural state a plankton-feeder. In the aquarium, small pieces of food.
Biology *Behavior:* same as that of other species of the genus. *Reproduction:* similar to that of *Dascyllus* species, but always within reach of the protecting anemone. *Social life:* in pairs or small schools close to *Stoichactis* anemones. *Compatibility:* only together with other anemone fishes.

132 BLACK-BACKED ANEMONE FISH
Amphiprion frenatus

Family Pomacentridae.
Distribution Andaman Sea and adjacent coasts.
Description *Shape:* body short and deep. *Color:* the body is glowing orange all around and black in the center, the colors merging into each other like those of a live coal. A fairly wide whitish vertical band, rounded at the bottom, behind the eye. Young specimens often have a second and even a trace of a third bar; in adults, as they grow considerably darker, the head bar may be lost. *Size:* 4–6 in (10–15 cm). *Sexual differences:* not clear.
Environment See also *A. ocellaris* and the other species. *Temperature:* 77–86 °F (25–30 °C). *pH:* 8.2–8.6. *Density:* 1.020–1.023. *Illumination:* good light. *Furnishings:* stones and built-up structures as supports for *Stoichactis* and similar giant sea anemones. Will also accept *Actinia equina.*
Feeding Eats small living creatures; see *A. ocellaris.*
Biology *Behavior:* very lively and interesting. In natural surroundings stays at a distance of several yards (meters) from the sea anemones. *Reproduction:* this species has been bred in captivity. *Social life:* always keep a surplus of sea anemones and a small school of *Amphiprion. Compatibility:* only together with other anemone fishes.

133 CLOWN ANEMONE FISH
Amphiprion ocellaris

Family Pomacentridae.
Distribution Widespread in the tropical Indo-Pacific.
Description *Shape:* short, squat. *Color:* body orange-red with three black-edged white vertical bars: the first curving from the nape backward past the eye to the throat; the second behind the spiny and soft-rayed parts of the dorsal fin, with a triangular extension toward the front; the third on the caudal peduncle. *Size:* up to 4 in (10 cm). *Sexual differences:* almost none.
Environment *Temperature:* 77–82 °F (25–28 °C). *pH:* over 8 (8.2–8.5). *Density:* about 1.023. *Illumination:* strong light. *Substrate and furnishings:* some sand; firm structures for the giant sea anemones.
Feeding Small live creatures.
Biology *Behavior:* the remarkable symbiosis between two different organisms and the mechanism of chemical protection are already widely known. *Reproduction:* spawning within reach of the protecting anemone. *Social life:* like all members of its genus, it lives in huge sea anemones of the genus *Stoichactis* and others, and cannot thrive without them; it is best for each pair or each individual to occupy its own sea anemone. *Compatibility:* can be kept only with other anemone fishes. The giant sea anemones are too dangerous for some other species; conversely, many trigger-fishes and others would feed on the sea anemones.

134 RED-GIRDLED ANEMONE FISH
Amphiprion rubrocinctus

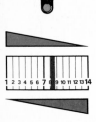

Family Pomacentridae.
Distribution Indo-Pacific from Japan to Australia.
Description *Shape:* body more rectangular, less slender than *A. ocellaris*, not so deep as *A. chrysopterus. Color:* body orange, the head slightly paler; a black-edged broad white vertical bar on head behind the eye; fins yellowish. *Size:* up to 3 in (8 cm). *Sexual differences:* none.
Environment See also *A. ocellaris. Temperature:* 75–86 °F (24–30 °C). *pH:* 8.3–8.6. *Density:* between 1.020 and 1.023. *Illumination:* good light. *Furnishings:* stones and support for giant sea anemones essential.
Feeding Small living creatures and other animal food.
Biology *Behavior:* comparable to other *Amphiprion* species. *Reproduction:* this species has already been bred in the aquarium for two generations. *Social life:* provide more anemones than fish; these are best kept in a small school. *Compatibility:* only together with other anemone fishes.

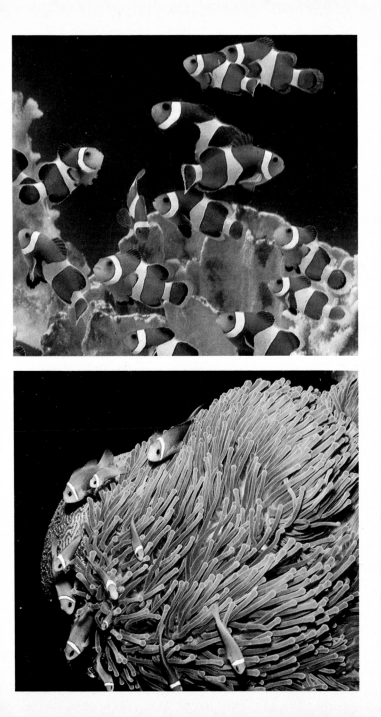

135 YELLOW-TAILED ANEMONE FISH
Amphiprion clarkii

Family Pomacentridae.
Distribution From Sumatra to East Africa.
Description *Shape:* a rather more robust, deep-bodied *Amphiprion. Color:* black to dark brown (the latter in ill health) with two or three broad white vertical bars, the second continuing into the dorsal fin and hardly growing any broader. The third bar, on the caudal peduncle, disappears with age, the back edge breaking up first. Dorsal, anal and pelvic fins black (the last only in front). Pectoral and caudal fins yellow, the latter especially uniform in color. The snout also yellow. *Size:* up to 5 in (12 cm). *Sexual differences:* not clear except during spawning.
Environment See also *A. ocellaris. Temperature:* 75–86 °F (24–30 °C). *pH:* 8.2–8.6. *Density:* between 1.020 and 1.023. *Illumination:* good lighting. *Furnishings:* stones and supports for giant sea anemones essential.
Feeding Small live and prepared food.
Biology *Behavior:* similar to other *Amphiprion* species. Stays nearer the bottom. *Reproduction:* spawns near its sea anemone. *Social life:* always keep more sea anemones than fish. *Compatibility:* keep only with other anemone fishes.

136 FROGFISHES
Antennarius spp.

Family Antennariidae.
Distribution This genus is widespread in all the warmer seas.
Description *Shape:* fantastic-looking, squat and clumsy. Thick skin, often with growths on it. All have a fishing rod, often with slender appendages, above the sloping-to-vertical upward-opening mouth. *Color:* varied; often colorful but more or less camouflaged. *Size:* 5–8 in (12–20 cm) according to species (among those so far imported). *Sexual differences:* unknown.
Environment Requirements differ widely according to geographical origin or depth at which it normally lives. Your supplier may be able to advise you.
Feeding Catches its food by lurking in the rocks; can overpower fish as big as or even bigger than itself. Once settled in, will eat well. At first the substitute diet (strips of fish or meat) should be moved about so that it seems alive.
Biology *Behavior:* territorial, does not move much; often walks with the aid of its jointed pelvic fins. *Reproduction:* unknown. *Social life:* it is advisable to experiment first with single specimens. *Compatibility:* keep only with peaceable larger fishes.

137 PAJAMA CARDINAL FISH
Sphaeramia nematoptera

Family Apogonidae.
Distribution Indo-Australian seas, China Sea.
Description *Shape:* body short and deep; two widely separated dorsal fins, the first two rays of the second dorsal fin elongated like threads. Large head with very big eyes and large mouth. *Color:* ground color, especially on head and front of body, yellowish brown. A broad vertical bar from the base of the first dorsal fin to the belly, in which the centers of the scales are often light-colored. Behind this bar, the hind part of the body and the caudal peduncle are covered with brown or red-brown spots. *Size:* up to 5 in (12 cm). *Sexual differences:* unknown.
Environment Likes to live in shady waters. *Temperature:* 75–82 °F (24–28 °C). *pH:* at least 8. *Density:* about 1.025. *Illumination:* subdued lighting. *Furnishings:* many hiding places.
Feeding Very predatory, feeding in nature on large plankton, crustaceans, small fishes.
Biology *Behavior:* a peaceable schooling fish, active chiefly at twilight. *Reproduction:* unknown. *Social life:* best in schools. *Compatibility:* species tank.

138 THREE-SPOT ANGELFISH
Holacanthus trimaculatus

Family Pomacanthidae.
Distribution Indian Ocean, western Pacific.
Description *Shape:* very similar to the butterfly fishes but with gill-cover spines as in *Pomacanthus. Color:* almost uniform gold to orange-yellow on body and fins, with rather darker edges to scales. Only snout and throat dark blue; the dark iris and two dark patches on the upper edge of the operculum and on the top of the head give this species its name. Inner half of the anal fin white, outer edge generally contrasting black. *Size:* up to 10 in (26 cm). *Sexual differences:* unknown.
Environment Comparable to butterfly fishes.
Feeding Browser, feeding on plant food, small animals and larvae. Requirements similar to *Pomacanthus imperator.*
Biology *Behavior:* territorial. *Reproduction:* probably not possible in aquaria. *Social life:* keep as individuals. *Compatibility:* take care in acclimatization.

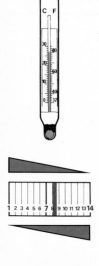

139   BOXFISHES or TRUNKFISHES
Ostracion spp.

Family Ostraciidae.
Distribution The genus is widespread in the tropical Indo-Pacific and represented by several species.
Description *Shape:* the shape of the boxfishes is unmistakable. *Color:* the species are often very pretty and colorful, some of them with very distinctive coloring. Photograph is of *O. cubicus*, the spotted trunkfish. *Size:* differs according to species. *Sexual differences:* not always known.
Environment *Temperature:* 75 to 82–86 °F (24 to 28–30 °C). *pH:* always more than 8. *Density:* 1.018–1.030. *Illumination:* generally good lighting. *Substrate:* sandy bottom, stone structures with hiding places.
Feeding Omnivorous; only in some cases specialized feeders.
Biology *Behavior:* very interesting, gently swimming fishes. They can move their eyes independently, but they focus both eyes together when necessary. *Reproduction:* no report yet of any species breeding in captivity. *Social life:* some species and individuals are very vicious and unsociable, but some are quite peaceable. In any case, care should be taken in putting them into a tank with other fish.

140   PUFFERFISH
Arothron hispidus

Family Tetraodontidae.
Distribution India, Indonesian archipelago, Philippines, New Guinea, northern Australia to the Fiji Islands.
Description *Shape:* clublike, elongated oval shape. Between the eyes and the tip of the snout there are a pair of nasal tentacles. *Color:* a few light markings on a brownish-gray background. The base of the pectoral fins is distinguished by a black spot surrounded by yellow. Generally, regular dark spots along the sides. *Size:* up to 17 in (42 cm). *Sexual differences:* unknown.
Environment *Temperature:* 75–82 °F (24–28 °C). *pH:* over 8. *Density:* 1.020–1.025. *Illumination:* good. *Substrate:* sand; rocks and stones for hiding places.
Feeding Omnivorous.
Biology *Behavior:* easy to acclimatize and to tame. Amusing and interesting. *Reproduction:* unknown. *Social life:* peaceable and sociable. *Compatibility:* can be kept with other species.

141 UNDULATE TRIGGERFISH
Balistapus undulatus

Family Balistidae.
Distribution Widespread in tropical regions of Indo-Pacific.
Description *Shape:* very much like the genus *Balistes*. *Color:* ground color green, darker when fish is at rest; a pattern of diagonal orange stripes. The whole of the caudal fin, the rays of the vertical and pectoral fins and spots on the head are orange. *Size:* 12 in (30 cm). *Sexual differences:* unknown.
Environment *Temperature:* 75–82 °F (24–28 °C). *pH:* about 8. *Density:* about 1.023. *Illumination:* good lighting. *Furnishings:* hiding places where the fish can withdraw at night.
Feeding Eats anything it can catch: sea urchins, snails, mussels, calcareous algae, pieces of coral and bits of passing fishes.
Biology *Behavior:* territorial, lively, unsociable. *Reproduction:* unknown. *Social life and compatibility:* one of the least sociable species of triggerfish; definitely to be kept as single specimen in a large tank.

---

142 WHITE-LINED TRIGGERFISH
Sufflamen bursa

Family Balistidae.
Distribution Widespread in tropical Indo-Pacific.
Description *Shape:* large-headed; eyes near dorsal-fin spines; also typical of the species are the opposite dorsal and anal fins. *Color:* olivaceous to dark brown, partly clouded and with darker longitudinal stripes. Snout light; a light-colored stripe leading from its upper side to the gill opening and below it is a blue or greenish band to the anus; the lower parts lighter, partly with a reddish flush. Fin rays brownish; fin membrane almost transparent. *Size:* up to 10 in (25 cm). *Sexual differences:* unknown.
Environment *Temperature:* 75–79 °F (24–26 °C). *pH:* about 8. *Density:* about 1.020. *Illumination:* bright or moderate lighting. *Furnishings:* plenty of room to swim, and some hiding places.
Feeding Omnivorous; not fastidious once acclimatized.
Biology *Behavior:* lively and intelligent. Very interesting pets. *Reproduction:* probably not possible in aquarium, since in the natural state they live solitarily or in pairs. *Social life:* must be kept singly in a large tank. *Compatibility:* very unsociable; cannot be kept together with other triggerfishes or surgeonfishes.

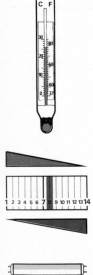

143 GRAY TRIGGERFISH
Balistes capriscus

Family Balistidae.
Distribution Tropical Atlantic and Mediterranean.
Description *Shape:* body compressed, high, ellipti-cal. Eyes set very high near forehead. Small mouth, fleshy lips, big teeth. Scales rough, biggest below the pectoral fins, smallest near the bases of the vertical fins. *Color:* more colorful in young stage; the light patches on the head, two round patches on the upper part of the flanks and the vertical fins are bluish or sometimes whitish. Adults brownish, paler below. American specimens differ somewhat from the European ones. *Size:* up to 24 in (60 cm) in the Atlantic, 16 in (40 cm) confirmed in the Mediterranean. *Sexual differences:* unknown.
Environment Is almost pelagic. *Temperature:* Amer-ican specimens 64–75 °F (18–24 °C); Mediterranean 64–68 °F (18–20 °C). *pH:* at least 8. *Density:* 1.020–1.025. *Illumination:* good light. *Substrate and furnishings:* sandy bottom, a lot of swimming room, a few hiding places.
Feeding Eats almost anything.
Biology *Behavior:* active, curious; adults easy to acclimatize. *Reproduction:* has spawned in big tanks. *Social life:* lively, sociable, but needs plenty of room. *Compatibility:* quite sociable, but be careful.

144 QUEEN TRIGGERFISH
Balistes vetula

Family Balistidae.
Distribution Tropical Atlantic and Indian Ocean.
Description *Shape:* typical of the genus. The front tip of the dorsal fin and outermost rays of the caudal fin in mature fish are elongated into points. *Color:* ground color yellowish, with two striking, curved light-blue stripes on either side of the head. Light blue stripes on dorsal, anal and caudal fins. Occasionally an irregular star-shaped pattern. Young fish have some diagonal black lines along the rows of scales. *Size:* over 20 in (50 cm). *Sexual differences:* unknown.
Environment *Temperature:* 71–79 °F (22–26 °C). *pH:* about 8. *Density:* about 1.020–1.025. *Illumination:* good lighting. *Furnishings:* plenty of swimming room, some hiding places.
Feeding In the wild state it likes to crunch sea urchins; in the aquarium it accepts various kinds of meat.
Biology *Behavior:* an interesting fish that grows tame enough to hand-feed. *Reproduction:* probably im-possible in the aquarium. *Social life:* one individual to a tank. *Compatibility:* can be kept with members of other genera and families.

145 YELLOW-BLOTCHED or CLOWN TRIGGERFISH
Balistoides niger

Family Balistidae.
Distribution Tropical Indo-Pacific.
Description *Shape:* upper profile straight. A group of enlarged scales near the pectoral fin. A depression in front of the eye, the interorbital space almost flat. Three rows of spines on the caudal peduncle. *Color:* coloring variable (brown or dark blue); a light-colored saddle with vermiculations on the forward part of the back; the lower half of the body adorned with large oval white spots; caudal peduncle also white, as are a stripe below the eyes and a narrower stripe around the brilliant red or orange mouth. *Size:* 20 in (50 cm). *Sexual differences:* unknown.
Environment *Temperature:* 75–82 °F (24–28 °C). *pH:* over 8. *Density:* 1.023. *Illumination:* good light. *Substrate and furnishings:* sandy bottom; plenty of swimming room; one or two good shelters, in which the fish wedges itself with its dorsal spine when in deep sleep.
Feeding When accustomed, eats almost anything.
Biology *Behavior:* very curious but extremely vicious. *Reproduction:* unknown. *Social life:* must be kept singly. *Compatibility:* hardly ever possible to keep with other fishes.

---

146 TOMPOT BLENNY
Blennius gattorugine

Family Blenniidae.
Distribution Mediterranean and eastern Atlantic, north to the Irish Sea.
Description *Shape:* usual for a blenny (see *B. ocellaris*). Body robust but quite compressed. Dorsal-fin spines not much higher than the soft-rayed section. Cirrus above eye, irregularly fringed. *Color:* generally with six darts, broad vertical bars which continue into the vertical fins. *Size:* up to 10 in (25 cm). *Sexual differences:* male bigger than female.
Environment Lives in shallow water on rocky shores, where it is easy to observe, but also at greater depths. Also lives in beds of *Posidonia* and near harbors. *Temperature:* room temperature, unheated tank. *pH:* 8 and over. *Density:* about 1.023. *Illumination:* good light. *Substrate:* stone structures, little sand.
Feeding Omnivorous; will feed from the hand.
Biology *Behavior:* lively, territorial, interesting to observe. *Reproduction:* breeding probably not difficult, but it is not known whether the fry, which swim on hatching, can be raised with the appropriate plankton. *Social life:* similar to *B. ocellaris*. *Compatibility:* not to be kept with very small fishes (which they will eat) or with big fishes (which might injure them).

147 BUTTERFLY BLENNY
Blennius ocellaris

Family Blenniidae.
Distribution Mediterranean, eastern Atlantic, English Channel.
Description *Shape:* elongated, large-headed fish; dorsal and anal fins long, pectoral fins broad. Skin scaleless and slimy. Body robust, with a cirrus over the eye longer than the eye and fringed at the end; the first spine of the dorsal fin elongated. At the base of the elongated first spine is a short, broad fringed flap on either side, strong in the male. *Color:* back and sides pale reddish or gray-green, with broad brown vertical bars. Between the fifth and eighth dorsal spines is a blue-black eyespot. *Size:* up to 7 in (17 cm). *Sexual differences:* see above; male bigger than female.
Environment On rocky bottoms in fairly deep water. *Temperature:* 59–70 °F (15–21 °C). *pH:* about 8. *Density:* about 1.025. *Illumination:* subdued light. *Substrate:* deep sandy bottom with mussel and snail shells together with pots and stones.
Feeding All sorts of live food and meat.
Biology *Behavior:* active, territorial. *Reproduction:* no report of breeding of this species. *Social life:* the need for individual territories limits the number of specimens in the tank. *Compatibility:* only together with much smaller, or much larger, fishes.

148 SPANISH HOGFISH
Bodianus rufus

Family Labridae.
Distribution Tropical Atlantic waters: Bermuda and Florida to Brazil.
Description *Shape:* relatively short, but streamlined. Very much compressed, especially the caudal peduncle. Dorsal and anal fins drawn out to points. Snout conical; mouth terminal; lips fleshy. Large scales, like the others of its family. *Color:* red-brown or violet-red from top of head to underside of eye, back as far as the soft-rayed portion of the dorsal fin; the rest of the body, including fins, is yellow or orange. Only one color phase seems to be known for this species. *Size:* 14–20 in (35–50 cm) or more. *Sexual differences:* unknown.
Environment *Temperature:* 68–82 °F (20–28 °C), according to origin. *pH:* over 8. *Density:* 1.020–1.023. *Illumination:* good light. *Substrate:* sandy bottom, a few stone structures.
Feeding In natural surroundings feeds chiefly on small animals; the young act as cleaner-fishes.
Biology *Behavior:* interesting swimmer. *Reproduction:* unknown. *Social life:* swims about rather violently. *Compatibility:* can be kept happily with other species.

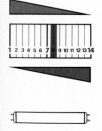

149 BLUE-SPOTTED LONGFIN
Calloplesiops altivelis

Family Plesiopidae.
Distribution Indian Ocean, from the East African coast to the Indonesian archipelago.
Description *Shape:* perchlike; short and squat with large dorsal, caudal and anal fins; pelvic fins long and narrow. *Color:* head, body and fins blackish with a brownish tinge. Numerous tiny light blue dots. A large blue-edged black eyespot on the last five rays of the dorsal fin. A bright chrome-yellow area on the upper side of the caudal peduncle, extending onto the first two rays of the caudal fin. *Size:* up to 6 in (15 cm). *Sexual differences:* unknown.
Environment *Temperature:* 75–82 °F (24–28 °C). *pH:* about 8. *Density:* about 1.025. *Illumination:* subdued lighting. *Furnishings:* many hiding places; in natural state it lives in holes in coral reefs.
Feeding Feeds on small fishes; hunts from a set position.
Biology *Behavior:* peaceful lurker; active at twilight. *Reproduction:* unknown. *Social life:* solitary. *Compatibility:* test whether it will tolerate companions.

150 GOLDEN or BARRED JACK
Gnathanodon speciosus

Family Carangidae.
Distribution Pacific, Red Sea, Indian Ocean.
Description *Shape:* typical of a fast swimmer. Upper body outline rather more curved than belly outline. Pectoral fins large, pelvic fins small. Anal and dorsal fins opposite each other. Caudal fin deeply cleft. *Color:* on a yellow-silver ground a number of vertical bars, a broad one through the eye followed by an alternation of wide and narrow bars. This pattern is distinct on the young, but later disappears. *Size:* up to 3 ft 3 in (1 m). *Sexual differences:* unknown.
Environment High-seas long-distance swimmer, seldom near coasts. *Temperature:* 72–77 °F (22–25 °C). *pH:* about 8. *Density:* about 1.020. *Illumination:* strong lighting. *Substrate:* bottom of no significance, since the fish is generally near the surface.
Feeding Live food; lives on fish and large plankton.
Biology *Behavior:* long-distance swimmer. *Reproduction:* probably impossible. *Social life:* schooling fish. *Compatibility:* peaceable. Can be kept in a home aquarium only when young.

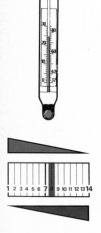

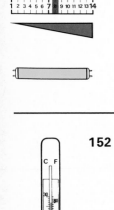

151 CENTROPYGE ANGELFISHES
Centropyge spp.

Family Pomacanthidae.
Distribution Rare, in central and western Pacific.
Description *Shape:* elongated oval, with spine on operculum typical of the genus. *Color:* uniform chrome yellow on body and fins, often slightly orange. *C. heraldi*, the species illustrated, is often confused with *C. flavissimus*, which has a blue ring around the eye and dark-blue edges to the vertical fins. Young *C. flavissimus* have a large black eyespot, often edged with blue, on the side of the body. *Size: C. flavissimus* to 5 in (12 cm); *C. heraldi* to 4 in (10 cm). *Sexual differences:* unknown.
Environment Data and requirements similar to butterfly fishes.
Feeding *C. flavissimus* in natural surroundings eats only algae; the food of *C. heraldi* is unknown. Offer plenty of plant food.
Biology *Behavior:* territorial. *Reproduction:* unknown. *Social life:* solitary. *Compatibility:* acclimatize carefully.

152 CORAL TROUT
Epinephelus miniatus

Family Serranidae.
Distribution Coastal regions of tropical Indo-Pacific.
Description *Shape:* body not so robust as in many other groupers. Caudal fin rounded, soft dorsal fin elongated. *Color:* ground color orange to cinnamon red, darkening toward the back. Head, body and fins covered with numerous round blue spots which are edged with brown. Spots on the young are fewer and relatively larger. The vertical and pelvic fins have blue markings; the pectoral fins are bright orange, unspotted. *Size:* up to 12 in (30 cm). *Sexual differences:* unknown, but presumably a protogynous hermaphrodite.
Environment *Temperature:* 75–82 °F (24–28 °C). *pH:* about 8. *Density:* about 1.025. *Illumination:* subdued to moderately bright lighting. *Furnishings:* possibilities for shelter.
Feeding Easily accustomed to substitute meat diet.
Biology *Behavior:* territorial, predatory. *Reproduction:* unknown in aquaria. *Social life:* solitary. *Compatibility:* keep only with fishes of the same size.

153 PRICKLY LEATHERJACKET
Chaetoderma penicilligera

Family Balistidae.
Distribution Tropical Indo-Pacific.
Description *Shape:* body almost diamond-shaped, with thin, prominent caudal peduncle. The whole body is covered with flaps of skin branched like little trees. *Color:* on a golden-brown ground a dozen very dark horizontal lines, partly broken and partly bordered with shining dots. The same lines appear in an irregular pattern on the head. Vertical fins have transparent membranes and darkly ringed rays; pectoral fins completely transparent. *Size:* 10 in (25 cm). *Sexual differences:* unknown.
Environment The species is thought to live among seaweed and/or algae above a sandy bottom. *Temperature:* 79 °F (26 °C). *pH:* 8. *Density:* between 1.020 and 1.025. A frequent slight change of water is good for the fish. *Illumination:* good lighting. *Substrate:* soft sandy bottom.
Feeding Very voracious, takes any live or dried food offered.
Biology *Behavior:* very hardy and sociable. *Reproduction:* unknown in aquaria. *Social life:* probably a schooling fish. *Compatibility:* sociable with other fishes and toward echinoderms and jellyfish.

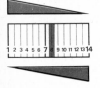

154 PAKISTANI BUTTERFLY FISH
Chaetodon collare

Family Chaetodontidae.
Distribution East African coast as far as Melanesia.
Description *Shape:* unmistakably a butterfly fish. *Color:* pearl-gray, edge of scales dark but their centers golden—more marked near the back. A broad, entirely black or dark gray vertical bar extends from the beginning of the dorsal fin through the eyes to the lower edge of the gill cover; a white line in front of this, preceded by another dark patch, and in front of the dark stripe a narrower white line. Dorsal fin lined with black, red, white and red again, and the anal fin similarly striped blue, black, red-brown. The caudal peduncle and caudal fin orange to red, then a black and a transparent zone. *Size:* up to 6 in (16 cm). *Sexual differences:* unknown.
Environment *Temperature:* 75–82 °F (24–28 °C). *pH:* about 8. *Density:* about 1.025. *Illumination:* plenty of light. *Furnishings:* rocks, with room to swim.
Feeding As varied a diet as possible.
Biology *Behavior:* territorial; only young fish in schools. *Reproduction:* unknown. *Social life:* living in pairs; only newly captured pairs or schools of young fish can be kept. *Compatibility:* in general, butterfly fishes cannot be kept with other butterfly fishes unless they are quite different in size; they can, however, be kept with unrelated fishes.

155 SADDLE BUTTERFLY FISH
Chaetodon ephippium

Family Chaetodontidae.
Distribution Pacific, from Indo-Australian archipelago to Hawaii.
Description *Shape:* typical butterfly fish, dorsal fin coming to a point. *Color:* ground color of the body pure light pearl gray. A black vertical bar through the eyes. A black saddle from the beginning of the fifth spine of the dorsal fin down to the beginning of the caudal peduncle, covering about a quarter of the body and almost the whole of the dorsal fin. The saddle is separated from the pearl gray of the body by a wide white border, and on the dorsal fin is followed by an orange-red band, a narrow black line, a bright light blue stripe and a smoky, opaque border. The point of the dorsal fin is orange-yellow. Caudal-fin base, outermost rays and a quite narrow outer border are orange-yellow. *Size:* up to 12 in (30 cm). *Sexual differences:* unknown.
Environment *Temperature:* 75–82 °F (24–28 °C). *pH:* over 8. *Density:* about 1.023. *Illumination:* good lighting. *Furnishings:* reproduction of reef.
Feeding Feeds on algae and plant food. It should be given as varied a diet as possible.
Biology See *C. collare.*

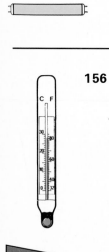

156 HOODED BUTTERFLY FISH
Chaetodon larvatus

Family Chaetodontidae.
Distribution Red Sea.
Description *Shape:* characteristic of the *Chaetodon* species. *Color:* a brown cowl or mask from the beginning of the dorsal fin over the head and gill cover and as far as the beginning of the pelvic fins. In sharp contrast behind, a white field extending upward, becoming brilliant blue farther back. This field includes nearly all the body and much of the vertical fins, and grows darker toward the rear. Over this blue ground color are a large number of herringbone lines, white, narrow and bent in the middle. A white line extends from the tip of the dorsal fin over the caudal peduncle and a little way into the anal fin. Behind this the vertical fins, caudal peduncle and caudal fin are pure black. The blue of the ground color becomes black in the anal fin. Dorsal, caudal and anal fins have shining blue edges. *Size:* 4 in (10 cm). *Sexual differences:* unknown.
Environment *Temperature:* 79–82 °F (26–28 °C). *pH:* about 8. *Density:* about 1.025. *Illumination:* good lighting. *Furnishings:* reproduction of reef.
Feeding A specialized feeder.
Biology See *C. collare.*

157 PEARL-SCALE BUTTERFLY FISH
Chaetodon chrysurus

Family Chaetodontidae.
Distribution Indian Ocean.
Description *Shape:* has very large scales. *Color:* ground color light orange, with dark blue edges to the scales. A dark band through the eye, gray to brown. On the rear third of the dorsal fin, caudal peduncle and tip of the anal fin, an irregular orange-yellow patch. Finally, at the base of the caudal fin, a pale blue and an orange band, and a dark blue edge. The front dorsal-fin spines have projecting yellow tips; orange-colored parts of the fin are striped dark and bright blue. Several geographical forms with different coloring and patterns. *Size:* up to 5 in (12 cm). *Sexual differences:* unknown.
Environment *Temperature:* 75–82 °F (24–28 °C). *pH:* about 8. *Density:* about 1.025. *Illumination:* good lighting. *Furnishings:* reproduction of reef.
Biology See *C. collare.* Live in pairs as soon as they are half-grown.

158 SIX-SPINED BUTTERFLY FISH
Parachaetodon ocellatus

Family Chaetodontidae.
Distribution Coasts of India, southern China, the Philippines and the Indo-Australian archipelago.
Description *Shape:* similar to *Chaetodon.* The dorsal fin is high and roughly triangular. *Color:* characteristic orange-yellow vertical bars, darker than the rest of the body. The thinnest of the bars cuts across the eye and has black borders. At the base of the dorsal fin there is a conspicuous black spot. Another dark spot decorates the caudal peduncle. *Size:* about 6 in (15 cm). *Sexual differences:* unknown.
Environment *Temperature:* 68–79 °F (20–26 °C). *pH:* greater than 8. *Density:* 1.020–1.023. *Illumination:* strong. *Furnishings:* should be ample room, with hiding places.
Feeding Algae and small animals. Should be fed mainly on brine shrimp to start with, so that it can become accustomed to aquarium food.
Biology *Behavior:* forms small groups in the natural state. Sedentary habits. *Reproduction:* unknown in aquaria. *Social life:* young specimens especially can live together without any problems. *Compatibility:* can easily be kept with, for example, damselfishes (pomacentrids).

159 EIGHT-BANDED BUTTERFLY FISH
Chaetodon octofasciatus

Family Chaetodontidae.
Distribution Tropical Indo-Pacific.
Description *Shape:* typical butterfly fish. *Color:* on a silvery ground, six regular dark brown vertical bars near one another on the body; two similar bars on the caudal peduncle and the base of the caudal fin. *Size:* up to 4 in (10 cm). *Sexual differences:* unknown.
Environment Probably reefs. *Temperature:* 75–77 °F (24–25 °C). *pH:* about 8. *Density:* about 1.020. *Illumination and furnishings:* see *C. triangulum*. Good aeration needed.
Feeding Easily looked after once accustomed to substitute diet.
Biology *Behavior and social life:* territorial and unsociable; it is not known whether, like most brilliantly colored butterfly fishes, *C. octofasciatus* live in pairs. *Reproduction:* not yet bred in captivity.

160 CORAL BUTTERFLY FISH
Chaetodon plebeius

Family Chaetodontidae.
Distribution Eastern Indian Ocean, Indo-Australian archipelago, western Pacific north to Japan.
Description *Shape:* a rather elongated butterfly fish. *Color:* almost uniform color—light, shiny yellow as far as a broad vertical bar through the eye, edged in front and behind with turquoise. The scales of the body are partly edged with darker yellow, giving the impression of dusky lines along the body. A light blue smudge in the upper part of the body. The rear half of the caudal fin bright blue. A black or dark brown eyespot edged with turquoise on the caudal peduncle. Tips of the dorsal fin slightly greenish. *Size:* up to 5 in (12 cm). *Sexual differences:* unknown.
Environment *Temperature:* 75–82 °F (24–28 °C). *pH:* about 8. *Density:* about 1.025. *Illumination:* plenty of light. *Furnishings:* many hiding places and ample room for swimming.
Feeding Eats only polyps of corals; difficult to get it to take a substitute diet.
Biology See *C. collare*.

161 GOLDEN BUTTERFLY FISH
Chaetodon semilarvatus

Family Chaetodontidae.
Distribution Red Sea.
Description *Shape:* body almost circular, with the usual slightly projecting snout. *Color:* almost uniform orange-yellow with somewhat darker narrow vertical bars. A blue patch on eye and gill cover; a narrow stripe in the soft-rayed sections of the dorsal and anal fins with another line outside tracing the outline. Pectoral fins transparent, pelvic fins yellow. *Size:* up to 8 in (20 cm). *Sexual differences:* unknown.
Environment *Temperature:* 79–82 °F (26–28 °C). *pH:* over 8. *Density:* about 1.023. *Illumination:* good light. *Furnishings:* reproduction of reef.
Feeding Offer all sorts of substitute food based on algae and plankton.
Biology See *C. collare.*

162 BENNETT'S BUTTERFLY FISH
Chaetodon bennetti

Family Chaetodontidae.
Distribution Tropical Indo-Pacific.
Description *Shape:* typical of the genus: deep, compressed, more or less oval body; snout small, often protruding; dorsal and anal fins very scaly. *Color:* almost uniform yellow with the following pattern: dark vertical bar as narrow as the iris, dark gray or brown, passing through the eye, with a light gray-blue or gray line in front and behind. Two stripes, equally light and somewhat concave toward the top, start near the top of the gill cover and extend to the anal fin, one in front of the base of the pectoral fins and one behind. A large black eyespot, edged with light blue like the eye bar, on the upper part of the flank under the last spiny ray of the dorsal fin. *Size:* up to 6 in (15 cm). *Sexual differences:* unknown.
Environment *Temperature:* 75–82 °F (24–28 °C). *pH:* about 8. *Density:* about 1.025. *Illumination:* plenty of light. *Furnishings:* ample swimming space, narrow hiding places, reproduction of reef.
Feeding Like many butterfly fishes, likes to nibble at its food; dislikes small pieces of food.
Biology *Behavior:* active, keen swimmer, territorial. *Reproduction:* unknown in captivity. *Social life:* to be kept singly. *Compatibility:* do not keep with similarly patterned relatives.

163 TRIANGLE BUTTERFLY FISH
Chaetodon triangulum

Family Chaetodontidae.
Distribution Tropical Indo-Pacific.
Description *Shape:* typical butterfly fish. *Color:* see photograph. Has several geographical subspecies. *Size:* 5–6 in (12–15 cm). *Sexual differences:* none known.
Environment Probably coral reefs. *Temperature:* 75–77 °F (24–25 °C). *pH:* about 8. *Density:* about 1.020. *Furnishings:* good ventilation; large tank with stone structures, coral, rock, etc. for the creation of territories and hiding places.
Feeding Like all butterfly fishes, very fastidious in choice of food; many kinds of varied live foods (also deep-frozen or freeze-dried).
Biology *Behavior and social life:* difficult; like other brilliantly colored butterfly fishes, can be kept in pairs only if they have paired off themselves and with other butterfly fishes only if they are of very different sizes. *Compatibility:* with unrelated fishes.

164 VERMICULATED ANGELFISH
Chaetodontoplus mesoleucus

Family Chaetodontidae.
Distribution Indo-Australian archipelago.
Description *Shape:* very much like butterfly fishes. *Color:* divided from front to back into six vertical zones of different breadth and coloring: tip of snout gray-brown, then a yellow band up to front of the eye. Through the eye, a chocolate-brown bar. Then a white zone from the first three spines of the dorsal fin to the belly, including the pectoral and pelvic fins. The next zone is not sharply divided; it is chocolate brown with light horizontal dotted lines. The caudal fin is a sharply contrasted chrome yellow. The soft-rayed portions of the dorsal and anal fins, after a broad chocolate-brown stripe, are edged with turquoise. *Size:* up to 6 in (16 cm). *Sexual differences:* unknown.
Environment Requirements and data similar to butterfly fishes.
Feeding Probably a very specialized plant-food feeder.
Biology *Behavior:* territorial. *Reproduction:* unknown in captivity. *Social life:* solitary. *Compatibility:* to be kept only with very similar species.

165 LONG-NOSED BUTTERFLY FISH
Chelmon rostratus

Family Chaetodontidae.
Distribution Indian Ocean, Indo-Australian archipelago.
Description *Shape:* a butterfly fish with a very long snout. *Color:* scales silvery with dark edges. Five orange crossbars, growing broader toward the tail. These stripes are dark-edged on both sides. The first and narrowest goes through the eye, the second from the first spine of the dorsal fin to the base of the pelvic fin. The third bar is in the middle of the body; the fourth runs from the soft-rayed part of the dorsal fin to the corresponding part of the anal fin. In this fourth bar, at the base of the dorsal fin, there is a velvety black and light blue eyespot with a dark rim. The fifth bar, on the caudal peduncle, is a velvety black stripe. *Size:* up to 7 in (17 cm). *Sexual differences:* male has steep forehead and horizontal snout, female more sloping forehead and sloping snout.
Environment As for *Chaetodon* species.
Feeding Extracts small creatures from cracks and crannies. Feed often.
Biology Similar to *Chaetodon* species.

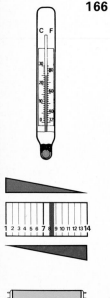

166 BICOLOR PARROT FISH
Bolbometopon bicolor

Family Scaridae. The notes that follow cover the entire family.
Distribution Family represented in all warm seas.
Description *Shape:* generally elongated, with long vertical fins. Very big scales. *Color:* a change from the immature coloring to an often totally different mature coloring. The change is generally common to both sexes. *Size:* differs according to species; many over $6\frac{1}{2}$ ft (2 m).
Environment Typical coral fish. *Temperature:* according to species; one must make the adjustments indicated for fish of similar origin. *pH:* over 8. *Density:* in accordance with temperature. *Illumination:* good lighting, but for some species a subdued light is sufficient. *Substrate:* deep sandy bottom.
Feeding In natural surroundings, they feed on hard corals. Pieces are bitten off with the "parrot's bill" and ground up with the solid teeth in the throat. The family thus plays a very important role in the destruction of coral reefs. Many parrot fishes sleep in a coating of mucus, buried in sand.
Biology *Behavior:* active swimmers, always in motion. *Reproduction:* no reports of breeding in aquaria. *Social life:* mostly sociable, at any rate as young fish. *Compatibility:* the most sociable parrot fish species can be kept with other fishes.

167 POLKA-DOT GROUPER
Chromileptes altivelis

Family Serranidae.
Distribution Tropical Indo-Pacific.
Description *Shape:* very elegant variation of normal grouper shape: snout elongated, its upper profile concave. Very large dorsal fin. *Color:* ground color pale brown; round dark spots on whole body and all fins. *Size:* 20 in (50 cm). *Sexual differences:* unknown.
Environment *Temperature:* 73–77 °F (23–25 °C). *pH:* about 8. *Density:* about 1.020. *Illumination:* good lighting. *Furnishings:* large tank with plenty of opportunity for shelter.
Feeding Predatory, fish-eater.
Biology *Behavior:* continually on the move with a very graceful gliding motion. Propulsion mainly by the big, paddlelike pectoral fins, which are constantly in motion when the fish is stationary. *Reproduction:* unknown in captivity. *Social life and compatibility:* territorial, solitary; but can be kept in a tank with companions that are not too small.

168 BLUE DAMSELFISH
Chromis chromis

Family Pomacentridae.
Distribution Mediterranean.
Description *Shape:* characteristic perchlike silhouette with swallow tail and large pectoral fins. *Color:* ground coloring, at a short distance, gold-brown with dark edges to the scales; at a greater distance blue-black with appearance of particularly deeply forked caudal fin owing to a white border on the cutout. Young, intense blue-violet. *Size:* 5 in (12 cm). *Sexual differences:* unknown.
Environment Rocky coasts, piers, the steep shores of islands. *Temperature:* 62–70 °F (17–21 °C). *pH:* about 8. *Density:* about 1.025. *Illumination:* subdued lighting. *Furnishings:* vertical structures with caves.
Feeding Plankton feeder. Will do well in the aquarium on chopped meat.
Biology *Behavior:* territorial schooling. In July the males occupy nests of 3–3½ in (8–9 cm) between medium-sized stones on pebbly bottoms and sparse growths of *Zostera* at depths of 3–20 ft (1–6 m). *Reproduction:* not yet achieved in the aquarium. The males clean stones and display before the approaching females. *Social life:* lively, peaceable. *Compatibility:* can be kept only with other fishes that are not too large; best in species tank.

169 GAIMARD'S WRASSE
Coris gaimardi

Family Labridae.

Distribution Tropical Indian and Pacific oceans.

Description The species changes its coloration during development. Young specimens have a red background color decorated with a few white spots with thin black borders (see top right). When fish has grown to $3\frac{1}{2}$–4 in (9–10 cm) long, its transitional coloring is indicated by the fading red background and the growing black borders around the white spots (center). In the adult fish, only a portion of the dorsal and anal fins is red. The rest is brown to olive green decorated with small black spots and greenish stripes (see bottom right). *Size:* up to 8 in (20 cm). *Sexual differences:* unknown.

Environment *Temperature:* 75–80 °F (24–27 °C). *pH:* over 8. *Density:* around 1.023. *Illumination:* good. *Substrate and furnishings:* structures of stone and rock fragments over a thin layer of sand.

Feeding Small animals. The young fish easily get used to aquarium food. In their natural state the adults feed mainly on mollusks and crustaceans.

Biology *Behavior:* lively fish, living alone when adult. Sometimes, as in the case of the Mediterranean rainbow wrasse, *C. julis,* wrasses spend their time buried under the sand, with only the mouth and eyes showing. However, if a fish stays buried too long, it means that it is ill. *Reproduction:* unknown in captivity. *Social life:* very peaceable. *Compatibility:* can be kept happily with other species.

170 RAINBOW WRASSE
Coris julis

Family Labridae.

Distribution Mediterranean; eastern Atlantic from the Gulf of Guinea to the coasts of Europe.

Description *Shape:* fusiform, elongated body, slightly compressed. In old males the first three spiny rays of the dorsal fin are longer than the rest of the fin. *Color:* the fish first goes through a prolonged female phase, then a short transitional phase, to finish up with a long male phase. The male coloring is greatly different from that of the female—so much so that at one time the two sexes were thought to belong to different species: the males to *C. julis* (bottom photo) and the females to *C. giofredi.* The young and female fish are multicolored: brown, greenish or orange on top, with a longitudinal red or orange band. This has wavy or zigzag edges and is interrupted by a long black, blue or brown marking behind the pectoral fins. *Size:* up to 10 in (25 cm). *Sexual differences:* protogynous; see above.

Environment Coastal fish, down to 400 ft (120 m) over algae, sand and mud. *Temperature:* 64–70 °F (18–21 °C). *pH:* about 8. *Density:* about 1.025. *Illumination:* soft. *Substrate and furnishings:* smooth layer of sand and hiding places.

Feeding Mainly on mollusks and crustaceans. Occasionally takes organic detritus from the bottom.

Biology *Behavior:* territorial; will frequently clean up its surroundings. Sometimes it will bury itself in the bottom. *Reproduction:* spawning time is in June and July. The eggs are pelagic; hence breeding in the aquarium is impossible. *Social life:* should be kept as single specimens in a tank, or in small numbers. *Compatibility:* can be kept easily with other species.

171 AXILLARY WRASSE
Crenilabrus mediterraneus

Family Labridae.
Distribution Mediterranean and in the Atlantic from Morocco to Portugal, off Madeira and the Azores.
Description *Shape:* body elongated, rather compressed, with deep caudal peduncle. Snout broad and thick. Thick lips, upper jaw having two large, prominent teeth. *Color:* both sexes have a large black or dark red-brown patch on the base of the pectoral fins and a large but indistinctly bordered brown patch on the caudal peduncle. Male brightly colored: back brown with green luster, sides red-brown or red with pale longitudinal stripes, belly and throat blue. Cheeks red with some blue and yellow lines. Vertical fins yellow, orange at the base, green-blue at the tips, with a number of blue and green eyespots. Females less bright. *Size:* up to 6 in (16 cm). *Sexual differences:* urogenital papilla small and colorless in males, prominent and black in females.
Environment Feeds on vegetation in shallow water. *Temperature:* 64–70 °F (18–21 °C). *pH* about 8. *Density:* about 1.025. *Illumination:* plenty of light. *Furnishings:* swimming room and sheltering places.
Feeding Eats echinoderms, other invertebrates.
Biology *Behavior:* active, territorial, quite peaceable. *Reproduction:* spawns end of spring into summer. *Social life:* territorial but sociable. *Compatibility:* can be kept successfully with other peaceable fishes.

172 PEACOCK WRASSE
Crenilabrus tinca

Family Labridae.
Distribution Mediterranean, Black Sea and Atlantic off the coasts of Morocco and the Iberian peninsula.
Description *Shape:* body elongated, much compressed; head long, with pointed snout and flat dorsal profile. *Color:* the male is brighter and more colorful: body dark green with golden sheen, belly yellow, cheeks similar, generally with golden sheen. Body and gill covers have red and blue spots in three or four longitudinal rows. A large bluish spot in front of the eye, a large greenish-brown or black patch below the pectoral fins and on the caudal peduncle a black patch that turns blue in summer. In maturity five dark spots on the back, three on the pelvic fins. Female has a dark back, light red-brown flanks, gray belly. Cheeks and the lower area of the gill covers silver-gray, lips gray-white. A small red-brown spot on the caudal peduncle. *Size:* up to 14 in (35 cm). *Sexual differences:* see above.
Environment Seaweed and algae. *Temperature:* 64–70 °F (18–21 °C). *pH:* about 8. *Density:* about 1.025. *Furnishings:* swimming room and hiding places.
Feeding Thought to feed mainly on echinoderms and other small invertebrates. Not many reports from aquaria.
Biology *Behavior:* territorial, very peaceable. *Reproduction:* nests in algae. *Social life:* keep in a small group. *Compatibility:* can be kept together with other fishes.

173 THREE-SPOT DAMSELFISH
Dascyllus trimaculatus

Family Pomacentridae.
Distribution Tropical Indo-Pacific.
Description *Shape:* perchlike fish, almost circular; mouth small, eyes large; the greatly curved profile of the upper part of the head gives it a snub-nosed look. Spiny part of the dorsal fin very long, anal fin broad. *Color:* dark, nearly black, with a white spot on the forehead and one on each side below the rear section of the spiny dorsal fin. *Size:* up to 6 in (15 cm). *Sexual differences:* unknown.
Environment Reef-dweller. *Temperature:* 75–82 °F (24–28 °C). *pH:* over 8. *Density:* about 1.023. *Illumination:* good light. *Furnishings:* plenty of hiding places in stone and coral structures.
Feeding In the reef eats mainly plankton. Accustom to brine shrimps; then quite easy to look after.
Biology *Behavior:* lives over crevices in branched coral. Sometimes also goes into sea anemones. When frightened turns pale. *Reproduction:* becomes reddish gray when spawning. The eggs are laid in clumps of coral or on stones, and one parent guards the spawn until hatching occurs. No report yet of a successful brood in captivity. *Social life:* quite peaceable but needs plenty of space. *Compatibility:* not to be put together with larger fishes.

---

174 ZEBRA TURKEY FISH
Brachirus zebra

Family Scorpaenidae.
Distribution Indian Ocean and in the Pacific as far as the China Sea and Polynesia.
Description *Shape:* perchlike, with very high, long fins; spiny dorsal fin with the membrane divided down to the base. A long cirrus above the eye. *Color:* ground color reddish, with reddish-black or brown vertical stripes—two or three on the head, six or seven on the body and caudal peduncle. At least five rows of dark-brown spots on all unpaired fins; membranes otherwise transparent. Several rows of half-moon or chevron-shaped spots or stripes on pectoral fins. White spot on shoulder. *Size:* up to 8 in (20 cm). *Sexual differences:* unknown.
Environment *Temperature:* 75–79 °F (24–26 °C). *pH:* at least 8.2 to 8.6. *Density:* about 1.023. *Illumination:* good light. *Furnishings:* stone structures with hiding places.
Feeding Voracious predator, fish-eater. Very easily accustomed to substitute diet.
Biology *Behavior:* similar to that of the large fire-fishes (*Pterois*). *Reproduction:* unknown in captivity. *Social life:* sociable with others of the same species. *Compatibility:* small fishes, except cleaner-fishes, will be eaten; tolerant of fishes of same or larger size.

175 SPINY PUFFER
Diodon holacanthus

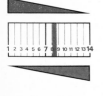

Family Diodontidae.
Distribution Cosmopolitan, in the tropical regions of the three oceans and expanding into their subtropical regions.
Description *Shape:* oval; the anal and dorsal fins a long way back in line with the caudal peduncle; the whole head and body covered with erectile, double-rooted spines. *Color:* quite variable; the upper side either completely dark or spotted with brown, the spots having a more or less distinct outline or being edged with white or light blue. *Size:* up to 16 in (40 cm). *Sexual differences:* female has much shorter spines, closer together. The young when $\frac{3}{4}$–2 in (2–4 cm) long have very long spines, as thin as bristles.
Environment *Temperature:* 75–82 °F (24–28 °C). *pH:* over 8. *Density:* about 1.023. *Illumination:* bright lighting. *Substrate and furnishings:* sandy bottom, room to swim, hiding places.
Feeding Eats virtually any animal food.
Biology *Behavior:* generally a slow, deliberate swimmer; may also bury itself in the sand to rest. *Reproduction:* unknown. *Social life:* quite sociable. *Compatibility:* takes very little notice of other fishes. When in danger, can very quickly pump itself full of water, and is then fully protected. (Never let it fill itself with air.) Very tolerant of other fishes.

176 PORCUPINE FISH
Diodon hystrix

Family Diodontidae.
Distribution Nearly all warm seas.
Description *Shape:* unmistakable balloon-shaped body. Large head, narrow gill opening behind the endlessly moving pectoral fins. The caudal fin is used as a brake and for rapid swimming. Very large eyes, which can also be moved separately. The long spines normally lie flat on the thick skin. *Color:* ground color yellowish, with brown spots or vertical bars. *Size:* up to 36 in (90 cm). *Sexual differences:* unknown.
Environment Requirements differ according to origin. You should find out both about the origin and about the water in which it was last kept. *Temperature:* 71–82 °F (22–28 °C).
Feeding In natural state crunches mollusks and crustaceans, but in captivity will take anything readily and in good quantities. Can be hand-fed.
Biology *Behavior:* constantly in motion, especially when young. When disturbed can blow itself up like a football with water; empties itself with belching and grunting noises. Make sure the fish does not pump itself full of air. *Reproduction:* unknown in captivity. *Social life:* generally peaceable. *Compatibility:* easily kept once acclimatized.

177 CLOUDED MORAY
Echidna nebulosa

Family Muraenidae.
Distribution Tropical Indo-Pacific.
Description *Shape:* extremely elongated body characteristic of eels; very strong, with naked, thick, rough skin. No pectoral or pelvic fins. Gill openings small, round, wide apart. Mouth opening wide, with powerful teeth. *Color:* ground color on the back light brown to orange, whitish down to the belly, tip of caudal fin orange. A group of two rows of star-shaped spots, consisting of a light (often orange) central spot and a network of connected dark lines. *Size:* 30 in (75 cm) long. *Sexual differences:* unknown.
Environment Lives in flat coastal zones in cracks, caves and coral blocks with plenty of crevices. *Temperature:* 72–82 °F (22–28 °C). *pH:* over 8. *Density:* about 1.025. *Illumination:* subdued lighting.
Feeding Predatory lurker, crepuscular, normally a-sleep during the day. Does well on aquarium food.
Biology *Behavior:* restful species not generally disturbed by sharing its tank. Be careful: the bite of all moray eels is painful. *Reproduction:* unknown in captivity. *Social life:* territorial, hence individuals best kept singly. *Compatibility:* easily grows accustomed to other occupants of the tank.

178 GROUPERS
Epinephelus spp.

Family Serranidae.
Distribution This genus is widely distributed in the subtropical and tropical zones of all the oceans, and also in the Mediterranean. Many species are recognized, from coastal waters to great depths.
Description *Shape:* see *E. aeneus. Color:* species vary from very colorful to almost monochrome. *Size:* medium-sized to huge. *Sexual differences:* all *Epinephelus* species are protogynous hermaphrodites — female when young and later becoming male; consequently, very large specimens are always male.
Environment Requirements differ according to species.
Feeding Mostly predatory, feeding on fish, large crustaceans and mollusks.
Biology *Behavior:* solitary and peaceable; active swimmers when young. *Reproduction:* does not take place in aquaria. *Social life:* generally only one individual in a tank. *Compatibility:* to be kept only with larger fishes. Exception: they readily allow themselves to be cleaned by cleaner-fishes.

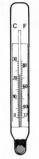

179 ALEXANDRIA GROUPER
Epinephelus alexandrinus

Family Serranidae.
Distribution Mediterranean, especially African coast, rarely south European; Atlantic along west coast of Africa.
Description *Shape:* typical grouper, resembling *E. aeneus*. Caudal fin rounded at the end. *Color:* ground color brown to violet, with four or five distinct longitudinal stripes on the back. *Size:* up to 16 in (40 cm). *Sexual differences:* unknown; protogynous (first female, then male).
Environment *Temperature:* 71 °F (22 °C). *pH:* about 8. *Density:* about 1.025. *Illumination:* subdued lighting. *Furnishings:* ample shelter.
Feeding Predatory; eats fish by preference but also crustaceans.
Biology *Behavior:* lurker, waiting in ambush for passing prey. In the swift attack the victim is overcome by being bitten or sucked in. *Reproduction:* probably not possible in the aquarium. *Social life:* solitary and territorial. *Compatibility:* can overpower fish three or four times its own length. Not really suitable for an indoor tank.

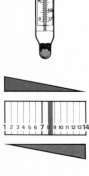

180 DUSKY PERCH or MEROU
Epinephelus guaza

Family Serranidae.
Distribution Mediterranean, eastern Atlantic.
Description *Shape:* grouper shape (see *E. aeneus*), fairly deep. Gill covers with three spines, no longitudinal bony ridge. Lower jaw very protruding. *Color:* olivaceous to red-brown, marbled, with a pattern of whitish dots on back and flanks. Two diagonal lines on the gill covers. Belly yellow; fins nearly black, almost always with a light edge. *Size:* up to 4 ft 7 in (140 cm). *Sexual differences:* unknown; protogynous hermaphrodite.
Environment Lives on rocky coasts, also on the edge of *Posidonia* beds; goes down to depths of several hundred feet. *Temperature:* 61–73 °F (18–23 °C), according to origin. *pH:* 8 or more. *Density:* 1.020 to 1.025. *Illumination:* subdued lighting. *Furnishings:* plenty of room for cover.
Feeding Lurker. Does not hunt for prey but captures it at the last moment by a sudden attack or by sucking it in.
Biology *Behavior:* large specimens particularly are quite peaceful. The younger fish are more mobile. With suitable feeding they grow very quickly and become too big for the home aquarium. *Reproduction:* does not take place in aquaria. *Social life:* unsociable, solitary. *Compatibility:* can be kept only with larger fishes.

181 BLUE-GIRDLED ANGELFISH
Euxiphipops navarchus

Family Pomacanthidae.
Distribution Indo-Australian archipelago, Philippines.
Description *Shape:* very similar to *Pomacanthus* but without the long point on the dorsal fin. *Color:* young are blue-black with bright blue vertical lines; the color becomes orange on the back. Remarkable contrast between the two ground colors: snout, throat and breast dark yellow to light brown with dark spots; a broad zone on the body and also on the dorsal and caudal fins bright orange with dark spots on the scales; the rest of the body dark blue. *Size:* up to 12 in (30 cm). *Sexual differences:* unknown.
Environment Requirements and data similar to *Chaetodon* species.
Feeding Probably lives on plant food.
Biology *Behavior:* territorial. *Reproduction:* probably not possible in aquaria. *Social life:* solitary. *Compatibility:* introduce with other fishes carefully, at first separating them by a pane of glass.

182 YELLOW-FACED ANGELFISH
Euxiphipops xanthometopon

Family Pomacanthidae.
Distribution Indo-Australian archipelago and surroundings as far as the Caroline Islands.
Description *Shape:* body shape much like that of *Pomacanthus*, but more elongated. *Color:* pectoral and pelvic fins, together with a narrow area round the eye and nostrils, golden brown; snout, chin and cheeks marked with a strong blue network pattern. Nape dark olive, ground color of the body light olive, each scale marked with dark olive to blue in the center. Dorsal fin yellow, toward the back orange like the caudal fin. At the base of the last ray of the dorsal fin a black patch generally edged with light blue. *Size:* up to 16 in (40 cm). *Sexual differences:* unknown.
Environment *Temperature:* 73–84 °F (23–29 °C). *pH:* over 8.2. *Density:* 1.020–1.023. *Illumination:* good light. *Furnishings:* very big tank with a lot of good hiding places.
Feeding Plant food. Reckoned one of the most difficult species to adapt; it is best to begin with brine shrimps.
Biology *Behavior:* territorial, living individually or in pairs. *Reproduction:* unknown in captivity. *Social life:* only one individual per tank. *Compatibility:* together with other angelfishes and butterfly fishes.

183 LONG-NOSED BUTTERFLY FISH
Forcipiger flavissimus

Family Chaetodontidae.
Distribution Tropical Indo-Pacific.
Description *Shape:* the most extreme pincerlike snout in the family. Normal *Chaetodon* body shape. *Color:* markedly bright colors. A velvety black triangle from the tip of the snout through the eye to the beginning of the (colorless) pectoral fin, thence vertically to the first spine of the dorsal fin. Snout and throat below this triangle to the beginning of the pelvic fins bluish green; pelvic fins, rest of the body, caudal peduncle and vertical fins bright chrome yellow or golden, apart from a narrow blue-and-green line at the back and a black eyespot in the anal fin just under the caudal peduncle. *Size:* up to 6 in (16 cm). *Sexual differences:* unknown.
Environment Requirements and data similar to *Chaetodon* species.
Feeding Not a true polyp-eater; digs its food (animal) out of the narrowest crevices.
Biology *Behavior:* territorial. *Reproduction:* unknown in captivity. *Social life:* in natural state lives in pairs; keep singly in aquarium. *Compatibility:* introduce carefully and observe the reactions of companions.

184 FAIRY BASSLET
Gramma loreto

Family Grammidae.
Distribution Bermuda, Bahamas to Venezuela.
Description *Shape:* small, perchlike fish with round outline to top of head and elongated pelvic fins. *Color:* its double coloring makes it unmistakable: the front two-thirds of the body (including the spiny sections of the anal and dorsal fins) is bright magenta, the rear third lemon yellow. A black stripe extends diagonally from the snout backward through the eye. There is a black spot on the foremost spine of the dorsal fin. *Size:* up to 2 in (5 cm). *Sexual differences:* unknown.
Environment Lives in hiding in caves and cracks and under rocky ledges. *Temperature:* 79–82 °F (26–28 °C). *pH:* at least 8. *Density:* about 1.025. *Illumination:* subdued lighting. *Furnishings:* many hiding places.
Feeding Needs small, live food; generally very particular. Try brine shrimps.
Biology *Behavior:* shy and territorial, very unsociable; few specimens in one tank. *Reproduction:* well cared for, they will soon begin their mating displays and spawning; but there are problems in their care. They easily get sick and are sensitive to acid water. *Social life:* test how many individuals will share a territory. *Compatibility:* best in species tank.

185 SIX-LINE GROUPER
Grammistes sexlineatus

Family Grammistidae.
Distribution Tropical Indian and Pacific oceans.
Description *Shape:* body high-backed and squat, scales very small, skin very slimy. *Color:* ground color very dark brown, almost black, often with a slight bluish cast. Fish is easily distinguished from almost all other groupers by its pattern: three to nine yellowish longitudinal stripes from head to caudal peduncle, their number increasing with age. *Size:* up to 10 in (25 cm). *Sexual differences:* unknown.
Environment *Temperature:* 75–82 °F (24–28 °C). *pH:* about 8. *Density:* about 1.025. *Illumination:* subdued lighting. *Furnishings:* many opportunities for hiding places.
Feeding Predatory, extremely voracious; can swallow fishes as long as its own body. In captivity readily accepts fish and beef heart.
Biology *Behavior:* territorial. In captivity tough and long-lived; specimens of this species have been kept in an aquarium for more than ten years. *Reproduction:* unknown in captivity. *Social life:* solitary. *Compatibility:* can be kept with larger fishes only.
Warning When caught can exude a poisonous secretion which quickly kills other fishes.

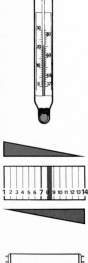

186 MADEIRA ROCKFISH
Scorpaena maderensis

Family Scorpaenidae.
Distribution Azores, Madeira, and Canary and Cape Verde Islands.
Description *Shape:* typical for a scorpion fish (see *Scorpaena scrofa*); body fairly compressed. A deep pit at back of head. Preoperculum with five strong spines, and two very distinct spines on the gill cover. Caudal fin short and square-cut. Wide fan-shaped pectoral fins. *Color:* pale red, with irregular vertical stripes of red or a mixture of red and brown from the front of the dorsal fin to the front of the anal fin. The soft-rayed section and the front edges of the pelvic and anal fins lined with white. Head light red, gill covers with a blue-black spot. *Size:* about 5 in (13 cm). *Sexual differences:* unknown.
Environment *Temperature:* 68–71 °F (20–22 °C). *pH:* over 8. *Density:* about 1.023. *Illumination:* subdued lighting. *Furnishings:* stones, hiding places.
Feeding In natural surroundings eats fish and shellfish.
Biology *Behavior:* an inshore fish of the sea bottom, peaceable, generally lying on its favorite resting place; seldom swims. Young more active. *Reproduction:* does not take place in aquaria. *Social life:* territorial but sociable if given enough room. *Compatibility:* not to be kept with smaller species.

187 PENNANT BUTTERFLY FISH
Heniochus acuminatus

Family Chaetodontidae.
Distribution Tropical Indo-Pacific.
Description *Shape:* similar to *Chaetodon* but with longer forceps-like snout, and in young fish elongated dorsal-fin spines drawn out like a pennant. *Color:* ground color of head, body and dorsal-fin pennant white; caudal fin and soft part of dorsal fin yellow; pectoral fins yellowish. Two black or dark brown vertical bars, the first from the front part of the dorsal fin over the base of the pectoral fins to the belly and over the pelvic fins, the second parallel with it over the rear part of the spiny dorsal fin to the rear of the body and the hind section of the anal fin. The belly often completely dark. *Size:* up to 8 in (20 cm). *Sexual differences:* unknown.
Environment *Temperature:* 75–82 °F (24–28 °C). *pH:* over 8. *Density:* about 1.023. *Illumination:* strong lighting. *Furnishings:* reproduction of reef; especially plenty of free space for swimming.
Feeding Similar to the *Chaetodon* species but also animal plankton.
Biology *Behavior:* active school fish, living more in open water than the reef-bound butterfly fishes. *Reproduction:* unknown in captivity. *Social life:* live in large schools. *Compatibility:* a small school alone can fill an ordinary commercial tank.

---

188 COMMON SEA HORSE
Hippocampus guttulatus

Family Syngnathidae.
Distribution In the Mediterranean (forms a separate geographical species in the Black Sea) and the tropical and temperate zones of the Atlantic.
Description *Shape:* unmistakable—the universally known sea horse. Snout as long as the head; head and body covered with numerous threadlike flaps of skin. *Color:* normally gray-black or gray-brown to brown, with darker or lighter dots, patches or marbling. Occasional red specimens. *Size:* up to 5 in (12 cm); rarely, as much as 6 in (15 cm). *Sexual differences:* see *H. kuda.*
Environment Eelgrass and algae near coasts. *Temperature:* room temperature, 68–71 °F (20–22 °C). Fish from the Black Sea (i.e., *H. microstephanus* Slastenenko) are much hardier and can withstand temperatures ranging between 50 and 86 °F (10–30 °C). *pH:* over 8. *Density:* about 1.025. *Illumination:* not-too-harsh lighting. *Furnishings:* vertical and horizontal structures for the fish to cling to absolutely essential.
Feeding Feeds on plankton and should be given this in small portions.
Biology *Behavior:* similar to *H. kuda. Reproduction:* breeding and raising of young has been successful. At spawning time this sea horse turns light yellow-ocher. *Social life and compatibility:* comparable to *H. kuda.*

189 SEA HORSE
Hippocampus hudsonius

Family Syngnathidae.
Distribution West Atlantic from Florida north to New York.
Description *Shape:* sea horse shape; body surrounded by numerous hard, bony rings; threadlike attachments to body in young are lost in adults. All sea horses are very hard to see in natural surroundings. *Color:* normally dark grayish or brownish; rarely, red, yellow or white specimens. *Size:* 6 in (15 cm); rarely, as much as 8 in (20 cm). One of the larger species. *Sexual differences:* see *H. kuda*.
Environment Eelgrass and patches of algae. *Temperature:* 69–75 °F (20–24 °C). *pH:* over 8. *Density:* about 1.023. *Illumination:* not-too-intense lighting. *Furnishings:* vertical or horizontal structures in the aquarium for the fish to attach itself to.
Feeding Feeds on plankton; like all sea horses, must have living food.
Biology See *H. kuda*. Very easy to keep.

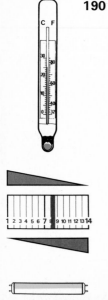

190 GOLDEN SEA HORSE
Hippocampus kuda

Family Syngnathidae.
Distribution Tropical Indo-Pacific.
Description *Shape:* sea horse shape. Characteristics of the species: snout of medium length; a low, five-pointed crest on the head; spines of various lengths on the body rings; generally entirely without skin flaps. *Color:* ground color changes from ivory white to yellow ocher, often with light or dark spots or stripes. In intense light the fish gradually turns pale. *Size:* up to 10 in (25 cm); most individuals considerably smaller. *Sexual differences:* males have brood pouch.
Environment Lives in seaweed beds in fairly calm water. *Temperature:* about 77 °F (25 °C). *pH:* at least 8. *Density:* about 1.023. *Illumination:* bright to moderate lighting. *Substrate:* needs bottom growth to which it can attach itself (stalks of algae, etc.).
Feeding Needs plenty of food in relation to its size — e.g., 10 young guppies a day.
Biology *Behavior:* mostly swimming upright, propelling itself with dorsal fin. Color change is also an indication of "mood." *Reproduction:* the female lays its eggs in a brood pouch on the belly of the male. *Social life:* several specimens can be kept well together. *Compatibility:* only with equally peaceful species such as other sea horses and pipefishes or the still more delicate shrimpfishes (Centriscidae).

191 RED SQUIRRELFISH
Holocentrus ruber

Family Holocentridae.
Distribution Tropical Indo-Pacific.
Description *Shape:* perchlike, the spiny section of the dorsal fin having widely separated spines. Snout short and pointed, eyes very large. Gill cover has several spines, the longest on the preoperculum. *Color:* occasionally bright red, more commonly dark red-brown, with silvery longitudinal stripes. The top third of the spiny dorsal fin is dark, as is the anal fin. *Size:* 8 in (20 cm). *Sexual differences:* unknown.
Environment Lives in coral reefs under overhanging coral branches or in caves. *Temperature:* 73–82 °F (23–28 °C). *pH:* at least 8. *Density:* about 1.020. *Illumination:* subdued lighting. *Furnishings:* many refuge holes.
Feeding Predatory; in natural state feeds on crustaceans and small fishes. Also accepts substitute foods.
Biology *Behavior:* crepuscular lurkers; they will actively search for food if the lighting is dimmed. They should in any case be given caves and crevices, preferably made to open out toward the display side. *Reproduction:* unknown in captivity. *Social life:* quite sociable; several individuals can be kept together. *Compatibility:* since they are predators, small fish and shellfish should not be kept in the same tank.

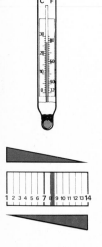

192 SPINY SQUIRRELFISH
Holocentrus spinifer

Family Holocentridae.
Distribution Tropical Indo-Pacific.
Description *Shape:* plump, high-backed and compressed; caudal peduncle slender. Spines on the preoperculum greatly elongated. *Color:* mostly brilliant red, underside silver-orange. Spiny section of dorsal fin uniform ruby red, soft part red-orange to yellowish. Caudal fin dark red, turning to orange at the back edge. Pectoral, pelvic and anal fins yellowish. *Size:* up to 18 in (45 cm). *Sexual differences:* unknown.
Environment *Temperature:* 75–82 °F (24–28 °C). *pH:* over 8. *Density:* something over 1.020. *Illumination:* subdued lighting. *Furnishings:* plenty of hiding places in and under which this crepuscular fish can shelter.
Feeding Predatory; see *H. ruber.*
Biology *Behavior:* in natural state lives under shelter all day; a crepuscular and nocturnal predator that eats crustaceans, mollusks and fishes. *Reproduction:* unknown in captivity. *Social life:* best kept in a school. *Compatibility:* quite sociable, but not with smaller fishes.

193 GREEN WRASSE
Labrus viridis

Family Labridae.
Distribution Mediterranean; Atlantic coast as far as the Bay of Biscay.
Description *Shape:* head and body a very long oval. Both the dorsal fin and the anal fin are quite long. *Color:* generally a yellowish green, more or less dark on the back and top of the head. Flanks, belly and throat increasingly yellowish, with white spots. A shining white or silvery stripe, which disappears with increasing age, from eye to caudal fin. Occasionally with reddish tinge and brownish clouding, and yellow or orange vermiculations enclosing green patches on flanks, throat and belly. *Size:* up to 18 in (47 cm). *Sexual differences:* females not so highly colored.
Environment Lives on rocks and in coastal vegetation. *Temperature:* 64–70 °F (18–21 °C); unheated tank. *pH:* about 8. *Density:* about 1.025. *Illumination:* plenty of light. *Furnishings:* adequate refuge holes and generous swimming room.

Feeding Carnivorous; in natural surroundings eats fishes and crustaceans. Easy to feed.
Biology *Behavior:* territorial. *Reproduction:* spawns in winter and spring, on algae. *Social life:* aggressive when in territorial state. *Compatibility:* not to be kept together with small fishes.

---

194 LONG-HORNED COWFISH
Lactoria cornuta

Family Ostraciidae.
Distribution Tropical Indo-Pacific.
Description *Shape:* unique, with bony armor, leaving only the snout, eyes, fins, gill opening and anus uncovered. Cross section of body at the middle point almost triangular; in front of and above the eyes two long, pointed bony cones pointing forward and upward, and two similar bones in extension of the lower side of the body in front of the anal fin. The caudal fin grows relatively longer as the fish grows older. Midline of the back may or may not have a very short spine. *Color:* ground color yellow to olivaceous, with turquoise spots. *Size:* up to 20 in (50 cm) long. *Sexual differences:* unknown.
Environment *Temperature:* 75–86 °F (24–30 °C). *pH:* over 8. *Density:* 1.020–1.025. *Illumination:* bright lighting. *Substrate:* sandy with rocks or coral skeleton.
Feeding At first will accept only fresh, live food (*Artemia*, small fishes, etc.); after a difficult period of training will become tame enough to feed from the hand.
Biology *Behavior:* always moving, maneuvers like a little helicopter. *Reproduction:* unknown in captivity. *Social life:* peaceable but sensitive; see also *Ostracion.* *Compatibility:* not to be kept with curious or aggressive fishes.

195 FOX-FACE
Siganus vulpinus

Family Siganidae.
Distribution Southwest Pacific.
Description *Shape:* shows relationship to the surgeonfishes (Acanthuridae) —oval, strongly laterally compressed, with long anal and dorsal fins—but lacks the spines on the caudal peduncle. A peculiarity is that the snout is prominent and has a small mouth at the end of it. *Color:* upper part of the body and dorsal, anal and caudal fins vary from bright yellow to orange; the rest plain yellow but with diverse light and dark patterns. *Size:* up to 10 in (25 cm). *Sexual differences:* unknown.
Environment *Temperature:* 77–86 °F (25–30 °C). *pH:* over 8. *Density:* 1.018–1.023. *Illumination:* good lighting. *Substrate:* perhaps a sandy bottom.
Feeding Many kinds of live food, plus algae and lettuce. No special requirements.
Biology *Behavior:* lively, peaceable. When disturbed it points its dorsal fin toward the attacker; the spines are connected with venom glands at the base which make wounds painful. *Reproduction:* unknown in captivity. *Social life:* aggressive toward its own species. *Compatibility:* very sociable with other fishes.

196 BLUE-STRIPED SNAPPER
Lutjanus kasmira

Family Lutjanidae.
Distribution Tropical Indo-Pacific.
Description *Shape:* body perchlike but elongated. Dorsal fins connected. Very large head, forehead profile slightly curved, belly line almost horizontal. *Color:* ground color of body and fins canary yellow; from the area of the cheeks to the back and as far as the caudal peduncle four or five bright cobalt blue horizontal stripes, and a similar stripe in the middle of the dorsal fin. *Size:* 13–16 in (35–40 cm). *Sexual differences:* unknown.
Environment *Temperature:* 73–80 °F (23–27 °C). *pH:* about 8. *Density:* 1.020. *Illumination:* moderate lighting. *Furnishings:* lives on many kinds of coast, also on outer reefs, etc., so ledges and refuge holes required.
Feeding In natural surroundings, fishes and many kinds of crustaceans.
Biology *Behavior:* not very active, with feeding territory; in the wild state lives in loose schools under cover from the surf. *Reproduction:* unknown in captivity. *Social life:* in the aquarium often very vicious toward individuals of its own species. *Compatibility:* can be kept only with other fishes of the same size. Be careful when introducing to tank.

197 EMPEROR SNAPPER
Lutjanus sebae

Family Lutjanidae.
Distribution Tropical Indo-Pacific.
Description *Shape:* powerful and compact, large head. Belly profile horizontal, head profile rising fairly steeply. *Color:* ground color whitish to reddish, with three broad red to dark brown vertical bands sweeping obliquely over the body. *Size:* up to 39 in (1 m). *Sexual differences:* unknown.
Environment Lives in calm areas of reef. *Temperature:* 75–82 °F (24–28 °C). *pH:* over 8. *Density:* about 1.025. *Illumination:* moderate to strong lighting. *Furnishings:* shelters and hiding places; be careful during acclimatization.
Feeding Predatory but by no means exclusively fish-eating; feeds also on crustaceans and other invertebrates. In the tank they will accept any kind of meat; easy to raise, but grow very quickly and are soon too big for the average tank.
Biology *Behavior:* fairly quiet; swim little and not far. *Reproduction:* probably not possible in aquaria. *Social life:* best in a school, but then of course only in a large (display) tank. In captivity become aggressive if cramped for room and are a danger to weaker fishes. *Compatibility:* not to be kept with much smaller fishes.

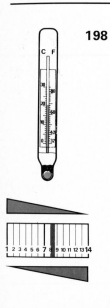

198 COMMON MORAY
Muraena helena

Family Muraenidae.
Distribution Whole Mediterranean, subtropical coasts of the eastern Atlantic.
Description *Shape:* powerful body, characteristically eel-shaped; lacks scales. Mouth large, snout pointed. The nostrils open just in front of the eyes; their raised flaps of skin look like little horns. *Color:* ground coloring brown to blackish brown, yellow marbling over the whole body. *Size:* 39–60 in (1–1.5 m) long. *Sexual differences:* unknown.
Environment Lives in caves and openings in rocks. *Temperature:* 64–70 °F (18–21 °C). *pH:* at least 8. *Density:* about 1.025. *Illumination:* subdued lighting. *Furnishings:* plenty of hiding places, such as jars, which it would also occupy in natural surroundings.
Feeding In ancient times it was kept in properly adapted pools on the coast. Becomes tame enough to take food (fish) from forceps.
Biology *Behavior:* crepuscular; sleeps by day, but can easily be roused to feed. *Reproduction:* does not take place in aquaria. *Social life:* best kept singly, and only in very roomy display tanks. Grows too big for the home aquarium. *Compatibility:* must be carefully accustomed to other occupants of the tank.

199 COMB GROUPER
Epinephelus ruber

Family Serranidae.
Distribution East and west coasts of the tropical and subtropical zone of Atlantic, western Mediterranean as far as Sicily.
Description *Shape:* characteristic grouper shape. *Color:* when immature, somewhat similar to the painted comber, *Serranus scriba*, but the vertical bars are broken up by round spots. Also three or four diagonal stripes, sloping down and back, from the eye to the edge of the gill cover. When mature, almost uniform in color. *Size:* up to 32 in (80 cm). *Sexual differences:* unknown.
Environment Rocky bottom. *Temperature:* 64–75 °F (18–24 °C) according to origin. *pH:* about 8. *Density:* up to 1.020. *Illumination:* moderate lighting. *Furnishings:* stones and holes for concealment.
Feeding Predatory; solely a fish-eater.
Biology *Behavior:* young very lively, but adults prefer to remain in the same spot. *Reproduction:* unknown in captivity. *Compatibility:* easily kept with larger fishes that do not form part of its diet.

200 BIGEYE SQUIRRELFISH
Myripristis murdjan

Family Holocentridae.
Distribution Tropical Indo-Pacific.
Description *Shape:* notably deep, much-compressed perchlike body; differs from *Holocentrus* in having no spine on the preoperculum. Huge eyes. *Color:* almost red; above the lateral line a suggestion of dark longitudinal lines. Fins reddish, the soft-rayed section of the dorsal and anal fins white and a black line behind. The front edge of the pelvic fins also white. A broad black vertical bar through the eye. *Size:* up to 12 in (30 cm). *Sexual differences:* unknown.
Environment Coral reefs. *Temperature:* 75–82 °F (24–28 °C). *pH:* at least 8. *Density:* about 1.025. *Illumination:* subdued lighting. *Furnishings:* many hiding places (caves, cracks, jars, etc.).
Feeding Predatory, in nature nocturnal. In dim light they will also take food by day.
Biology *Behavior:* nocturnal, schooling predators. *Reproduction:* unknown in captivity. *Social life:* several individuals can be kept together. *Compatibility:* quite peaceable, but not with small fishes.

201 FRECKLED or BLUE-SPOTTED BOXFISH
Ostracion meleagris

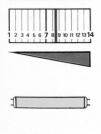

Family Ostraciidae.
Distribution Tropical Indo-Pacific.
Description *Shape:* body rectangular, confined in a suit of armor made of polygonal bony plates which leave openings only for the following parts: mouth, gills, eyes, fins and anus. No pelvic fins. *Color:* ground color variable, brown, green or dark brown, but always with a pattern of white dots. *Size:* up to 9 in (22 cm). *Sexual differences:* mature males have a convex, unspotted snout; the white spots on the sides are either larger than those on the back or absent altogether. Mature females (as in photograph) have a concave, spotted snout and similar small white spots on the back, sides and belly.
Environment *Temperature:* 75–82 °F (24–28 °C). *pH:* over 8.2 *Density:* 1.020–1.023. *Illumination:* good light. *Substrate and furnishings:* sandy bottom, plenty of swimming room and good shelter.
Feeding Difficult at first; eats small creatures mostly from the sand. Offer brine shrimps and other live crustaceans at first.
Biology *Behavior:* lively, always moving. *Reproduction:* unknown in captivity. *Social life:* peaceable and very sociable. *Compatibility:* suitable for keeping with companions, but skin is very thin and fragile.

---

202 BEAKED LEATHERJACKET
Oxymonacanthus longirostris

Family Balistidae.
Distribution Tropical Indo-Pacific.
Description *Shape:* elongated, compressed body. Snout very long, small mouth set on top. Two spines in front of the soft-rayed dorsal fin; the first, above the eye, has barbs, giving it a rough edge. Pelvic-fin spines erectile. Very small scales, with tiny spines pointing backward. *Color:* ground color gray-blue; three or four orange-yellow or orange-red longitudinal stripes over the snout; some six rows of orange-yellow or orange-red spots with dark borders along the body and caudal peduncle, a similarly colored patch in the area of the pelvic fins dotted with small, light-colored blue-framed spots. *Size:* up to 4 in (10 cm). *Sexual differences:* unknown.
Environment *Temperature:* 75–82 °F (24–28 °C). *pH:* 8.2–8.6. *Density:* about 1.023. *Illumination:* good lighting. *Substrate and furnishings:* sandy bottom, plenty of room to swim and shelters in the coral setting.
Feeding Specialized feeder on coral polyps. Very difficult to keep for any time.
Biology *Behavior:* in natural state adults live in pairs and young in small groups. *Reproduction:* unknown in captivity. *Social life:* even pairs keep their distance in natural state. *Compatibility:* tolerant of other fishes.

203 FLAG-TAIL SURGEONFISH
Paracanthurus hepatus

Family Acanthuridae.
Distribution Tropical Indo-Pacific.
Description *Shape:* body oval and compressed. Spikes on caudal peduncle erectile and very sharp. Very long dorsal fin and quite long anal fin. *Color:* much blue, black and yellow. Caudal fin yellow with black edge, the yellow extending onto the caudal peduncle in a wedge shape. A black mask over the eyes is connected with a palette-shaped black patch that includes the whole back and flanks down to the caudal peduncle. The rest of the body and the vertical fins are blue, paler toward the belly. Once the fish is 8 in (20 cm) long, the yellow gradually takes over; the belly may change through gray-violet to yellowish. The formerly blue vertical fins become olive green, the face greenish. *Size:* up to 10 in (25 cm). *Sexual differences:* unknown.
Environment *Temperature:* 75–82 °F (24–28 °C). *pH:* about 8. *Density:* about 1.025. *Illumination:* good lighting. *Furnishings:* plenty of free swimming space, some hiding places.
Feeding A grazer; needs plenty of vegetable food.
Biology *Behavior:* very fond of swimming and so often visible. *Reproduction:* probably impossible in captivity (see *Zebrasoma xanthurum*). *Social life:* intolerant of other members of its species and genus. *Compatibility:* be careful when putting with other fishes.

204 MUDSKIPPERS
Periophthalmus spp.

Family Gobiidae.
Distribution Red Sea, Indian Ocean, the Sunda Islands, Australia.
Description *Shape:* elongated, compressed at the caudal peduncle. Prominent spherical eyes. *Color:* different according to species, origin, age and sex. Generally marbled with white, gray, black and brown. *Size:* 5–10 in (12–25 cm) or more, according to species. *Sexual differences:* mostly evident in fin characteristics.
Environment Lives in estuaries and mangrove swamps. Amphibious. The related *Boleophthalmus* and *Periophthalmodon* live similarly; others (*Scartelaos*, etc.) live submerged at the waterline. *Temperature:* 79–86 °F (26–30 °C). *pH:* 8 or more. *Density:* brackish water, 1.010–1.015. *Illumination:* plenty of light. *Substrate and furnishings:* large, roomy, level tank, meticulously cleaned out, with a few inches of water, a thick bottom of soft sand and some flat islands of stone and branches (no sharp edges).
Feeding Eats mostly worms, and in natural surroundings many crustaceans. Needs a lot of food.
Biology *Behavior:* very active creatures. *Reproduction:* no species has yet bred in an aquarium. *Social life:* very quarrelsome; need plenty of room. *Compatibility:* can sometimes be kept with *Boleophthalmus*.

205 ROUND BATFISH
Platax orbicularis

Family Ephippidae.
Distribution Red Sea, Indian Ocean, western Pacific.
Description *Shape:* unmistakable shape, very much like the freshwater *Pterophyllum;* on a deep, oval body, huge dorsal and anal fins opposite each other. *Color:* uniform coloring broken only by irregular spots, little dots and a suggestion of vertical bars. Generally a dark brown or black vertical band through the eye. In adults the first two bars become very distinct. *Size:* up to 20 in (50 cm) long. *Sexual differences:* unknown.
Environment Prefers to live in the sea but can also penetrate into the brackish waters of estuaries. Salinity levels of no great importance. *Temperature:* 71–80 °F (22–27 °C).
Feeding Voracious and omnivorous; very long-living and trouble-free (specimens have been kept in captivity up to fourteen years).
Biology *Behavior:* very peaceful and calm, but easily scared. Should be given a tall tank and hiding places. *Reproduction:* unknown in captivity. *Social life:* preferably a few specimens together. *Compatibility:* preferably in a species tank.

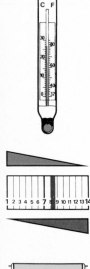

206 HARLEQUIN SWEETLIPS
Plectorhinchus chaetodonoides

Family Pomadasyidae.
Distribution Indo-Australian archipelago, west and central Pacific.
Description *Shape:* head large and round, body powerful. Spiny and soft-rayed dorsal fins joined, the spines greatly developed. Small mouth with noticeable lips, teeth narrow. Eleven or twelve spines in dorsal fin. *Color:* young and mature fishes have very different coloration. Young coloring: dark brown with large round white patches marked off with blackish brown. The brown coloring extends also to the fins. Caudal fin white with two brown spots. Adults are a uniform mid-brown with dark brown dots. *Size:* up to 36 in (90 cm). *Sexual differences:* unknown.
Environment *Temperature:* 75–82 °F (24–28 °C). *pH:* at least 8. *Density:* about 1.025. *Illumination:* moderate to subdued lighting. *Furnishings:* hiding places absolutely essential.
Feeding In natural surroundings live mainly on crepuscular invertebrates. Feed on small pieces.
Biology *Behavior:* crepuscular, often very quiet by day. *Reproduction:* unknown in captivity. *Social life:* sociable, at least when young. *Compatibility:* can be kept very successfully with peaceable companions.

207 RINGED EMPEROR ANGELFISH
Pomacanthus annularis

Family Chaetodontidae.
Distribution Indo-Australian archipelago; eastern Indian Ocean as far as Sri Lanka and India.
Description *Shape:* deep-bodied, compressed, dorsal and anal fins long, dorsal fins in adults extending to a point. *Color:* coloring of young practically indistinguishable from *P. maculosus* (q.v.). In the transition stage to adult coloring the fish first lose the thin vertical lines; instead there appear blue horizontal lines on the flanks. The stripes on the head of the young fish are the last to disappear. The final coloring has a yellow-brown to olivaceous ground. From the base of the dorsal fin obliquely over the side of the body to the hindmost corner of the dorsal fin run five or six bright blue longitudinal stripes. Between the pectoral fins and the front of the dorsal fin is a bright blue ring (from which the species gets its name). *Size:* up to 15 in (37 cm). *Sexual differences:* unknown.
Environment Reef-dweller. Data and requirements similar to *Chaetodon* species.
Feeding Browser. Special diet, especially the adults.
Biology *Behavior:* solitary, territorial. *Reproduction:* probably impossible in captivity. *Social life:* single specimen. *Compatibility:* be careful when introducing into already occupied tank.

208 EMPEROR ANGELFISH
Pomacanthus imperator

Family Chaetodontidae.
Distribution Wide areas of the tropical Indo-Pacific from east Africa and the Red Sea in the west to Polynesia in the east.
Description *Shape:* very much like that of *P. annularis*. *Color:* young fish deep blue with white or light blue concentric bands, the last of which forms a closed ring on the caudal peduncle. A similarly colored network pattern on the soft-rayed sections of the dorsal and anal fins. Adult fish have purple-brown to blue-green ground color, a black patch behind the head and a similarly colored band over forehead, eye and cheek, both edged with bright blue. A number of yellow horizontal lines along the flanks. Caudal fin bright orange. *Size:* up to 14 in (35 cm) long. *Sexual differences:* unknown.
Environment Reef-dweller. Data and requirements similar to *Chaetodon* species.
Feeding Browser. Will more easily adapt to substitute diet when young.
Biology *Behavior:* territorial. *Reproduction:* probably impossible to breed. *Social life:* solitary. Keep individually. *Compatibility:* take care when introducing to other species.

209 SPOTTED ANGELFISH
Pomacanthus maculosus

Family Chaetodontidae.
Distribution Red Sea, east African coast, Arabian coast as far as Persian Gulf.
Description *Shape:* typical of the genus; deep-bodied. *Color:* young are almost indistinguishable from the ringed emperor angelfish, *P. annularis*: dark blue with many differently marked light blue vertical bars; caudal fin light. A light sickle-shaped mark on the upper half of the flank appears when fish reaches 1½ in (4 cm) length. The bars may be retained up to a length of 6 in (15 cm). Exceptionally colored specimens have gray-blue or gray-violet ground color, dark blue-violet toward the tail. On the neck, back of the head and front of the body, small dark blue spots like commas. On the sides of the body a large, irregularly edged, rather crescent-shaped patch from the middle of the dorsal fin to the belly. *Size:* up to 12 in (30 cm). *Sexual differences:* unknown.
Environment *Temperature:* 75–82 °F (24–28 °C). *pH:* about 8. *Density:* about 1.025. *Illumination:* good lighting. *Furnishings:* reproduction of reef.
Feeding In natural surroundings small pieces of sponge and algae. Difficult to keep.
Biology *Behavior:* territorial, solitary. *Reproduction:* probably impossible in the aquarium. *Compatibility:* angelfishes are almost impossible to keep with one another.

210 ZEBRA ANGELFISH
Pomacanthus semicirculatus

Family Chaetodontidae.
Distribution Indian Ocean, Red Sea, Indo-Australian archipelago, western Pacific.
Description *Shape:* very similar to *P. maculosus*. *Color:* the immature coloring changes. White and some light blue curved stripes, convex toward the front, on a dark brown to dark blue ground change into an entirely different pattern: body yellowish with dark spots, head black, lips white, unpaired fins dark blue with small white dots. The vertical bars may also still be present in this transitional stage. In mature fish the ground coloring is vivid green to brownish, the head often lighter. A number of spots on the flanks, half-moon-shaped, circular or rhomboidal. *Size:* over 12 in (30 cm). *Sexual differences:* unknown.
Environment *Temperature:* 75–82 °F (24–28 °C). *pH:* 8.2–8.5. *Density:* about 1.025. *Illumination:* good lighting. *Furnishings:* provide hiding places.
Feeding Browser; young fish are easier to accustom to substitute diet.
Biology *Behavior:* if it is to be seen much, needs plenty of swimming room. Territorial and aggressive. *Reproduction:* unknown in captivity. *Social life:* only single specimens or possibly one adult and a more immature specimen together. *Compatibility:* carefully accustom to companions in tank.

211 BLUE DAMSELFISH
Pomacentrus caeruleus

Family Pomacentridae.
Distribution Tropical Indo-Pacific.
Description *Shape:* very much like *Chromis chromis* but more elongated. Edge of the operculum is toothed. *Color:* orange-yellow, brown to bluish, in good health a beautiful blue, the scales having light lines. Caudal fin yellowish white to yellow. Damselfish species are very hard to distinguish alive. *Size:* up to 5 in (12 cm). *Sexual differences:* unknown.
Environment *Temperature:* 75–82 °F (24–28 °C). *pH:* over 8. *Density:* 1.023. *Illumination:* lighting medium to strong. *Furnishings:* structures of dead branched coral, stones, etc.
Feeding Feeds on small living food, still necessary during acclimatization; later many kinds of animal food.
Biology *Behavior:* active; quick to take refuge under cover, but can often be seen. *Reproduction:* unknown in captivity. *Social life:* quick to bite. *Compatibility:* can be kept with other fishes of the same size.

212 BROWN TRIGGERFISH
Pseudobalistes fuscus

Family Balistidae.
Distribution Tropical Indo-Pacific.
Description *Shape:* typical triggerfish, somewhat elongated, throat profile slightly rounded, caudal fin extending to a point. *Color:* various ground colors, mostly light brownish to orange, but also light green. Light blue horizontal stripes running in and out of one another to form a labyrinthine pattern over the whole body and fins. Lips and tips of pectoral, dorsal and anal fins striped yellowish. Can also be uniform in color or speckled. *Size:* 20 in (50 cm). *Sexual differences:* unknown.
Environment *Temperature:* 75–77 °F (24–25 °C). *pH:* about 8. *Illumination:* good lighting. *Furnishings:* plenty of swimming room; hiding places essential.
Feeding Carnivorous; crunches mollusks, crustaceans and sea urchins.
Biology *Behavior:* active swimmer. *Reproduction:* impossible in tank. *Social life and compatibility:* some specimens are extremely unsociable; best therefore to try them singly before experimenting with tank companions.

213 ORANGE-TOP PSEUDOCHROMIS
Pseudochromis flavivertex

Family Pseudochromidae.
Distribution Tropical Indo-Pacific.
Description *Shape:* elongated, perchlike shape, compressed, with very long dorsal and anal fins. *Color:* distinctly bicolored: from the lower lip, the mouth and the forehead over the whole of the back including the dorsal fin and the upper edge of the caudal peduncle and caudal fin, a brilliant chrome yellow; all parts of the body and fins below that blue, sides of the belly paler or greenish, also the pelvic and anal fins and the bottom of the caudal fin. Pectoral fins very long and colorless. *Size:* under 4 in (10 cm). *Sexual differences:* unknown.
Environment In natural surroundings lives mostly in large numbers in bushy, branched coral skeletons. *Temperature:* 75–82 °F (24–28 °C). *pH:* at least 8. *Density:* 1.020–1.025. *Furnishings:* must have shelters in the form of bushy coral skeletons with many small cavities.
Feeding In natural surroundings, plankton; in the tank it will take finely chopped mussel or fish meat, *Mysis*, *Tubifex* and similar animal foods.
Biology *Behavior:* lives in schools under cover. Very active. *Reproduction:* unknown in captivity. *Compatibility:* not to be kept with very large fishes. Very peaceable.

214 LONG-HORNED LION-FISH
Pterois radiata

Family Scorpaenidae.
Distribution Tropical Indo-Pacific.
Description *Shape:* perchlike body with long, high fins, similar to *Brachirus* but with the rays of the pectoral fins unbranched and only the inner third joined with fin membrane. *Color:* from the snout to the throat, dull pinkish white or yellowish; ground color of body generally dark brown (sandy to blackish brown); sides of the body with six thin, shining white bars, partly forked on the back; two similar horizontal stripes on the caudal peduncle. A dark brown line through the eye from the eye cirrus to the interoperculum, also edged with white, and a similar line along the nape. Soft-rayed part of the dorsal and anal fins, and the caudal fin, spotted. *Size:* up to 8 in (20 cm). *Sexual differences:* unknown.
Environment *Temperature:* 75–78 °F (24–26 °C). *pH:* 8.2 and higher. *Density:* 1.027. *Illumination:* good light. *Furnishings:* stone structures.
Feeding Predatory, fish-eater.
Biology see under *P. volitans.*

215 RED FIRE-FISH; TURKEY FISH; LION-FISH
Pterois volitans

Family Scorpaenidae.
Distribution Tropical Indo-Pacific.
Description *Shape:* generic characteristics as for *P. radiata*. Species characteristics: long eye cirrus, twelve dorsal-fin spines as long as the body. *Color:* ground color pale reddish, numerous broad brown vertical bars on the body, three or four narrower bars on the head. Rows of black-brown spots on the unpaired fins; four or five rows of brown spots on the spiny section of the dorsal fin. A chalky white spot on the shoulder; often three or four similar spots on the lateral line. *Size:* up to 14 in (35 cm). *Sexual differences:* unknown.
Environment *Temperature:* 75–79 °F (24–26 °C). *pH:* about 8.2. *Density:* about 1.027. *Illumination:* good light. *Furnishings:* stone structures with holes.
Feeding A fiercely predatory fish-eater. Will soon get used to substitute diet if it is moved about as if alive.
Biology *Behavior:* a free swimmer. Forces small fishes into a corner with the help of its spread pectoral fins and then sucks them in and swallows them. *Reproduction:* unknown in captivity. *Social life:* several specimens can be kept together in a roomy tank. *Compatibility:* only with fishes of the same size or larger; voracious.

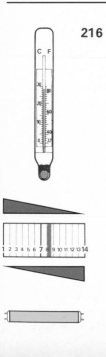

216 REGAL ANGELFISH
Pygoplites diacanthus

Family Chaetodontidae.
Distribution Tropical Indo-Pacific.
Description *Shape:* very similar to *Pomacanthus*. *Color:* the coloring of the young differs from that of the adult; the young fish have four light bars with dark outlines vertically across the flanks; on the rear part of the soft-rayed portion of the dorsal fin is a large dark patch. As the fish matures, the number of body bars increases and this patch disappears. Mature coloring: head blue-gray; snout, chin and breast area yellowish; ground color of the body bright orange-yellow with five to nine light blue vertical bars with dark outlines from back to belly; caudal fin bright yellow. *Size:* up to 10 in (25 cm). *Sexual differences:* unknown.
Environment *Temperature:* 79–84 °F (26–29 °C). *pH:* over 8. *Density:* 1.020–1.023. *Illumination:* good lighting. *Furnishings:* as for all angelfishes, very large tank with ample swimming room and plenty of shelter.
Feeding In natural state feeds on mollusks. Offer mainly mollusks, also crustaceans and *Tubifex*, etc. Plenty of vegetable foods. Vitamins once a week.
Biology *Behavior:* solitary, territorial. Very aggressive in the aquarium. *Reproduction:* unknown in captivity. *Social life:* single individual in very large tank. *Compatibility:* can be kept well with butterfly fishes and *Paracanthurus hepatus*.

217 PICASSO FISH
Rhinecanthus aculeatus

Family Balistidae.
Distribution Tropical Indo-Pacific.
Description *Shape:* head very large; typical triggerfish. Several rows of black spikes on caudal peduncle, curved toward the rear. *Color:* ground color variable but pattern constant: Generally a white, yellowish or yellow stripe from the opening of the mouth toward the back, giving the impression of a larger mouth. At its end this meets a vertical bar which leads over the eye and in front of which a yellow stripe extends. Iris and lips yellow, blue stripes on upper lip. A number of light diagonal stripes on the lower part of the flanks. Center of the body cloudy dark gray or dark brown; two indistinct diagonal lines. *Size:* 12 in (30 cm). *Sexual differences:* unknown.
Environment Likes calm water and sandy bottom. *Temperature:* 75–82 °F (24–28 °C). *pH:* about 8. *Density:* about 1.025. *Illumination:* good lighting. *Furnishings:* plenty of swimming room.
Feeding Once acclimatized eats various animal foods.
Biology *Behavior:* becomes tame enough to hand-feed, but a sudden shock may send it into a frenzy. Sleeps on its side. Blows food out of the sand. *Reproduction:* probably impossible in a tank. *Social life:* keep singly. *Compatibility:* best not together with other triggerfishes.

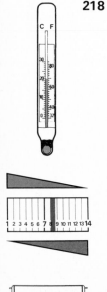

218 SMALL-SCALED SCORPION FISH
Scorpaena porcus

Family Scorpaenidae.
Distribution Mediterranean and eastern Atlantic.
Description *Shape:* oval, compressed body. Snout stumpy, convex, as broad as it is long. Mouth wide, lower jaw slightly projecting. A fleshy flap of skin above the eye. A number of bony spines on top of the head. *Color:* back and flanks brown, darkly marbled and spotted; underside paler. Three broad dark, marbled saddle patches over the back; often a dark spot between the seventh and ninth dorsal spines. Caudal fin has three dark vertical bars. The very broad pectoral fins, and the unpaired fins, marbled or having concentric rings of spots; pelvic fins light. *Size:* up to 12 in (30 cm). *Sexual differences:* unknown.
Environment *Temperature:* 64–73 °F (18–23 °C). *pH:* over 8. *Density:* 1.020–1.025. *Illumination:* subdued light. *Substrate:* sandy bottom with stones.
Feeding Predatory. In captivity takes only live food at first, but later any substitute diet that is moved about (strips of fish and lean meat, etc.).
Biology *Behavior:* adults stay almost continuously in the same place. *Reproduction:* spawns like *S. scrofa*. Breeding in captivity not recorded. *Social life:* quite sociable. *Compatibility:* can be kept successfully with fishes of similar size.

219 LARGE-SCALED SCORPION FISH
Scorpaena scrofa

Family Scorpaenidae.
Distribution Eastern Atlantic, Mediterranean.
Description *Shape:* body oval, compressed, somewhat elongated. Many spines on the head, and small flaps of skin on the chin and lower jaw. *Color:* pink to bright red; much darker on the back, which has four dark marbled patches, and lighter on the belly. Head marbled; jaw and underside with close-set dark spots and white vermiculations; shining white on chest and gill cover. All fins have irregular pattern of dark spots; spiny portion of the dorsal fin has a blackish patch. *Size:* up to 12 in (30 cm). *Sexual differences:* unknown.
Environment *Temperature:* 62–75 °F (17–24 °C). *pH:* at least 8. *Density:* about 1.020–1.025. *Furnishings:* stone structures with hiding places.
Feeding Predator, fish-eater, easy to feed in aquarium.
Biology *Behavior:* peaceful when adult. In natural surroundings it lies motionless. The young are more active, moving about and swimming more readily. *Reproduction:* has been known to spawn in large aquaria. Lays several thousand eggs in gelatinous strips. *Social life:* quite sociable. *Compatibility:* only with fishes of the same size and not too active.
Note The dorsal-fin spines have venom glands at their base. Their secretion causes very painful wounds.

---

220 AENEUS GROUPER
Epinephelus aeneus

Family Serranidae.
Distribution Mediterranean, West Africa.
Description *Shape:* longish; laterally compressed, most deeply in area of pectoral fins; caudal peduncle compressed; snout conical. Eyes as large as the mouth, those of the young positioned in the first third of the head. Mouth large, lower jaw protruding. Preoperculum with three or four sharply divergent spines, gill cover with two strong spines, the upper one longer. *Color:* brown, fins with some darker marbling or indistinct spots overall. Six dark vertical bands, wider than the spaces between them. A diagonal line from the eye backward to the preoperculum and suboperculum and a shorter, parallel line over the lower cheek area. *Size:* up to 32 in (82 cm). *Sexual differences:* unknown.
Environment *Temperature:* 64–74 °F (18–24 °C), according to origin. *pH:* above 8. *Density:* 1.020–1.025. *Illumination:* subdued light. *Furnishings:* plenty of hiding places.
Feeding Predatory, feeds on fishes and crustaceans.
Biology *Behavior:* young more active, older solitary. *Reproduction:* does not take place in captivity. *Social life:* best separately. *Compatibility:* only together with larger fishes.

221 PAINTED COMBER
Serranus scriba

Family Serranidae.
Distribution Mediterranean and eastern Atlantic from western France to Senegal.
Description *Shape:* highly elongated body shape, caudal fin slightly rounded. *Color:* a group of four to seven brownish vertical bands on a yellowish to reddish ground, growing darker toward the back. A large pale bluish to blue-violet patch on the belly. On snout, cheeks and gill cover, bluish and yellow-red flourishes which suggest Arabic writing. *Size:* 6–8 in (15–20 cm), according to origin. *Sexual differences:* unknown; hermaphrodite.
Environment Inhabits algae-covered rocks of the upper coastal zone. *Temperature:* 64–70 °F (18–21 °C). *pH:* about 8. *Density:* about 1.026. *Illumination:* moderate lighting. Needs hiding places.
Feeding Fish-eater; in natural state eats small fishes and also crustaceans.
Biology *Behavior:* peaceful, rather shy. *Reproduction:* does not take place in aquaria. *Social life:* solitary and territorial; to be kept singly. *Compatibility:* tolerant of not-too-small fishes.

222 BLACK-BLOTCHED TURRET FISH
Rhinesomus gibbosus

Family Ostraciidae.
Distribution Tropical Indo-Pacific
Description *Shape:* body cross-section distinctly triangular, coming to a point in the middle of the back. The side edges of the body have five distinct points angled backward: the first below the gill opening, the last from the front of the movable caudal peduncle. Another pair, over the eyes, form two small horns. Back rather arched, sides almost flat, sides of the belly somewhat concave. Very small gill slit. Lips thick, teeth brown. *Color:* gold-brown, often with darker marbling. The exterior structure and joints are clearly shown by the polygonal armor plates. *Size:* up to 10 in (25 cm). *Sexual differences:* unknown.
Environment *Temperature:* 77–86 °F (25–30 °C). *pH:* over 8. *Density:* about 1.023. *Illumination:* bright lighting. *Substrate and furnishings:* sandy bottom, stone or coral structures.
Feeding See *Lactoria cornuta*.
Biology *Behavior:* similar to *Lactoria cornuta*. *Reproduction:* unknown in captivity. *Social life:* peaceable but sensitive. *Compatibility:* not to be kept with rough or aggressive fishes.

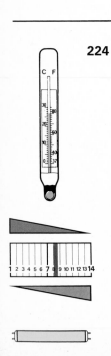

223 GUINEA-HEN WRASSE
Anampses meleagrides

Family Labridae.
Distribution Red Sea, Indian Ocean and western Pacific Ocean.
Description *Shape:* similar to *Thalassoma lunare*. Caudal fin cut off straight. *Color:* female coloration shown in photograph. In males, the dorsal and anal fins have several wavy horizontal blue lines, these fins lacking the eyespot in the soft portion; the caudal fin has a vertical, narrow, blue crescent-shaped mark, with an orange region and blue spots in front of it and a colorless area behind. *Size:* up to 12 in (30 cm). *Sexual differences:* see under *Color.*
Environment *Temperature:* 75–82 °F (24–28 °C). *pH:* over 8. *Density:* about 1.023. *Illumination:* good light. *Substrate and furnishings:* sandy bottom; stone structure or branched coral skeleton.
Feeding Feeds on small marine animals; best to accustom to live food and then add to the diet.
Biology *Behavior:* gliding swimming motion with tail dragged behind. *Reproduction:* unknown in captivity. *Social life:* apt to chase one another. Provide plenty of shelter. *Compatibility:* very peaceable toward other fishes.

224 MOON WRASSE
Thalassoma lunare

Family Labridae.
Distribution Tropical Indo-Pacific.
Description *Shape:* rather like the Mediterranean *T. pavo.* Caudal fin with extended outer rays making the shape of a crescent moon. *Color:* ground color blue-green. The caudal fin, except for the blue-green outer rays, brilliant yellow or orange, often divided by brown or red stripes. On the head, green, green-blue or blue stripes on a red ground, radiating from the eye. Pectoral fin blue, a red patch over the upper rays; pelvic fin greenish. The vertical fins, from the outer edge toward the middle of the body, green; bright blue and orange or red stripes. *Size:* up to 12 in (30 cm). *Sexual differences:* unknown.
Environment *Temperature:* 77–80 °F (25–27 °C). *pH:* over 8. *Density:* about 1.023. *Illumination:* good light. *Substrate and furnishings:* deep sandy bottom, some structures for shelter by day.
Feeding Feeds on small animals; quite easily adapted to substitute diet.
Biology *Behavior:* in nature found even in tidal pools, thus very resistant. Sleeps in the sand like *T. pavo,* but only at night. *Reproduction:* unknown. *Social life:* very peaceable, though territorial. *Compatibility:* easily kept in tank with other fishes.

225 PEACOCK WRASSE
Thalassoma pavo

Family Labridae.
Distribution Tropical and subtropical eastern Atlantic; Mediterranean.
Description *Shape:* body long and compressed. Upper profile from snout to the base of the dorsal fin strongly convex. Body covered with large, thin scales; no scales on head. *Color:* ground color light green or greenish blue, many scales having a red line. Head and gill covers decorated with azure stripes. Dorsal fin has either a pink or a blue band at its beginning, followed by a dark chestnut or black band and finally a white or bluish marginal stripe. The caudal fin is striped red and green-blue; pectoral fins green or yellow with a black patch at the tip. There are many color variations. *Size:* up to 8 in (20 cm) long. *Sexual differences:* not well understood.
Environment Coastal vegetation and beds of seaweed. *Temperature:* 64–71 °F (18–22 °C). *pH:* about 8. *Density:* 1.023–1.025. *Illumination:* good lighting. *Furnishings:* plenty of hiding places.
Feeding Almost exclusively carnivorous.
Biology *Behavior:* active swimmer. *Reproduction:* in nature spawns in June and July; eggs pelagic. *Social life:* territorial. *Compatibility:* very tolerant of other species.

226 MOORISH IDOL
Zanclus cornutus

Family Zanclidae.
Distribution Tropical Indo-Pacific.
Description *Shape:* unmistakable. Body circular, strongly compressed; snout very prominent; mouth very small; caudal fin cut off square. Third spine of the dorsal fin extremely elongated, forming a pennant. Young have a small "horn" in front of each eye. *Color:* ground color white to yellowish; all unpaired fins yellow posteriorly; three wide black vertical bars outlined in blue across the body; brown saddle patch on the snout. *Size:* up to 10 in (25 cm). *Sexual differences:* unknown.
Environment *Temperature:* 78–84 °F (23–29 °C). *pH:* 8.2–8.6. *Density:* about 1.020–1.023. *Illumination:* plenty of light, sun if possible. *Furnishings:* plenty of free room to swim.
Feeding Very difficult to accustom. A plant-food picker; needs small live food and additional vegetable food.
Biology *Behavior:* swims with alternate strokes of the pectoral fins. Lives near the coast as well as offshore. *Reproduction:* unknown in captivity. *Social life:* peaceable schooling fish, but can launch sudden unpredictable attacks. *Compatibility:* sociable.

227 SAIL-FINNED SURGEONFISH
Zebrasoma veliferum

Family Acanthuridae.
Distribution Red Sea and tropical Indo-Pacific.
Description *Shape:* oval with rather prominent snout, strongly compressed. The anal and dorsal fins extremely high. *Color:* in maturity somewhat different from the young fish's coloring. Olive to dark blue ground color; head, throat and caudal fin with light spots in vertical lines; orange vertical bars on the body and unpaired fins. *Size:* up to 16 in (40 cm). *Sexual differences:* unknown.
Environment *Temperature:* 73–79 °F (23–26 °C). *pH:* about 8. *Density:* 1.020. *Illumination:* good lighting. *Substrate and furnishings:* deep sand, plenty of free swimming space and cover. Installation of ozonizer and ultraviolet radiation recommended.
Feeding Much vegetable food—a browser in natural surroundings. Large quantities of lettuce should be included in the substitute diet. Acclimatization is difficult.
Biology *Behavior:* territorial. *Reproduction:* unknown in captivity. *Social life:* probably live in pairs in natural state. *Compatibility:* very aggressive, even against fish of other species its own size or larger.

---

228 BLUE SURGEONFISH
Zebrasoma xanthurum

Family Acanthuridae.
Distribution Red Sea, Gulf of Aden, Sri Lanka.
Description *Shape:* snout strikingly elongated in this genus, and has the tall fins of the rest of this family. *Color:* deep blue with black bars and partly speckled; caudal fin bright yellow. *Size:* up to 16 in (40 cm). *Sexual differences:* unknown.
Environment Coral reefs. *Temperature:* 79–82 °F (26–28 °C). *pH:* about 8. *Density:* about 1.025. *Illumination:* good lighting. *Furnishings:* plenty of free swimming space and potential hiding places.
Feeding Grazes on plant growth. Add plenty of vegetable foods (lettuce and other soft leaves) to the substitute diet.
Biology *Behavior:* relatively peaceable when single. *Reproduction:* probably impossible in aquaria, since they most likely have planktonic eggs and larval stages (acronurus). *Social life:* to be kept separately. *Compatibility:* only a few, fairly large and peaceable tank companions.

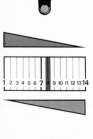

AMPHIBIANS
AND REPTILES

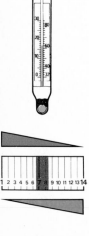

229 MARBLED SALAMANDER
Ambystoma opacum

Classification Class Amphibia, family Ambystomidae.

Distribution U.S.A., from New England to Texas and Florida.

Description Large head, small eyes, conspicuous costal ridges, tail flattened in a vertical plane. Gills are absent in the adult. The male of the species may be distinguished by its larger cloaca and tail. The upper aspect of the animal is dark, often black, with regular whitish markings, particularly at the sides. Overall length 4–5 in (10–12 cm).

Habitat Humid, sandy areas or dry plains and hills near water.

Feeding Worms, insects, mollusks, crustaceans, spiders, etc.

Biology Mating occurs in autumn. In nature, the pair meet by accident without any attracting pheromones' being secreted by the female. It is the only species in the Ambystomidae that lays eggs on the ground, in hollows, pond banks, dried ponds, etc. The larvae, usually numbering 25–300, remain inside the eggs, watched by the female until they hatch or until they are flooded by rains or rising water.

Note Mainly nocturnal, living in humid air and at temperatures of 64–71 °F (18–22 °C).

---

230 AXOLOTL
Ambystoma mexicanum

Classification Class Amphibia, family Ambystomidae.

Distribution Lake Xochimilco, about 12 miles (20 km) southwest of Mexico City.

Description Short, stubby body; smooth skin; small legs with four fingers up front and five behind. The trunk bears twelve conspicuous costal grooves. The gills are large and conspicuous. Background color of the back is usually brown-black, sometimes black, while the sides and belly are usually yellow. In the laboratory it reproduces fairly frequently, and albino individuals (see photograph) are not uncommon. Length 10 in (25 cm).

Habitat Still, shallow or deep waters with or without vegetation.

Feeding Worms, mollusks, other invertebrates.

Biology The animals hide in their aquarium shelter to mate at the end of winter. The female lays several clutches of 50–100 jelly-enclosed eggs. These are oval, $\frac{3}{4}$–1 in (70–100 mm) long. The larvae hatch after 30 days. Axolotls become sexually mature after two years. Aquarium conditions sometimes cause the animals to metamorphose into adults lacking gills.

Note *Axolotl* means "water monster" in Aztec. The animal was long thought to be a separate genus (*Siredon mexicanum*) until it was identified as a neotenous form of salamander. It may live up to 25 years in the aquarium.

231 AMPHIUMAS
Amphiuma spp.

Classification Class Amphibia, family Amphiumidae.
Distribution U.S.A.: southwest Virginia south to Florida, west to southwestern Texas and north into the Mississippi Valley.
Description Long, cylindrical body; pointed snout; weak limbs, only a fraction of an inch (a few mm) long, bearing one, two or three toes. Tongue and gills are absent; lungs are present. Adult state reached through partial metamorphosis. Length up to $7\frac{1}{2}$ in (80 cm).
Habitat Ditches, rice fields, rivers, ponds, swamps.
Feeding Worms, insects, mollusks, crustaceans, small fishes, small snakes, frogs and young individuals of its own species.
Biology Usually nocturnal, almost exclusively aquatic. Mating season January to May. The spermatophore is directly inserted by the male into the female's cloaca. The eggs (up to 350 in number) are usually laid in a wet hollow in the ground and are watched over by the female. The larvae, $1\frac{1}{2}$ to $2\frac{1}{2}$ in (4–6 cm) long, have limbs and gills and hatch as soon as a neighboring stream or pond rises to their level.
Note The female becomes sexually mature when four years old and approximately 12 in (30 cm) long. Eggs are laid every other year. In the aquaterrarium, in water at 64–68 °F (18–20 °C), animals may live over 25 years. *Amphiuma* spp. should always be handled with caution because they may bite with considerable strength.

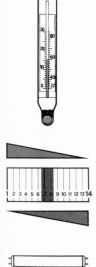

232 JAPANESE GIANT SALAMANDER
Andrias japonicus

Classification Class Amphibia, family Cryptobranchidae.
Distribution Japan: western Honshu and Kyushu.
Description Large, flattened head, wide mouth and small, lateral eyes. Thickened skin on its sides and on the posterior surface of its limbs. The skin is smooth and secretes a lot of mucus. A skin fold runs along the middle of the back, and two skin fringes are present at the sides. Length 40–57 in (100–144 cm).
Habitat Clear, running waters in streams and lakes; usually amid rocks in dark places near damp walls. Usually found at 1000–3300 ft (300–1000 meters) above sea level.
Feeding Usually crustaceans, annelids and insects; also fish, small frogs and young aquatic vertebrates.
Biology Sluggish, unable to move out of water, it uses its tail for locomotion. Largely nocturnal. Mating season in August and September. Soon after oviposition, the female is chased away by the male, who remains to guard the eggs until they hatch; this is because eggs take 8–10 weeks to hatch and the female often eats them. The newly hatched larvae are $1\frac{1}{2}$ in (3 cm) long and metamorphose in three years. The young usually live in shallow water; adult animals prefer deep, well-oxygenated water. This species adapts well to captivity.

233 YELLOW-BELLIED TOAD
Bombina variegata

Classification Class Amphibia, family Discoglossidae.

Distribution Central, western and southern Europe (except Spain, Portugal, Corsica and Sardinia).

Description The male bears black, horny protuberances on the lower surface of the forearm, on the internal side of the first three fingers of the hand and on the lower surface of some of the toes. Maximum length 2 in (5 cm). The male makes flutelike sounds depending on temperature.

Habitat Small ponds, woods or fields, at altitudes of up to 5900 ft (1,800 m).

Feeding Insects such as flies, dragonflies and stone flies, but also worms and particularly mollusks, both aquatic and terrestrial.

Biology Mating occurs 2–3 times a year from May to October. Amplexus is of the lumbar type, and the eggs are laid one by one or in small groups at intervals of several hours, 80–100 at a time. The egg sticks to the bottom or to plants. The larva is at most 2 in (5 cm) long, hatches after 7 days and metamorphoses after 2–3 months. Sexual maturity is reached after two years.

Note When disturbed or otherwise stimulated, *Bombina* emits an irritant whitish secretion (which is volatile, thus acting at a distance).

234 LOGGERHEAD TURTLE
Caretta caretta

Classification Class Reptilia, family Chelonidae.

Distribution Tropical and subtropical, Atlantic, Pacific and Indian oceans, Mediterranean.

Description Carapace with five pairs of lateral laminae; lateral bridge between carapace and plastron with three (rarely, four to seven) laminae below the margin, touching both plastron and marginal laminae. Adult carapace 32–48 in (80–120 cm) or more in length. Adult weight 176–814 lbs (80–370 kg). The male has a longer tail and longer claws on its hind limbs than the female, which, however, is usually larger.

Habitat Shallow or deep slow-moving waters. Bays and large river estuaries, in sea and brackish water.

Feeding Mollusks, crustaceans, gastropods, echinoderms, sometimes fish and algae.

Biology Oviposition occurs every two or three years, usually on deserted beaches above the high-water line, at dusk or after dark. The female leaves a characteristic "tank" track on the sand. It lays from 60 to 200 eggs in one hour in a hole 16–30 in (40–75 cm) deep and 8–12 in (20–30 cm) wide. When the young hatch after 6–8 weeks, their carapace is $1\frac{1}{2}$–2 in (4–5 cm) long. The animal reaches sexual maturity when body weight about 187–220 lbs (85–100 kg).

Note This species is threatened with extinction. The animal has not yet reproduced in captivity.

235 MATAMATA
Chelys fimbriatus

Classification Class Reptilia, family Chelyidae.
Distribution Venezuela, the Guyanas, central and northern Brazil.
Description Flat head, with a flexible proboscis and two wide lateral skin flaps which make it look triangular. The neck, which is likewise flattened, is very long and also carries numerous skin appendages. Three series of large tubercles run longitudinally on the carapace. Carapace may reach 16 in (40 cm) in length.
Habitat Fresh and stagnant waters, clay or mud bottom, rich vegetation wth plant detritus.
Feeding Fishes, amphibian larvae, invertebrates and plants.
Biology Its bizarre appearance enables it to blend in with its environment. When a fish passes within reach, it rapidly opens its mouth, thereby sucking in water which carries the prey into its jaws. *C. fimbriatus* is usually active at dusk or at night. Its reproductive habits are not known.
Note In the aquaterrarium, water temperature should be in the 79–86 °F (26–30 °C) range and air temperature at ground level 80–86 °F (27–30 °C). The animal lives from ten to twenty years in captivity.

236 SNAPPING TURTLE
Chelydra serpentina

Classification Class Reptilia, family Chelydridae.
Distribution From southwestern Canada to the Gulf of Mexico and from the Atlantic coast to the Rocky Mountains.
Description The small plastron is joined to the carapace by a narrow bridge and the two are not entirely ossified. The nose is hook-shaped. Plastron length up to $6\frac{1}{2}$ in (47 cm).
Habitat Stagnant or slow-moving waters with dense vegetation, often on clay bottoms.
Feeding Omnivorous, preferably carnivorous. It will sometimes eat dead animals.
Biology On land, it is often aggressive. Not a particularly good swimmer, it avoids open waters. It usually lies in mud in shallow water, its head half-submerged, ready to capture its prey. Algae grow on its shell and help it to merge with its surroundings. It spends the winter submerged in mud or in abandoned rodent holes. Mating season is from April to November. The eggs are laid on the ground, usually in June, in places exposed to sunlight. Their number is usually from 12 to 30 and does not exceed 52. They resemble table-tennis balls, with white shell, diameter $1–1\frac{1}{2}$ in (2.5–3 cm).
Note *Chelydra serpentina* is easily kept in an aquater-rarium, with a water temperature of 70–73 °F (21–23 °C).

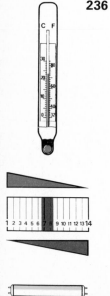

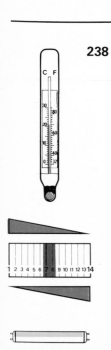

237 JAPANESE NEWT
Cynops pyrrogaster

Classification Class Amphibia, family Salamandridae.

Distribution Japan: Honshu, Shikoku, Kyushu, Yaku.

Description A shortish tail compared with the trunk. The male bears a conspicuous filament at the tip of its tail. It is an extremely polymorphic species. Length $3\frac{1}{2}$–$4\frac{3}{4}$ in (9–12 cm).

Habitat Ponds with still, clear water and small mountain streams up to 4900 ft (1500 m) above sea level. Terrestrial habits, but mating season is spent in water.

Feeding *Tubifex,* mud and stone insects, spiders, mollusks, crustaceans.

Biology After a spring courting "dance," the male lays a spermatophore which is taken up by the female in its cloaca. Each female lays up to 200 eggs. The larvae hatch 20 days after oviposition and metamorphose from July to September. Sexual maturity is reached at 2–3 years.

Note Lives very well in captivity with almost exclusively aquatic habits. In the aquaterrarium the water proportion must be high, optimal water temperature 77 °F (25 °C). To ensure spring reproduction, it is advisable to bring water temperature down to 39 °F (4 °C) in winter for short periods. The aquatic plants best suited to retain the eggs are *Elodea, Ceratophyllum, Vallisneria* and *Myriophyllum.*

---

238 EUROPEAN POND TORTOISE
Emys orbicularis

Classification Class Reptilia, family Emydidae.

Distribution North Africa, Europe and western Asia.

Description Smooth, oval carapace, small joint between abdominal and pectoral areas of the plastron. Separate webbed fingers with sharp, visible nails. Older individuals are darker, whereas young adults usually bear light, often yellowish spots and stripes on carapace, neck and head. Adult carapace is 7–14 in (18–36 cm) long and weighs $1\frac{1}{4}$–$2\frac{1}{4}$ lb (600–1000 g). The female is larger.

Habitat Still or slowly moving waters, with or without vegetation, from sea level to altitude of 5580 ft (1700 m).

Feeding Fishes, amphibians and their larvae, insects, mollusks, crustaceans, worms, young snakes, small mammals and occasionally plants.

Biology Mating may occur from March through October but is most frequent in March and April. The female, usually in June, lays from 3 to 16 eggs, each less than an ounce (4–6 g) in weight and measuring 1–$1\frac{1}{2}$ in (31–39 mm) x $\frac{3}{4}$ in (19–22 mm) in holes dug in the ground. The young hatch from August to September. The male reaches sexual maturity after 12–13 years (sometimes 6–8); the female does so after 15–20 years.

Note In the aquaterrarium, the tortoise may live for over 120 years. *Emys* is an active digger and may damage aquarium plants. Watch out for eye infections, colds, rickets, tuberculosis and avitaminosis.

239 ERPETON TENTACULATUM
Erpeton tentaculatum

Classification Class Reptilia, family Colubridae.
Distribution Thailand, Cambodia and Vietnam.
Description Easily distinguishable from other snakes by the pair of scaly appendages on either side of the nose, resembling antennae, with which it presumably senses its prey when swimming. Overall length 28–31 in (70–80 cm).
Habitat Clear or turbid brackish waters in estuaries of richly vegetated rivers.
Feeding Fishes, amphibians and plants.
Biology This species is almost exclusively aquatic, although it lays its eggs (usually 9 to 13) on land among plants. Little is known about its life history.
Note Water temperarure should be kept above 73–79 °F (23–26 °C).

240 MALAYSIAN WATER TURTLE
Malayemys subtrijuga

Classification Class Reptilia, family Emydidae.
Distribution Malaysia, particularly in the Sunda Archipelago.
Description Brown-black carapace, yellow-orange plastron, black around the sutures and on the lower surface of the plastron. Head, neck and legs are dark, with longitudinal light bands that disappear with age. Carapace length 8 in (20 cm).
Habitat Richly vegetated swamps, stagnant or slow-moving waters.
Feeding Eats mollusks almost exclusively.
Biology Similar to *Emys orbicularis* and *Chrysemys scripta*.
Note In the aquaterrarium, its activity is diurnal. Water temperature should be 75–82 °F (24–28 °C), soil temperature 79–86 °F (26–30 °C).

241 MUD PUPPY
Necturus maculosus

Classification Class Amphibia, family Proteidae.
Distribution U.S.A.: western New England southward to the confluence of the Tennessee and Missouri rivers.
Description Neotenous species with four-fingered limbs. The eye is often circled by a dark ring. Background color is gray to brown, with dark blue spots on the back. The tail is compressed and paddle-shaped. Overall length 3–5 in (8–13 cm), sometimes $6\frac{3}{4}$ in (17 cm)
Habitat Lakes, ponds, rivers, streams, provided water supply is continuous.
Feeding Crustaceans, insects, fishes, mollusks, microorganisms, plants, leeches and decaying matter in mud.
Biology Mating occurs in autumn, and the eggs, $\frac{1}{4}$ in (5–6 mm) in diameter, are laid a few months after fertilization. The larvae hatch after 40–60 days and are $\frac{3}{4}$–1 in (2–3 cm) long. Sexual maturation occurs in the fifth or sixth year of life. Essentially a nocturnal animal but sometimes has diurnal habits in muddy waters.
Note Its name is derived from an American tradition according to which the animal "barks." It is not easily kept in captivity; aquarium temperature should not exceed 64 °F (18 °C), with high oxygen content and pH around 6.5. *Necturus* may adapt to an aquarium with a putrefying mud bottom with or without vegetation.

242 RIBBED NEWT
Pleurodeles waltli

Classification Class Amphibia, family Salamandridae.
Distribution Portugal, western and south-central Spain, western Morocco.
Description The animal has sharp-pointed ribs which sometimes perforate the skin. The male has thickened humeri, callosities and pads on the inner side of its front limbs and a slightly protruding cloaca. Overall length 5–12 in (13–30 cm).
Habitat Stagnant waters and on land except in times of drought or during the mating season. Nocturnal habits in the wild. Found at up to 3600 ft (1100 m) above sea level.
Feeding Will eat anything it can swallow —freshwater crustaceans, *Tubifex,* etc.
Biology Reproduction occurs from September to May, and amplexus may last from several hours to several days without interruption. The eggs number from 150 to 800, depending on the age of the female. They are laid, in 10–15 minutes, 2 days after fertilization.
Note In captivity the animal is always aquatic and easily reproduces if the water temperature is kept at an optimum 64 °F (18 °C) and the water is frequently changed and kept fresh. It can live 8–12 years, exceptionally 20.

243   RED-EARED TURTLE
Chrysemys scripta elegans

Classification   Class Reptilia, family Emydidae.
Distribution   Eastern and central U.S.A., extending to northwestern Mexico.
Description   Bright green carapace, with plates decorated by a U-shaped concentric pattern in yellow and dark green, while those of the plastron carry two black concentric circles each. Legs and head are streaked with yellow and green. A red stripe on the side of the head extends from the snout to the rear of the eye, and there is a yellow stripe on the chin. There are also yellow lines along the sides of the tail. These colors are typical of young individuals and adult females. Adult males darken progressively and lose their characteristic dappling. Carapace length 10–12 in (25–30 cm).
Habitat   Strictly aquatic; found in lakes, ponds, swamps, rivers, canals and irrigation reservoirs. Prefers quiet waters, muddy bottoms and rich vegetation.
Feeding   Shrimps, amphipods, fishes, tadpoles, slugs, plants, etc.
Biology   Eggs are laid from April to June, each female laying from 5 to 22 eggs $\frac{3}{4} \times 1\frac{1}{2}$ in (21 × 36 mm) in size. The young hatch at the end of the summer or in autumn, sometimes even the following spring. Excellent and agile swimmer.
Note   This is one of the most common species in captivity. Water and soil temperature should be 68–82 °F (20–28 °C).

244   RED SALAMANDER
Pseudotriton ruber

Classification   Class Amphibia, family Plethodontidae.
Distribution   U.S.A. from New York to Ohio and south to north Alabama.
Description   Young and adult individuals are bright orange or orange-red with numerous irregular black spots on the upper side of trunk, legs and tail. Adult and old individuals become brownish on the back and sides. Overall length 7 in (18 cm).
Habitat   Under mosses, branches and stones near springs and streams with cold, running, well-oxygenated water. Sometimes on sand, pebble or rock bottoms.
Feeding   Worms; *Tubifex*; insect larvae, especially of flies and dragonflies; Daphnia.
Biology   In the summer, they stay out of water, moving among decaying vegetation and humid grass. As soon as the temperature falls, the animals move into clean stream waters or ponds. There the female lays up to 70 eggs, isolated or in small groups, $\frac{1}{4}$ in (6 mm) in diameter, which stick to stones or submerged objects. Newly hatched larvae are $\frac{5}{8}$ in (15 mm) long and are dark yellow. They leave the water when $\frac{1}{4}-\frac{3}{8}$ in (8–10 mm) long and are reddish brown with small black spots.
Note   In the aquarium they are active at night. Water and soil temperature should be 64–68 °F (18–20 °C).

245 GREATER SIREN
Siren lacertina

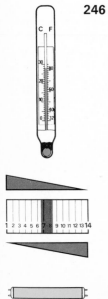

Classification Class Amphibia, family Sirenidae.
Distribution U.S.A.: Atlantic coast from Washington, D.C., to Florida and Alabama.
Description Neotenous species. Long, eel-like body with a short tail and without hind limbs. The eyes are small and lidless. Jawbones and cloacal glands are absent, and horny plates act as teeth. The head bears a gill slit, and the skin does not change throughout the animal's life. Overall length 39 in (1 m).
Habitat By day it lives in streams, ponds and swamps on muddy, richly vegetated bottoms. By night it slides rapidly on the ground, but never strays far from water.
Feeding Worms, shrimps, mollusks and plants.
Biology Mating habits are unknown. The female lays up to 500 eggs $\frac{1}{4}-\frac{3}{8}$ in (7—9 mm) in diameter, which it attaches individually or in small groups to underwater plants. The larvae, $\frac{3}{8}-\frac{3}{4}$ in (1—2 cm) long, hatch after a few weeks. *Siren* is an agile, quick and often aggressive animal. It burrows in mud during drought periods.
Note It lives up to twenty-five years in captivity. It exhibits a marked preference for *Eichhornia* roots, among which it settles. These plants should therefore be included in the aquaterrarium.

246 CLAWED FROG
Xenopus laevis

Classification Class Amphibia, family Pipidae.
Distribution Africa, from Kenya, Zaïre and Angola to South Africa.
Description The name *laevis*, meaning "smooth," refers to its very smooth, slippery skin, which makes it difficult to hold in one's hand. The toes are webbed and clawed. The small, superiorly placed eyes, streamlined body, lateral-line organs and absence of tongue reveal its adaptation to permanent underwater life. Overall length 3—5 in (8—12.5 cm), the female larger than the male.
Habitat Lakes, ponds, swamps, slow streams rich in vegetation.
Feeding Worms: *Tubifex*; dragonfly, fly and other insect larvae. The adults often eat their own tadpoles.
Biology During amplexus, the female lays the eggs one at a time; she holds each egg for a short instant in the lips of the cloaca, then pushes it to make it roll along the belly of the male past its cloaca, from which it settles on a plant. Ten to fifteen thousand eggs are laid. The tadpoles hatch 48 hours after oviposition. *Xenopus* takes 10—18 months to become sexually mature. It is able to "jump" backward both above- and underwater.
Note It is advisable to keep water temperature around 79—82 °F (26—28 °C) and to lay sand and pebbles on the aquarium bottom, plus some *C. alternifolios* plants.

FRESHWATER
INVERTEBRATES

247 CRAYFISH
Astacus fluviatilis

Classification Phylum Arthropoda, class Crustacea, subclass Malacostraca, order Decapoda, suborder Macrura.
Distribution Clear and well-aerated freshwater European habitat.
Description Typical crayfish morphology with large carapace, tapering abdomen and two large claws. Color varies with habitat; may be gray, greenish or brown. Body length rarely exceeds 4 in (10 cm).
Habitat Prefers quiet running waters in valleys, on muddy bottoms with dense vegetation. In the aquarium it prefers cold—64–68 °F (18–20 °C)—well-aerated water, with hiding places.
Feeding Varied, consisting mainly of animal detritus. In the aquarium it will eat most animal foods, fresh and preserved.
Biology Aggressive and solitary animal, particularly when adult. Nocturnal activity. Reproduction is sexual. The young have their final form upon hatching.

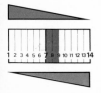

248 WATER FLEAS
Cyclops sp. and Daphnia

Classification Phylum Arthropoda, class Crustacea, subclasses Copepoda (*Cyclops*) and Branchipoda (*Daphnia*).
Distribution Numerous species belonging to these genera inhabit all types of freshwater habitats. Marine species belonging to related genera are equally common.
Description *Cyclops* gets its name from its single median eye; it carries two long characteristic antennae, and the females often carry egg sacs. *Daphnia* have two eyes, forward-pointing antennae and a globular body enclosed in two half-shells. These animals, which are big enough to be seen with the naked eye, are translucent, and the brown eggs may be seen inside.
Habitat Typical planktonic animals, they occur in most freshwater habitats. They live in aquaria when accidentally or purposely introduced as eggs.
Feeding On smaller plankton and organic detritus. They constitute a valuable food for other aquarium animals, especially small fishes.
Biology These animals are active swimmers, attracted by light. They exhibit sexual reproduction, following a seasonal cycle.

249 HYDRA
Hydra viridis

Classification Phylum Coelenterata or Cnidaria, class Hydrozoa, order Hydroida.
Distribution Small freshwater coelenterate; several species are found worldwide.
Description Small solitary polyp, a fraction of an inch (a few mm) long. The tubular body is attached by a foot to its substrate and carries five long, thin tentacles around the mouth. Buds sometimes appear on the body wall.
Habitat All types of freshwater habitat, mainly attached to plant stems. It adapts itself to any aquarium environment and because of its small size often goes unnoticed.
Feeding Small-sized plankton and organic detritus in suspension. It finds its own necessary food in any aquarium.
Biology Its tissues often contain microscopic algae (zoochlorellae) which give it a green color. It may reproduce both by budding and sexually. The buds are growing, newly formed individuals.

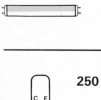

250 MELANOIDES TUBERCULATUS
Melanoides tuberculatus

Classification Phylum Mollusca, class Gastropoda.
Distribution Tropical species common in Southeast Asian waters.
Description This mollusk has an elongated spiral shell up to $\frac{1}{2}$ in (1.5 cm) long. The head carries the eyes, two narrow tentacles and a robust mouth apparatus (radula). The shell is brown, with small dark spots and tubercles.
Habitat Water temperature must not fall below 74 °F (23 °C).
Feeding Mixed diet, mainly detritus. Like *Planorbarius*, it eats aquarium detritus and encrustations and is useful in small numbers.
Biology A viviparous hermaphrodite. *M. tuberculatus* is normally an untiring burrower, but if the oxygen content of the water falls below acceptable levels or the aquarium becomes chemically or physically imbalanced, it tends to rise to the surface.
Note This animal can breed too freely and its numbers should be periodically controlled.

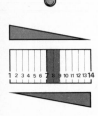

251 GREAT RAMSHORN SNAIL
Planorbarius corneus

Classification Phylum Mollusca, class Gastropoda.
Distribution Stagnant fresh water, in Europe and Asia; closely related species are widely distributed.
Description Easily recognizable species, brick red in color with a flat coiled shell. Color may be darker or more vivid. Shell diameter is usually near ½ in (1 cm), sometimes larger.
Habitat Still or slow-moving fresh water, depending on vegetation. Easily adapted to captivity, it may invade and damage aquarium vegetation.
Feeding *Planorbarius* is practically omnivorous and feeds on animal and vegetal detritus. Acts as a useful aquarium scavenger when not excessively numerous.
Biology It has gills as well as a lung, to ensure an efficient underwater respiration. A hermaphrodite, it lays eggs in characteristic disk-shaped clutches adhering to various substrates.

252 VIVIPARUS FASCIATUS
Viviparus fasciatus

Classification Phylum Mollusca, class Gastropoda.
Distribution Freshwater habitats in central and southern Europe, shared with *V. ater* and *V. contectus*.
Description Short spiral shell, light brown or greenish in color with darker longitudinal stripes. Average length around ¾ in (2 cm), sometimes larger. The shell can be closed with an operculum and may be covered with algae.
Habitat Stagnant water with mud bottom and rich vegetation. It survives with some difficulty in the aquarium, provided that water temperature does not exceed 71–75 °F (22–24 °C).
Feeding Like most other freshwater gastropods, it feeds on detritus and plants, which it grates with its radula.
Biology The species name refers to the viviparous character of this hermaphrodite species, in which every individual carries both male and female gonads. The young are born in their final form.

MARINE
INVERTEBRATES

253 BEADLET ANEMONE
Actinia equina

Classification Phylum Coelenterata or Cnidaria, class Anthozoa, subclass Hexacorallia, order Actiniaria.

Distribution Worldwide; common in Pacific and Indian oceans, Mediterranean and Atlantic Ocean.

Description Its body, easily recognizable, is dark red with lighter red tentacles. Some populations are more or less intensely colored, and the margins of the disk may be bluish. Body diameter is usually between $1\frac{1}{2}$ in (4 cm) and $3\frac{1}{2}$ m (8 cm).

Habitat Typically lives in tidal areas, firmly anchored to the rock. Presents no great problems in captivity and will survive in most aquarium environments.

Feeding Feeds on any organic detritus within reach of its tentacles. Will also feed on fresh and preserved animal foods.

Biology *A. equina* is adapted to live for hours abovewater with its tentacles completely retracted. It can reproduce by division, although sexual reproduction is the rule.

254 SOFT CORAL
Alcyonium palmatum

Classification Phylum Coelenterata or Cnidaria, class Anthozoa, subclass Octocorallia, order Alcyonaria.
Distribution Mediterranean.
Description Branched colonies 8–20 in (20–50 cm) high, solidly anchored to the substrate. The flexible but leathery body houses a large number of white polyps which protrude $\frac{1}{4}$ in (5–6 mm) from specialized thecae. The entire colony may vary in color from white to red and purple, and may expand or contract, thus absorbing or expelling water.
Habitat Lives in dimly illuminated areas on rocky walls or on sedimented detritus at depths exceeding 32 ft (10 m). This species has rather critical requirements and will not survive for very long in captivity. Aquarium temperature should be around 68 °F (20 °C).
Feeding The colony feeds on plankton and suspended animal foodstuffs. It will feed in this way in the aquarium when it survives.
Biology Its biology is similar to that of red coral, particularly as regards reproductive habits.

255 SNAKE-LOCKS ANEMONE
Anemonia sulcata

Classification Phylum Coelenterata or Cnidaria, class Anthozoa, subclass Hexacorallia, order Actiniaria.
Distribution Mediterranean and northern European Atlantic coast.
Description This sea anemone carries up to 200 tentacles, often with purple tips. The body is short and rarely exceeds $3\frac{1}{2}$–4 in (8–10 cm) in diameter. Basic color is whitish or cream.
Habitat Lives in very shallow waters as little as a few inches (cm) deep, inserted in rock crevices. It will stand temperatures slightly exceeding 71 °F (22 °C).
Feeding Any organic particle or small animal that comes in contact with the tentacles is captured and ingested. In the aquarium it will eat any fresh or preserved food. It likes live *Artemia*.
Biology The tentacles do not retract. Reproduction is mainly sexual, only rarely by division.

256 CUSHION STAR
Asterina gibbosa

Classification Phylum Echinodermata, class Asteroidea.

Distribution Common in the western Mediterranean, also widespread in the Adriatic.

Description Small starfish $1\frac{1}{2}$–2 in (3–5 cm) in diameter; short arms; upper side greenish and lower (oral) side yellow. The slender tube feet are situated at the tips of the arms.

Habitat Very common in shallow coastal waters, where it is found under stones. An extremely resilient animal, it easily tolerates water temperatures of up to 77 °F (25 °C).

Feeding A detritus eater, it will feed on any available organic matter. Efficiently cleans aquaria and does not require any additional feeding.

Biology *Asterina* is remarkably active and moves continuously in search of food. It reproduces sexually, and mature individuals hatch from its eggs. Like all other starfishes, it regenerates damaged arms.

---

257 WARTLET ANEMONE
Bunodactis verrucosa

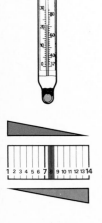

Classification Phylum Coelenterata or Cnidaria, class Anthozoa, subclass Hexacorallia, order Actiniaria.

Distribution Mediterranean. Similar species inhabit other seas.

Description Tentacles are short with annular light and dark stripes. Body is variable in color, ranging from gray to white and red, and bears twelve longitudinal rows of wartlike protrusions which extend from the tentacles to the foot. Average diameter approximately $2\frac{1}{2}$–$2\frac{3}{4}$ in (6–7 cm).

Habitat It shares its habitat with *Anemonia sulcata* in rock crevices in coastal waters. It adapts easily to aquarium life as long as the temperature remains around 71 °F (22 °C).

Feeding Similar to *Actinia equina*. It will eat fresh or preserved animal foods and living plankton (*Artemia*) from time to time.

Biology Shows little tendency to move if adequately placed. Will reproduce sexually, giving rise to large larvae.

258 CALAPPA GRANULATA
Calappa granulata

Classification Phylum Arthropoda, class Crustacea, subclass Malacostraca, order Decapoda, suborder Brachyura.

Distribution Mediterranean and neighboring Atlantic coastline.

Description This unusual crab has a compact humped body, white with red spots in a fanlike pattern. Its two very large, flat claws are toothed at their dorsal margins and cover its mouth parts when it is resting. The protruding eyes can retract into special cavities. Carapace width may reach 4 in (10 cm).

Habitat This species lives buried in bottom soil, at depths exceeding 65 ft (20 m). In captivity, it requires a sand layer at least ⅜ in (10 mm) deep and temperature below 71 °F (22 °C).

Feeding A carnivorous predator; feeds mainly on mollusks, but will readily accept any fresh or preserved animal food.

Biology One of the claws is modified for crushing gastropod shells. Reproduction is sexual (with separate sexes), and the larvae are planktonic.

259 EDIBLE CRAB
Cancer pagurus

Classification Phylum Arthropoda, class Crustacea, subclass Malacostraca, order Decapoda, suborder Brachyura.

Distribution Western Mediterranean and north Atlantic.

Description Large crab, smooth carapace, large claws and hairy walking legs. Dorsally, it is brown with small dark spots; ventrally, greenish yellow. Carapace may be as much as 8 in (20 cm) wide.

Habitat Sedentary inhabitant of sandy or rocky bottoms, 3–98 ft (1–30 m) deep with seasonal variation. Aquarium temperature should not exceed 71 °F (22 °C).

Feeding Feeds on mollusks and other benthic animals. In captivity will eat any animal food, fresh or preserved.

Biology Lays eggs which hatch as planktonic larvae.

260 HELMET SHELL
Cassis sulcosa

Classification Phylum Mollusca, class Gastropoda.
Distribution Mediterranean. Similar species populate other seas.
Description Attractive gastropod with a shiny, finely grooved shell, brown with lighter shades. The foot is brown on its upper side; the eyes are stalked. Shell size may exceed $2\frac{1}{2}$ in (6 cm).
Habitat Lives on sand or mud bottoms in coastal waters, where it may easily be seen in large numbers at night. It adapts satisfactorily to captivity at temperatures not exceeding 71 °F (22 °C).
Feeding Carnivorous predator; feeds on small bivalves, which it extracts from the sand and swallows whole. In captivity it will eat fresh or preserved animal foods.
Biology Nocturnal behavior. Reproduction is sexual; the animal is pictured atop a recently laid clutch of eggs.
Note Will feed on smaller mollusks.

261 CERIANTHUS MEMBRANACEUS
Cerianthus membranaceus

Classification Phylum Coelenterata or Cnidaria, class Anthozoa, subclass Hexacorallia, order Ceriantharia.
Distribution Mediterranean. Approximately fifty similar species inhabit all seas.
Description A double crown of narrow tentacles, white or brown, is attached to a wormlike body, which is enclosed in a membranous sheath formed by solidified mucus and small particles. Color is variable. Body may be as much as 12 in (30 cm) long.
Habitat Lives on muddy coastal bottoms. It must be carefully placed in the aquarium to avoid damage to the delicate body. Water temperature should be between 68 °F (20 °C) and 71 °F (22 °C).
Feeding Largely plankton. In captivity it will feed on dried animal food, but it needs live plankton (*Artemia*) from time to time.
Biology *C. membranaceus* is able to withdraw rapidly into the tubular body, which may be as much as 3 ft (1 m) long and serves as a shelter.

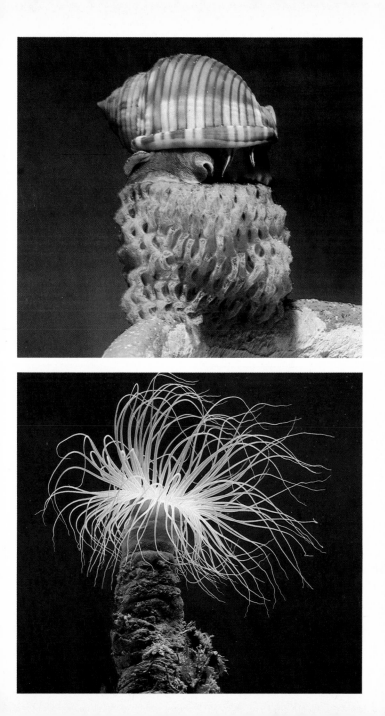

262 CLADOCORA CESPITOSA
Cladocora cespitosa

Classification Phylum Coelenterata or Cnidaria, class Anthozoa, subclass Hexacorallia, order Madreporaria.

Distribution Mediterranean. Many other similar corals inhabit tropical waters.

Description This colonial anthozoan often takes the form of a spheroidal mass of small individuals, $\frac{1}{2}$ in (1 cm) in diameter, with a calcium carbonate skeleton. Individual polyps are a diaphanous greenish yellow and carry a crown of tentacles covered with wartlike knobs. Each individual is distinct from its neighbors even as regards its skeleton.

Habitat The colonies live on flat rocky substrates, both in grottoes in coastal waters and at depths ranging from 50 to 2000 ft (15 to 600 m). They adapt easily to aquarium life, provided they are shielded from direct light and water temperature is kept below 71 °F (22 °C).

Feeding The colonies feed on plankton and other sedimenting organic foodstuffs. In the aquarium they will eat powdered food and living plankton (*Artemia*).

Biology Colonies sometimes exhibit a treelike appearance, depending on location. *C. cespitosa* is a sessile species—*i.e.*, it is firmly attached to its substrate. Reproduction is both sexual and asexual.

263 CONDYLACTIS AURANTIACA
Condylactis aurantiaca

Classification Phylum Coelenterata or Cnidaria, class Anthozoa, subclass Hexacorallia, order Actiniaria.

Distribution Mediterranean.

Description The body is cylindrical, bright orange with white undulated longitudinal ridges. The tentacles are purple-tipped, with brown and white rings. The body, $2\frac{1}{2}$–3 in (6–8 cm) long, is covered by small wartlike knobs.

Habitat Coastal waters 6–9 ft (2–3 m) deep. This animal attaches itself to stones or bivalve shells buried in at least 4 in (10 cm) of sand. In the aquarium it requires an appropriate substrate as well as a water temperature not exceeding 71 °F (22 °C).

Feeding Practically omnivorous, it feeds on any organic detritus. In the aquarium it will eat fresh and preserved animal foods and plankton.

Biology The body of this sea anemone is always buried in sand. Its reproduction is sexual.

264   RED CORAL
Corallium rubrum

Classification   Phylum Coelenterata or Cnidaria, class Anthozoa, subclass Octocorallia, order Alcyonaria.
Distribution   Mediterranean. Similar species populate other seas.
Description   A branching soft body containing calcium carbonate spicules, bright red in color, which tend to fuse and form a rigid central core. The constituent white polyps carry eight tentacles and are able to retract entirely into special cavities; colony size varies with age and environment.
Habitat   Red coral is becoming increasingly rare and now inhabits only inaccessible rocky walls and grottoes, at depths of 65–164 ft (20–50 m). It will live in the aquarium if the conditions are optimal and the temperature is kept below 64–68 °F (18–20 °C).
Feeding   The polyps gather food particles in suspension, both dead and living. It is necessary to use plankton and mollusk homogenates in the aquarium.
Biology   The individuals of this attractive colonial species reproduce sexually, giving rise to planktonic larvae which subsequently attach themselves to the substrate.

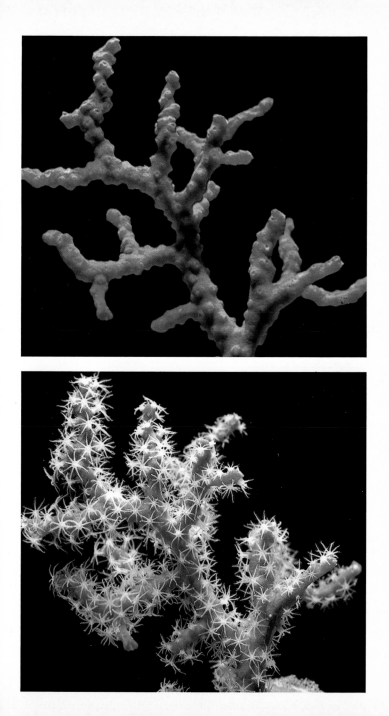

265 PEAR COWRIE
Cypraea pyrum

Classification Phylum Mollusca, class Gastropoda.
Distribution Mediterranean. Large numbers of similar species inhabit all other seas.
Description Small—1 in (3 cm)—but attractive gastropod; extremely shiny shell, golden brown on upper side and orange-red on its lower side. Body color is brown with small white spots.
Habitat Inhabits bottoms with coral or sea squirts, 65–164 ft (20–50 m) deep. Will adapt to aquarium life at temperatures not exceeding 71 °F (22 °C).
Feeding Carnivorous animal; will eat most fresh or preserved animal foods when in captivity.
Biology Little is known of the biology of this rare species. It reproduces sexually and is not completely hermaphroditic. It has nocturnal habits.

266 TIGER COWRIE
Cypraea tigris

Classification Phylum Mollusca, class Gastropoda.
Distribution Typically inhabits the Red Sea, but is also widespread in the Indian and Pacific oceans.
Description Like all the cowries, it has a shiny, globular shell, whose last spire wraps around and hides all the others. The shell is whitish, with numerous, sometimes confluent brown spots. Body color is brown, variegated, with white dots. The mantle may cover the entire shell. The animal may be up to 3–4 in (8–10 cm) long.
Habitat Lives on corals or rocks in shallow coastal waters and requires aquarium temperatures above 77 °F (25 °C). It is fairly tolerant of less-than-ideal aquarium conditions.
Feeding Essentially carnivorous, this gastropod will feed on fresh or dried animal food in the aquarium. It will occasionally eat plants.
Biology Cypraea tigris is a solitary, largely nocturnal animal, which, however, shows some diurnal activity. Reproduction is sexual, without larval stages.

267 DARDANUS ARROSOR with CALLIACTIS PARASITICA
Dardanus arrosor with Calliactis parasitica

Classification *Dardanus* phylum Arthropoda, class Crustacea, subclass Malacostraca, order Decapoda, suborder Anomura. *Calliactis* phylum Coelenterata, class Anthozoa, subclass Hexacorallia, order Actiniaria.
Distribution Mediterranean; similar species populate all other seas.
Description *D. arrosor* is the largest Mediterranean hermit crab—carapace length 1 in (3 cm)—and has large, curved claws. Body color is reddish orange, lighter ventrally. The sea anemone is variegated brown, with brown, sometimes white, tentacles. Its diameter seldom exceeds 2 in (5 cm).
Habitat These two animals are fairly common on sand or sediment bottoms at depths of 65 to 260 ft (20 to 80 m). They adapt easily to captivity if water temperature does not exceed 71 °F (22 °C).
Feeding The crab is carnivorous and will eat any fresh or dried animal food. The same holds for the sea anemone; drop food particles among its tentacles.
Biology The hermit crab inhabits an empty gastropod shell, onto which it actively carries the sea anemone. The crab reproduces sexually and the sexes are separate, whereas sea anemones may reproduce both sexually and asexually, according to the anthozoan alternating cycle.
Note It is advisable not to keep more than a single crab and its anemone per aquarium.

268 GNATHOPHYLLUM ELEGANS
Gnathophyllum elegans

Classification Phylum Arthropoda, class Crustacea, subclass Malacostraca, order Decapoda, suborder Macrura.
Distribution Mediterranean and neighboring Atlantic coasts.
Description Small shrimp, 1–1¾ in (25–35 mm) long, with short rostrum and claws. Brown, almost black body, with transparent external margins and diffuse yellow or pinkish dots.
Habitat Lives among colonies of marine plants or algae, at depths ranging from 6 ft (2 m) to 131 ft (40 m). Water temperature should not exceed 71 °F (22 °C). This animal prefers dark hiding places.
Feeding A detritus eater, it prefers animal foods; it readily accepts them, both fresh and dried, when in captivity.
Biology Shy, nocturnal animal. Sexes separate; eggs have a characteristic purple color.

269 SPONGE CRAB
Dromia vulgaris

Classification Phylum Arthropoda, class Crustacea, subclass Malacostraca, order Decapoda, suborder Brachyura.

Distribution Mediterranean. Other species belonging to the same genus populate all seas.

Description Near-spherical domed body covered with dense brown down. The claws are purple-tipped and are very strong. The third and fourth pairs of walking legs are flattened and displaced dorsally. Carapace width may reach 5 in (13 cm).

Habitat Lives on rocky coastal slopes at depths of up to 32 ft (10 m). It will easily adapt to captivity, but may cause extensive injury to other aquarium animals, particularly sessile ones. Water temperature should be kept below 71 °F (22 °C).

Feeding It will feed on organic detritus, mainly of plant origin. Will also eat fresh plant food.

Biology This species is well known for its habit of attaching live sponges and ascidians to its back, anchored with its specialized legs. Reproduction is sexual, with a planktonic larval stage.

270 ECHINASTER SEPOSITUS
Echinaster sepositus

Classification Phylum Echinodermata, class Asteroidea.

Distribution All coastal areas in the Mediterranean.

Description The upper side is bright red; the oral (lower) side is lighter in color. Its five equal arms are dotted with small depressions. Maximum diameter is usually 6–8 in (15–20 cm).

Habitat Lives on rocky slopes or among vegetation at depths of 26–32 ft (8–10 m). Its main requirement lies in the surrounding temperature, which should stay below 71 °F (22 °C).

Feeding Varied diet consisting mainly of animal fragments which it collects while sliding along the bottom. Small mollusks are easy prey for this starfish.

Biology It uses its tube feet to move along the bottom. These are moved by a complex hydraulic system which also controls the movement of the flexible arms. Reproduction is sexual.

271 GORGONIAN
Eunicella cavolinii

Classification Phylum Coelenterata or Cnidaria, class Anthozoa, subclass Octocorallia, order Gorgonacea. The white form is known as *E. verrucosa*.
Distribution Mediterranean.
Description Forms beautiful bright yellow branched colonies. The soft body contains numerous calcium carbonate spicules which help to give it some rigidity. The external surface of the colony is rough and corrugated, with small polyps.
Habitat This species prefers shady environments and grows by preference on vertical surfaces at depths exceeding 32 ft (10 m).
Feeding Members of this species feed on small planktonic organisms carried by currents. In the aquarium they will feed on plankton and powdered animal foods.
Biology The colony's branches usually extend in one plane like a fan. Reproduction of the individuals is sexual and gives rise to planktonic larvae.

---

272 SEA FAN
Eunicella stricta

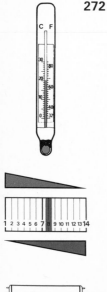

Classification Phylum Coelenterata or Cnidaria, class Anthozoa, subclass Octocorallia, order Gorgonacea.
Distribution Mediterranean.
Description Similar in morphology to the yellow gorgonian *Eunicella cavolinii*, but differing by its whitish color. *E. stricta* is considered by some authors to be a subspecies of *E. cavolinii*. Branched colonies are 10 in (25 cm) high on average, sometimes reaching 30 in (75 cm).
Habitat As for *E. cavolinii*, but at depths not exceeding 98 ft (30 m). Very delicate; requires low levels of illumination and temperature ranging from 64 to 68 °F (18 to 20 °C).
Feeding Feeds on small planktonic organisms carried by currents. In the aquarium this species will feed on plankton and other powdered animal foods.
Biology The branches of the colony are usually fan-shaped. Reproduction of the individuals is sexual and gives rise to planktonic larvae.

273 GLOSSODORIS VALENCIENNESI
Glossodoris valenciennesi

Classification Phylum Mollusca, class Gastropoda, order Nudibranchia.
Distribution Mediterranean; numerous other species in most seas.
Description Flat, oblong, shell-less gastropod, with a tuft of cutaneous appendages acting as secondary gills dorsally and posteriorly. Body color is brown, with white edges and many gold-colored skin flaps. Length is approximately $2\frac{1}{2}$ in (6 cm).
Habitat Lives in shallow water among plants. It will tolerate aquarium life, provided the temperature is kept below 71 °F (22 °C).
Feeding Diet is mainly vegetable; will eat detritus and fresh plants in captivity.
Biology Little is known about nudibranch biology. They are nocturnal animals, incomplete hermaphrodites, and sexual reproduction yields planktonlike larvae.

274 SEA SQUIRT
Halocynthia papillosa

Classification Phylum Tunicata, class Ascidiacea, order Stolidobranchiata.
Distribution Mediterranean. Other species live in temperate seas.
Description The small flask-shaped body carries two siphons (one inhaling, one exhaling). It is bright reddish orange in color and covered externally by small tubercles. Overall length from $2\frac{1}{2}$ in (6 cm) to 4 in (10 cm).
Habitat Normally anchors itself to rocks at depths exceeding 32 ft (10 m), or in caves at less depth. In the aquarium it prefers dark cavities and does not tolerate temperatures above 68–71 °F (20–22 °C).
Feeding A typical filter feeder, it uses its branchial basket to retain particles in suspension. Plankton and freeze-dried food are recommended for aquarium feeding.
Biology Reproduction may be either sexual (with a free-living larval stage) or asexual (by budding). A solitary species, it has striking regenerative abilities.

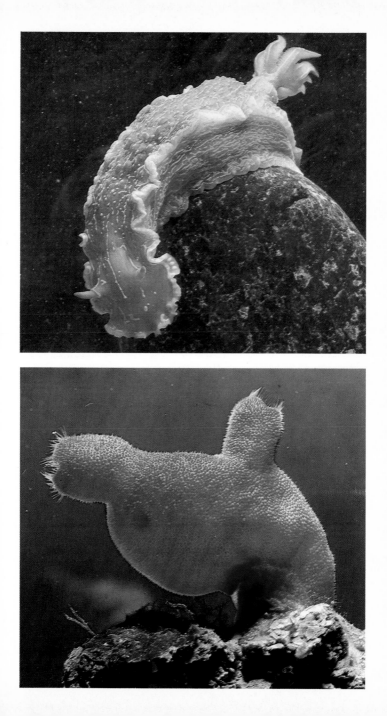

275 CLOWN SHRIMP
Hymenocera picta

Classification Phylum Arthropoda, class Crustacea, subclass Malacostraca, order Decapoda, suborder Macrura.

Distribution Indo-Pacific coral reefs.

Description One of the most beautiful crustaceans of the entire tropical fauna. Its color is pinkish white or white with large, purple-edged pink spots. Walking legs are striped in blue or indigo. The claws are tapered, the eyes are on stalks and the antennae are flattened and leaf-shaped. Maximum body length rarely exceeds 2–2½ in (5–6 cm).

Habitat Prefers a hard rocky or coral substrate, rich in hiding places. In captivity, it requires normal salinity and alkalinity, with temperatures above 77 °F (25 °C).

Feeding Mainly starfishes, but will accept other food in the aquarium.

Biology Marked territorial instincts; tends to form stable seasonal pairs, but rarely reproduces in the aquarium. Quick, sudden movements are typical of this species.

276 LYSMATA SETICAUDATA
Lysmata seticaudata

Classification Phylum Arthropoda, class Crustacea, subclass Malacostraca, order Decapoda, suborder Macrura.

Distribution Mediterranean and neighboring Atlantic areas.

Description Body shape is similar to that of *Palaemon serratus,* but *L. seticaudata* differs by its bright red color, distributed in horizontal stripes of small dots. The eyes, carried by short stalks, are black. Total body length does not exceed 2 in (5 cm).

Habitat The holdfasts of marine plants at depths ranging from 20 in to 49 ft (50 cm to 15 m). Adapts easily to captivity; temperature should be kept below 71 °F (22 °C).

Feeding Omnivorous; feeds largely on organic detritus. It will accept any fresh or dried food, but preferably animal rather than vegetable.

Biology Very active animal. Reproduction is sexual, the sexes being separate.

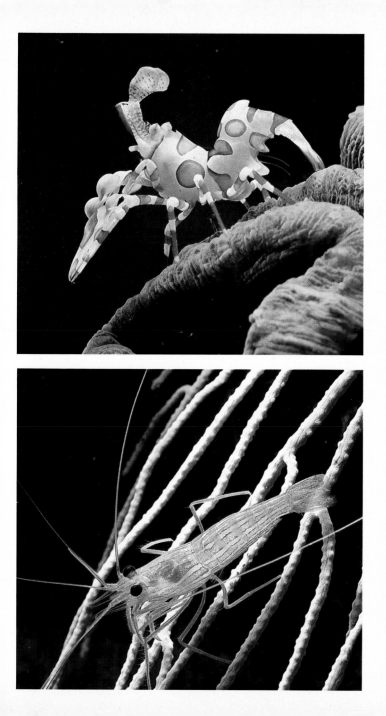

277 OCTOPUS
Octopus vulgaris

Classification Phylum Mollusca, class Cephalopoda, order Octopoda.
Distribution Widely distributed in tropical and temperate seas.
Description A short, bag-shaped body containing the viscera is joined to the head, which is provided with prominent eyes and carries eight tentacles, lined by double rows of suckers, around the mouth, which is on the lower surface. Has no fins. Color is variegated brown, with lighter and darker tones and very variable. The animal may be up to 10 ft (3 m) long.
Habitat *O. vulgaris* lives on rocky bottoms, with plentiful hiding places, in shallow coastal waters. Young individuals, better adapted to captivity, require optimal aquarium conditions and temperature not exceeding 71 °F (22 °C).
Feeding *O. vulgaris* is a predator, feeding on mollusks and crustaceans. In the aquarium it will tolerate most fresh animal foods.
Biology The octopus is probably the most intelligent invertebrate. Reproduction is sexual, the sexes are separate and the eggs, from which small octopuses will eventually hatch, are hidden and cared for in rocky cavities.

278 BRITTLE STAR
Ophiothrix fragilis

Classification Phylum Echinodermata, class Ophiuroidea.
Distribution Mediterranean waters. Similar species populate all seas.
Description Ophiuroids are easily distinguished from asteroid starfishes by their slender and extremely flexible arms. This very polymorphic species has a central oral disk, which bears five arms, covered by long brushlike bristles. Color may be green, black or reddish, usually variegated. Overall diameter usually ranges from $2\frac{1}{2}$ in (6 cm) to 4 in (10 cm).
Habitat Lives on rocky bottoms in shallow waters, or muddy bottoms at depths of up to 328 ft (100 m). In the aquarium, it lives constantly hidden among bottom rocks and does not tolerate temperatures above 71 °F (22 °C).
Feeding A detritus eater, it bases its diet on animal foods. In captivity it will eat sedimenting detritus.
Biology Brittle stars reproduce sexually and lay eggs from which hatch swimming planktonic larvae.

279 PAGURUS PRIDEAUXI with ADAMSIA PALLIATA
Pagurus prideauxi with Adamsia palliata

Classification *Pagurus* phylum Arthropoda, class Crustacea, subclass Malacostraca, order Decapoda, suborder Anomura. *Adamsia* phylum Coelenterata, class Anthozoa, subclass Hexacorallia, order Actiniaria.

Distribution Mediterranean. Similarly associated species populate other seas.

Description This hermit crab has a carapace length of $\frac{5}{8}$–$\frac{3}{4}$ in (15–18 mm). The animal has asymmetrical claws. The sea anemone wraps itself around the shell inhabited by the hermit crab. It is whitish in color with purple dots. Its white tentacles are placed ventrally with respect to *Pagurus*. The anemone's body measures approximately $\frac{3}{4}$ in (2 cm) in diameter at the base.

Habitat These symbiotically associated animals live on sand or mud bottoms at depths ranging from 98 to 328 ft (30 to 100 m). *Pagurus* is delicate and does not survive for very long in the aquarium. Water temperature must be kept below 68–71 °F (20–22 °C).

Feeding *Pagurus* is carnivorous and will eat any animal food, which will also feed its companion.

Biology The bond between these animals is strong; they accompany each other throughout their lives. It has been said, but never proved, that the *Pagurus* feeds its companion. For reproductive habits, see *Dardanus arrosor*.

280 COMMON PRAWN
Palaemon serratus

Classification Phylum Arthropoda, class Crustacea, subclass Malacostraca, order Decapoda, suborder Macrura.

Distribution Mediterranean. Other species belonging to the same genus are widely distributed in other seas.

Description This small shrimp, 3 in (7 cm) long, has a translucent body, with fragile legs and claws and thin antennae. The body bears narrow transverse bands of green or red. Internal organs are easily visible through the exoskeleton. The eyes are large, with short stalks.

Habitat Lives on rocky coastal bottoms and on the walls of reefs. It is able to withstand high temperatures and unfavorable environmental conditions (high salinity, high nitrite concentration, etc.).

Feeding Omnivorous; prefers organic detritus. In the aquarium, it acts as an efficient scavenger.

Biology An extremely active species, it moves continuously in search of food. Reproduction is sexual; the sexes are separate.

281 ZOANTHID
Parazoanthus axinellae

Classification Phylum Coelenterata or Cnidaria, class Anthozoa, subclass Hexacorallia, order Zoantharia.

Distribution Mediterranean.

Description Lives in small colonies. Has a calcium carbonate skeleton and protruding yellow polyps with smooth tentacles. Colony form is variable and influenced by substrate. Polyps are approximately $\frac{1}{2}$ in (1 cm) in diameter; $\frac{1}{4}$ in (.5 cm) when retracted.

Habitat Rocky substrates, rocks and steep slopes. The colony often grows on sponges (*Axinella*) or on encrusting red algae. Temperature should be kept below 71 °F (22 °C).

Feeding Planktonic animals and organic detritus. In the aquarium the colony will eat plankton and fresh or preserved marine animal homogenates.

Biology Dislikes light. Sexual reproduction, with planktonic larvae which swim to colonize new environments.

282 PILGRIM SCALLOP
Pecten jacobaeus

Classification Phylum Mollusca, class Bivalvia or Lamellibranchia.

Distribution Mediterranean and adjacent Atlantic coasts.

Description The shell comprises two valves, the left one flattened and brown, the right one curved and lighter in color. The valves are joined by a hinge. Numerous tentacles interspersed with iridescent eyes protrude between the half-opened valves. Shell diameter may reach 5 in (12 cm).

Habitat Usually lives at depths exceeding 32 ft (10 m) on sandy, rocky or detritus bottoms, sometimes on coral banks. Aquarium temperature should not exceed 71 °F (22 °C).

Feeding This species is a filter feeder, retaining organic particles suspended in the water. Feeding by scallops therefore filters the water in the aquarium.

Biology *P. jacobaeus* is able to swim by rapidly opening and closing its valves. Reproduction is sexual; it has small planktonic larvae.

283 PROTULA TUBULARIA
Protula tubularia

Classification Phylum Annelida, class Polychaeta, order Sedentaria, suborder Serpulimorpha, family Serpulidae.
Distribution Mediterranean and neighboring Atlantic. Many similar species inhabit other seas.
Description The segmented wormlike body is protected by a rigid calcium carbonate tube, which is three-sided in section, is up to $\frac{1}{2}$ in (1 cm) wide and has a lid to shut the opening. The gill crown is double and variously colored from yellow to reddish.
Habitat This animal lives alone or in groups on coral reefs in deep waters. Aquarium temperature should not exceed 71 °F (22 °C).
Feeding It normally feeds on plankton and suspended foods and will do so in the aquarium.
Biology The branchial tentacles may be folded and completely retracted into the chalky tube. Reproduction is sexual and yields eggs which hatch into planktonic larvae (trochophores).

284 PSAMMECHINUS MICROTUBERCULATUS
Psammechinus microtuberculatus

Classification Phylum Echinodermata, class Echinoidea.
Distribution Mediterranean coastal waters.
Description Small sea urchin, $\frac{3}{4}$–1 in (2–3 cm) in diameter, with short, numerous, dense spines. Color ranges from gray to green depending on background substrate color. Tubular zones are lighter in color.
Habitat Lives among *Posidonia* holdfasts at depths of up to 65 ft (20 m). It adapts better than other species to temperate aquarium environments.
Feeding Herbivorous; feeds on plants and detritus. In captivity it finds all its necessary nourishment on the bottom, but will readily eat fresh plants.
Biology Like all echinoids, it reproduces sexually. Planktonic larvae hatch from its eggs and eventually settle on the bottom to assume their adult form.

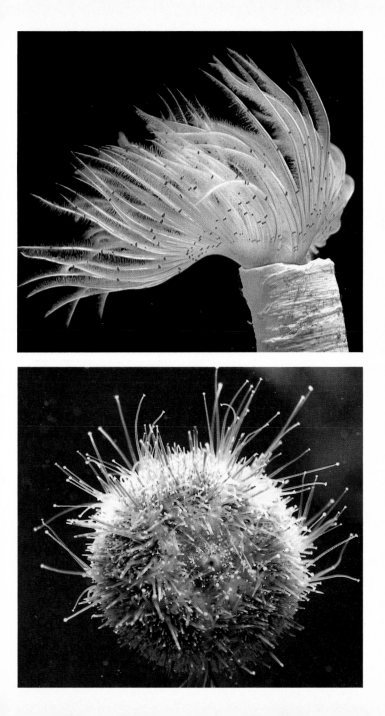

285 CUTTLEFISH
Sepia officinalis

Classification Phylum Mollusca, class Cephalopoda, order Decapoda.
Distribution Mediterranean, Atlantic Ocean.
Description The saclike body carries the head, with its large eyes and ten tentacles around the mouth. The whole body margin is lined by an undulating finlike structure. Body color, usually striped and dotted, varies according to the state of the animal. Body length may exceed 12 in (30 cm).
Habitat Bottom-dwelling animals in coastal waters; likes sandy or muddy bottoms as well as vegetation. It adapts to aquarium life if given sufficient space and temperatures not exceeding 71 °F (22 °C).
Feeding Very active predator; will feed on any small, swimming animal. In captivity, it will adapt to eat fresh or dried animal food.
Biology Reproduction is sexual and mating is preceded by a striking dance. The eggs, which are large and sessile, yield well-developed individuals.

1 2 3 4 5 6 7 8 9 10 11 12 13 14

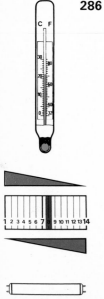

286 SEPIOLA RONDELETII
Sepiola rondeletii

Classification Phylum Mollusca, class Cephalopoda, order Decapoda.
Distribution Mediterranean. Similar species live in other seas.
Description Saclike body, containing the viscera, attached to the head, which has large eyes and ten tentacles around the mouth. Overall color is variable, depending on the state of the pigment cells (chromatophores). The siphon protrudes from the mantle beneath the head. Overall length approximately $1-2\frac{1}{2}$ in (3–6 cm). Two finlike structures extend horizontally from the body.
Habitat Sandy or rocky bottoms in shallow coastal waters. Adapts rather well to aquarium life if conditions are optimal and temperature does not exceed 71 °F (22 °C).
Feeding A small but efficient predator, this cephalopod is able to capture moving prey. It will reluctantly feed on dead animals, but prefers small, live fishes and crustaceans.
Biology Body color is basically reddish but varies, as mentioned above, according to the mood of the animal. Reproduction is sexual, and well-developed animals hatch from the eggs.

1 2 3 4 5 6 7 8 9 10 11 12 13 14

287 SIMIA
Simia spp.

Classification Phylum Mollusca, class Gastropoda.
Distribution Mediterranean; similar species in other seas.
Description Strikingly beautiful gastropod, with rounded shell somewhat slimmer than *Cypraea*. The shell, which is less than $\frac{1}{2}$ in (1 cm) long, is white but is covered by the spotted red mantle. The foot is also red, with shades of blue. The eyes lie at the base of two narrow, blue-tipped tentacles.
Habitat Lives among gorgonians, and is often found on them. Prefers low light levels and temperatures below 71 °F (22 °C).
Feeding Eats both plant and animal matter. In the aquarium it will eat standard fresh or dried foods.
Biology Phylogenetically closely related to cowries; the biology of this gastropod has not been extensively studied. Reproduction is sexual, and mature individuals hatch from the eggs.

288 PURPLE-SPINED SEA URCHIN
Sphaerechinus granularis

Classification Phylum Echinodermata, class Echinoidea.
Distribution Mediterranean and neighboring Atlantic coastline.
Description About $2\frac{1}{2}$ in (6–7 cm) in diameter. Bright purple with short, white-tipped spines. The young, which are $\frac{1}{2}$–1 in (1–2 cm) in diameter and white or reddish in color, adapt more easily to captivity.
Habitat Lives among algae and marine plants at depths ranging from 10 to 100 ft (3 to 30 m) along coastlines. Aquarium temperature should not exceed 71 °F (22 °C).
Feeding A detritus feeder, it eats any available organic matter as well as plants. In captivity, it requires fresh vegetable matter from time to time.
Biology In its natural habitat, it lives in isolation.

289 TUBE WORM
Spirographis spallanzanii

Classification Phylum Annelida, class Polychaeta, order Sedentaria, suborder Serpulimorpha.

Distribution Mediterranean. Similar tube worms are present in all seas.

Description The animal consits of a segmented wormlike body inserted in a soft, flexible tube fixed to the substrate. A single crown of spirally arranged tentacles protrudes from the tube, unevenly distributed between two supporting structures. The tentacles are yellowish with white, brown and reddish stripes. Tube diameter usually is between $\frac{1}{2}$ in (1 cm) and 1 in (2.5 cm).

Habitat Lives attached to rocks and artifacts in shallow coastal waters. It adapts itself easily to captivity and is able to withstand temperatures of up to 75 °F (24 °C).

Feeding Feeds on plankton and organic particles in suspension. In the aquarium it will feed on *Artemia* nauplii and other small plankton and on suspended organic materials.

Biology The crown of radioles can be folded and retracted when the animal is disturbed. Reproduction is sexual, with a planktonic larval stage (trochophore).

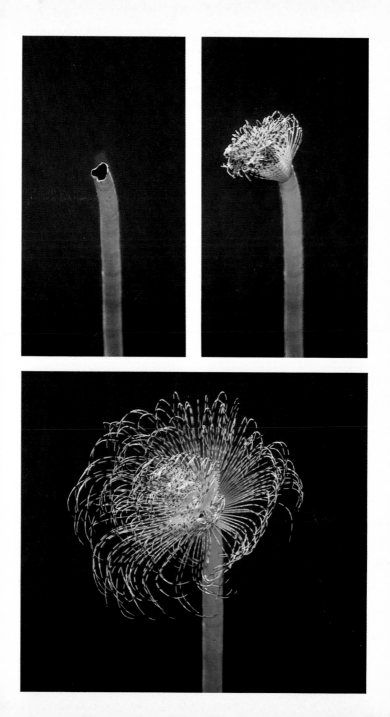

290 BANDED PRAWN
Stenopus hispidus

Classification Phylum Arthropoda, class Crustacea, subclass Malacostraca, order Decapoda, suborder Macrura.

Distribution Widely distributed in all tropical and subtropical seas.

Description Its appearance and behavior both make *S. hispidus* one of the most popular tropical shrimps. Its body is white, with wide, transverse red bands. The claws are strong, and the antennae are unusually long. The sharp angle between carapace and abdomen gives this animal its unusual "bent" appearance.

Habitat Lives in holes and crevices on hard or coral substrates in shallow waters. In the aquarium it requires high water temperatures—at least 77 °F (25 °C)—although it will tolerate somewhat lower temperatures.

Feeding A carnivorous animal, it will eat only fresh or dried animal food.

Biology The most outstanding behavioral characteristic of this animal is its highly developed territorial instinct, which makes it impossible for individuals of the same species to share an aquarium, but an individual may be kept with fishes. Sexes are separate, and the male is aggressive.

291 STOICHACTIS KENTI
Stoichactis kenti

Classification Phylum Coelenterata or Cnidaria, class Anthozoa, subclass Hexacorallia, order Actiniaria.

Distribution Widespread on coral or rocky bottoms in the Indian and Pacific oceans.

Description Large sea anemone with short tentacles and wavy margins, often over 20 in (50 cm) in diameter. Body color is pinkish brown variegated with white or green.

Habitat Anchors itself to hard substrates by its sturdy foot, but will sometimes move in the aquarium in search of a better location. It will tolerate less-than-optimal environmental conditions, but it needs temperatures above 77 °F (25 °C).

Feeding Feeds on live or dead animal food. Aquarium feeding is simple, provided that the food is placed in contact with the tentacles.

Biology This species is frequently associated with anemone fishes. The animal may reproduce by division or through the normal anthozoan reproductive cycle. The tentacles can sting weakly.

292 GIANT CLAM
Tridacna lamellosa

Classification Phylum Mollusca, class Bivalvia or Lamellibranchia.

Distribution Indo-Pacific coastlines. Various species belonging to the same genus inhabit all tropical seas.

Description The largest known bivalves belong to this genus. The two shells are strong and radially undulated to match each other exactly when shut. The lobed mantle protrudes outside the valves when the animal is undisturbed and bears a pattern of dots. *T. lamellosa* may be up to 3 ft (1 m) long.

Habitat Lives in shallow, brightly lit waters on coral or rocky beds. Young individuals tolerate captivity if well illuminated. Water temperature should not fall below 77 °F (25 °C).

Feeding Like most bivalves, *T. lamellosa* is a filter feeder and extracts particles in suspension from the water. It therefore presents no outstanding feeding problems in the aquarium.

Biology The presence of symbiotic algae often makes the mantle appear bright green. Sexual reproduction yields planktonic larvae.

293 KNOBBED TRITON
Tritonium nodiferum

Classification Phylum Mollusca, class Gastropoda.

Distribution Largely Mediterranean and adjacent Atlantic areas. Similar species in all seas.

Description Large mollusk, measuring up to 16 in (40 cm), with a long, narrow shell and a wide opening from which siphon and foot protrude, respectively, in front and below. The foot is large and is a spotted brown. The head carries two complex stalked eyes.

Habitat *T. nodiferum* lives on rocks and muddy bottoms in deep coastal waters. It has become rather rare and will require a large aquarium, preferably at temperatures not exceeding 71 °F (22 °C).

Feeding Large, carnivorous predator, which normally eats starfish and sea cucumbers. In captivity, it will eat corresponding amounts of animal foods, fresh or dried.

Biology Little is known of the biology of this rare and solitary species, which reproduces sexually.

Note It may seriously injure echinoderms in the aquarium.

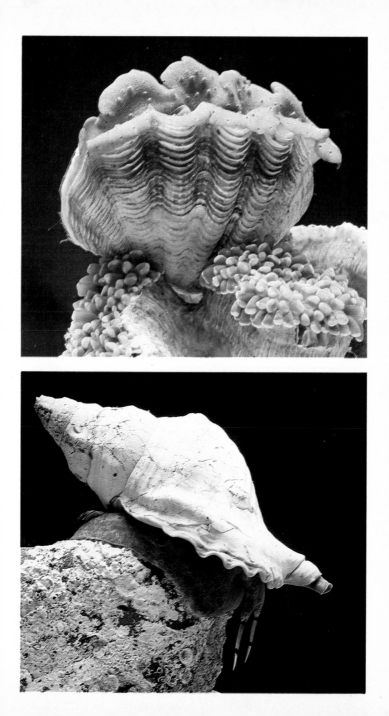

294 MADREPORIAN CORAL
Turbinaria mesentherina

Classification Phylum Coelenterata or Cnidaria, class Anthozoa, subclass Hexacorallia, order Madreporaria.

Distribution Tropical Pacific and Indian oceans.

Description Colonial coral, with a calcium carbonate skeleton which forms convoluted sheets. Protrusions on one face of the sheets are occupied by polyps. Colonies may cover large areas of sea floor.

Habitat Shallow tropical waters with moderate illumination. They require slightly moving waters and temperatures above 77 °F (25 °C).

Feeding Like all colonial madrepores, members of this species feed on plankton and organic food particles in suspension. In the aquarium, they prefer small planktonic animals such as *Artemia* nauplii and homogenized (by putting in a blender) fresh or dried mollusks.

Biology Reproduction is sexual, with planktonic larvae, but the colony may increase in size by growth.

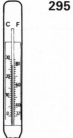

295 FIDDLER CRAB
Uca uca

Classification Phylum Arthropoda, class Crustacea, subclass Malacostraca, order Decapoda, suborder Brachyura.

Distribution Widely distributed along tropical Indo-Pacific coastlines.

Description Characterized, like many other species belonging to the same genus, by its bright, varied and uniform color. Typical crab shape, but this species has one small and one huge claw; the latter is rhythmically shaken up and down in social interactions between males of the species. The eyes are situated at the tips of conspicuous stalks.

Habitat Lives on mud or sand bottoms in tidal zones. Requires an aquaterrarium in which it can climb out of the water onto well-lit humid substrate. It tolerates sea water of varied salinity and is relatively insensitive to wide variations of alkalinity. However, it requires surrounding temperatures above 77 °F (25 °C).

Feeding It will eat any fresh or dried animal food.

Biology The behavior of this species has been extensively studied. The sexes are easily distinguished by the hypertrophied claw in the male. These animals inhabit holes dug out in the sand and live through several molts. The body is $\frac{3}{4}$ to $1\frac{1}{2}$ in (2.5 to 4 cm) wide, not including the legs.

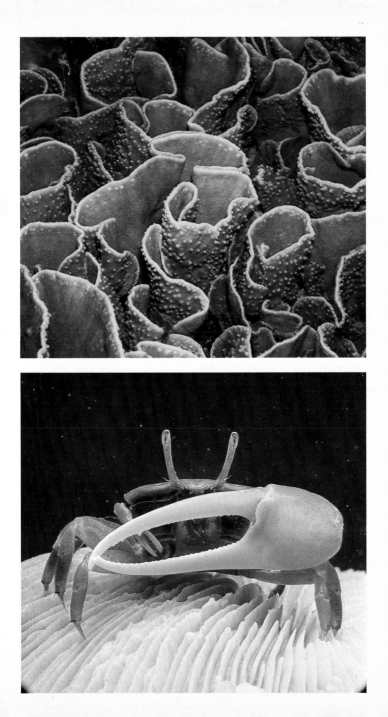

GLOSSARY

acid   a substance that in aqueous solution yields hydrogen ions. When combined with certain metals or bases the hydrogen forms salts. Acids have a sharp, sour taste and turn blue litmus paper red.

adipose fin   a small, fleshy, usually rayless fin found between the dorsal and caudal fins of some fishes.

aerobe   an organism that can survive only in the presence of oxygen.

albino   an animal that as a result of a hereditary anomaly has no pigment and is either white or transparent.

algae   a group of primitive aquatic plants including the seaweeds and allied forms.

alkaline   having the properties of a base.

amplexus   the male's grasp of the female during mating. Found among amphibians.

anal fin   an unpaired fin in a ventral position between the anus and the tail.

anesthetic   a substance that deadens feeling and produces a state akin to sleep without affecting the vital functions.

annual   living for a single year.

antenna   a sensory appendage found on the heads of crustaceans, insects, and other arthropods.

anterior   forward.

antibiotic   a substance that arrests growth or causes the death of pathogenic microorganisms. It is of great therapeutic value.

apex   farthest point of a leaf, branch, stalk, root, etc.

Artemia   a tiny crustacean that lives in very salty water; the brine shrimp.

arthropod   an invertebrate animal with segmented body and jointed limbs and an external skeleton in the form of a shell.

avitaminosis   a disease caused by a deficiency of vitamins.

axillary   pertaining to the hind part of the pectoral-fin base of fishes.

bacteria   unicellular organisms with no nucleus. They multiply mainly by division and live singly or in colonies.

barbel   fleshy beardlike appendage attached to the mouth of some fishes.

basal related to or situated at the base—e.g., leaves at the base of a stem.

basalt dark-colored igneous rock.

base a substance with the capacity to liberate hydroxyl ions in water. Bases have a bitter taste and turn red litmus paper blue. Thus they are the opposite of acids.

benthos the complex of aquatic organisms that live on the bottom of the sea; benthic: pertaining to the benthos.

biosphere that part of the earth and the atmosphere that contains living things.

biotic pertaining to living organisms.

brackish having a density between that of sea water and that of fresh water.

bud small, undeveloped part of a plant (flower, leaf, etc.), often protected by small leaves.

budding asexual form of reproduction which produces new organisms through budlike projections.

carapace the dorsal shell of crustaceans. Also applied to the dorsal shell of turtles and tortoises.

carnivorous flesh-eating.

catabolism the process of breaking down tissue used by organisms to produce energy.

caudal fin the tail fin of fishes.

caudal peduncle the tail stalk, where the tail fin joins the body.

caustic potash potassium hydroxide.

cephalothorax the fused head and thorax found, e.g., in crustaceans.

chromatophores the cells containing the pigment that gives animals their color.

ciliate having tiny mobile hairs, or cilia.

cirrus a small threadlike skin appendage sensitive to touch.

class a group of related orders. A group of classes forms a phylum.

claw pincer on the end of the front legs of crustaceans, used to catch food and for defense.

clay fine, impervious particles of earth, malleable when wet.

cloaca the common chamber in many animals into which intestinal, urinary, and generative canals discharge.

colony a sessile aggregation of individuals.

competition ecological relationship between

organisms that require the same food and other resources.

coral reef reef made of the calcareous skeletons of colonies of madrepores (q.v.). Found in tropical seas and usually parallel to coastal lines.

cordate heart-shaped.

corolla the ensemble formed by the petals of a flower.

cosmopolitan found nearly all over the world.

costal ridges ridges of skin over the ribs in some salamanders.

crenulated finely notched.

crepuscular animal one active at twilight.

crustacean any of a large class (Crustacea) of mainly aquatic animals with hard shells, such as crabs, lobsters, shrimps, water fleas, etc.

cutting (1) a stem cutting of a plant, capable of sending out roots and used for propagation; (2) way of propagating a plant. A branch or leaf is cut off the parent plant and inserted in soil. It then produces roots.

density the ratio of a mass of water to its volume. For sea water this varies between 1.020 and 1.030 grams per cubic centimeter and depends mainly on salt content and to a lesser degree on temperature.

denticulate notched.

detritus decomposing materials on the substrate that have been reduced to small fragments.

dichotomy division by an organ (such as a stem) into two equal parts which, in turn, divide into two more equal parts.

diet in a biological context, a detailed account of what an animal eats.

dilution the addition of solvent to a solution to diminish its concentration.

disinfectant a substance that kills pathogens.

diurnal animal one active by day.

dolomite a marblelike rock composed chiefly of carbonates of calcium and magnesium.

dorsal pertaining to the upper surface.

dorsal fin an unpaired fin on the back of fishes.

Drosophila a genus of small fruit flies used in genetic experiments.

echinoderms a group of marine animals that includes sea urchins, sea cucumbers, and starfishes.

ecosystem   the unit formed by a community of plants and animals and their environment.

ectoparasite   a parasite that lives outside the host.

embryology   the scientific study of the origin, structure, and development of the embryo.

enchytraeids   white worms readily eaten by small fishes, which should not be fed them too often, as worms are rather fattening.

endoparasite   a parasite that lives inside the host.

epidermis   the outer layer of skin.

equilibrium, biological   the balance established between various competing organisms and their environment.

erectile   capable of being raised.

essence   aromatic and volatile product extracted from plants.

ethology   the study of animal behavior.

family   a group of genera with common characteristics. A group of families forms an order.

febrifuge   a medicine that reduces fever.

foot   a muscular development on the ventral surface of mollusks that has various forms and functions.

frond   the leaf of a fern or seaweed.

fry   newly hatched fish.

gastropod   a member of the mollusk class Gastropoda, which includes snails, slugs, etc.

genus   a group of species with common characteristics. A group of genera forms a family.

gland   a small organ that produces secretions affecting the physiology of an organism.

gonopodium   an anal fin that has been transformed into the copulatory organ of some male fishes.

gorgonian   a type of sea fan that secretes a horny substance.

guanine   a fundamental constituent of nucleic acids, deposited in the genetic code. As a pigment it produces a silver coloring.

habitat   the physical environment of a species.

hermaphrodite   an organism with male and female genital organs.

homocercal   having symmetrical upper and lower lobes.

hormones   substances secreted by endocrine

glands and having particular physiological effects.

humerus   the bone of the upper part of the forelimb.

humus   the organic portion of soil composed of decayed plant or animal matter.

inert   not producing any chemical reaction.

infection   an injurious invasion of the body of a plant or animal by disease-producing organisms.

interoperculum   a bone between the pre-operculum and suboperculum in the gill cover of many fishes.

invertebrates   animals without bones. Some have no skeletal support at all, and others an external skeleton.

lacinia   a long, narrow lobe.

lamina   a leaf blade.

lanceolate   shaped like the point of a lance.

larva   a stage in the development of many animals when they are not yet mature and have a fundamentally different form from that of an adult.

lateral line   the sense organ extending longi-tudinally on each side of a fish.

limestone   a sedimentary rock composed of calcium carbonate.

linear   long and narrow with parallel sides.

litmus paper   a treated paper used to determine the acidity or alkalinity of a solution. Acids turn blue litmus paper red; bases turn red litmus paper blue.

madrepores   colonizing marine animals with stony, calcareous skeletons. They are the main constituent of coral reefs.

mangrove   a tree growing in tropical muddy estuaries, and characterized by its aerial roots.

mantle   a fold of tissue on the body of a mollusk which secretes the shell.

mesophyll   the tissues between the upper and lower surfaces of a leaf.

metabolism   the chemical processes that trans-form and break down organic materials inside organisms.

metameric   divided into segments.

metamorphosis   the process of transformation undergone by an animal at the larval stage in order to reach the adult stage.

methylene blue   a soluble dye used in prepar-ing microscope slides.

microfauna tiny animals, especially those invisible to the naked eye.

mimicry the superficial resemblance of one animal or plant to its surroundings or to other species for concealment, protection, or other advantages.

mollusk a member of the invertebrate phylum Mollusca, usually having a shell; examples are clams, octopuses, sea slugs, and snails.

morphology the form of an organism.

mucus a liquid secreted by membranes to moisten and protect the skin.

nape on a fish, the part of the back immediately behind the head.

naturalized adapted to living in a different region from that in which an organism originated.

neotenous sexually mature while retaining larval characteristics.

nervure the system of veins of a leaf.

node the point where a leaf is attached to a stem.

nitrates nitric acid salts, used by plants in the synthesis of proteins.

nitrification the chemical process carried out in the soil by bacteria that change salts of ammonia into nitrates and nitrites.

nitrites nitrous acid salts, produced by the action of bacteria on ammonia.

nocturnal animal one active at night.

ovoid egg-shaped.

omnivorous eating both animal and vegetable foods.

operculum the bony gill cover of fishes, or the horny plate covering the shell opening in many gastropods.

orbicular roughly circular or spherical.

order a group of related families. A group of orders forms a class.

osmosis the passage of a solute from a more concentrated solution to a less concentrated one through a semipermeable membrane.

ossified formed into bone.

oviparous egg-laying.

oviposition the act of depositing the ova, or eggs, during reproduction.

ovoviviparous producing eggs which are hatched, without the formation of a placenta, inside the mother's body.

ozone a gas whose molecules are composed of three oxygen atoms. It is a powerful oxidizing agent and acts as a disinfectant.

papilla a small projecting body part of an animal, similar to a nipple in form.

parasite an organism that lives at the expense of another and is usually incapable of an independent existence.

pathogen a microorganism that causes disease.

pathology the study of disease.

peat an acid soil derived from partially decomposed plant deposits, especially sphagnum moss.

pectoral fin a paired fin behind the gill opening.

peduncle a stalk connecting a part of a plant or animal with the main body.

pelagic living in the open sea, far above the seabed.

pelvic fin another name for a ventral fin (q.v.)

penicillin an antibiotic derived from the fungus *Penicillium notatum.*

pennate wing-shaped.

perciform perch-shaped.

perennial living more than a single year.

pH a number that expresses the acidity or alkalinity of a solution. A pH of less than 7 indicates an acid solution, 7 a neutral one, over 7 an alkaline one.

phanerogam a plant with flowers—that is, with distinct male and female organs.

photosynthesis the formation of sugars by green plants from carbon dioxide and hydrogen in cells containing chlorophyll and exposed to light.

phylum a group of related classes. A group of phyla forms a kingdom.

physiology the scientific study of the mechanisms that govern the vital functions of organisms.

phytophagous plant-eating.

pigment a substance that gives organisms their color.

pistil the female sex organ of a flower. It is divided into ovary, style, and stigma.

plankton the swimming organisms that live suspended in waters such as seas and lakes.

plastron the ventral shell of a turtle, tortoise, or crustacean.

Plexiglas (U.K.: Perspex) TM. a transparent, tough acrylic plastic often used in place of glass.

polyethylene a common plastic material.

polyp a single animal belonging to the phylum Coelenterata. It lives in fixed colonies (e.g., madrepores, corals).

polystyrene, expanded a very light plastic material.

posterior rearward.

preoperculum a bony plate at the front of the gill cover of most fishes.

proboscis a long snout or trunk.

propagation a form of plant reproduction that occurs when part of the vegetative organ of the plant detaches itself or is detached from the parent plant and forms a new individual.

protandrous sexually active first as a male and then as a female.

protein an organic compound essential to animal metabolism and consisting mainly of hydrogen, oxygen, and nitrogen.

prothallus a plant of the sexual generation in ferns and their allies. It has a small, heart-shaped structure, the prothallium, that produces male and female sex cells.

protogynous sexually active first as a female and then as a male.

radula the rasping "tongue" of a mollusk

rhizome a long underground rootlike plant stem that contains reserve substances and produces temporary roots.

rickets a disease of the bones caused by deficiency of calcium or vitamin D.

root a portion of a plant body, usually underground, that anchors the plant in the earth and through which it draws nutritive substances.

rosette the arrangement of leaves in a circle around the stem and close to the ground.

rostrum a beaklike process or part.

rotifers tiny freshwater animals with waving cilia around the mouth opening.

salts substances derived from the reaction of acids on the basic (alkaline) constituents of many rocks. In dissolved form they are necessary to both animals and plants.

savanna tropical or subtropical grassland with treeless vegetation.

scales thin, bony plates in the skin of most fishes.

schooling fish one that likes to swim with others of the same kind.

sediment particles that settle to the bottom of a liquid.

seed a multicellular structure derived from the fertilized ovule, and the means by which flowering plants usually reproduce.

sepal part of the outer set of leaves of a flower.

sessile (1) plants: without a stalk; (2) animals: anchored to the bottom.

shoal a number of fishes swimming together.

solute a dissolved substance.

solution a homogeneous mixture of two or more substances (one is usually liquid) in which the components cannot be distinguished.

spadix a fleshy spike of flowers.

spathe the large, sheathlike bract surrounding a spadix, q.v.

spawning the laying of eggs by aquatic animals.

species a group of similar, mutually fertile individuals, whose mating produces similar, fertile offspring and which cannot breed in nature with individuals of other such groups. A group of species forms a genus.

spermatophore a case produced by the male and containing sperm cells transferred to the female during fertilization.

spicule a minute, needlelike body. Spicules make up the skeleton of invertebrates such as sponges and sea cucumbers.

sprout a new shoot springing from the bottom of the plant.

stamen the male organ of a flower, formed of a filament whose end is called the anther.

stem the leaf-bearing part of a plant.

stigma the top part of the female sex organ of a flowering plant, which receives the pollen.

stolon a long shoot from the base of a stem or from a rhizome that produces roots.

style the middle section of the pistil, between the ovary and the stigma.

suboperculum the bony plate underneath the operculum in the gill cover of most fishes.

substrate the base on which plants and animals live. In an aquarium, the gravel or other covering on the bottom of the tank.

sucker   a shoot growing from the root of a plant and producing a new plant.

suspension   homogeneous   distribution   of microscopic particles within a liquid.

suture   the line of union between two parts forming an immovable joint.

symbiont   an organism living in symbiosis, q.v.

symbiosis   a mutually beneficial biological relationship between two or more dissimilar individuals, plants and/or animals.

territoriality   the tendency of many animals to occupy and defend a well-defined area.

thallus   a plant body not divided into leaf, stem, and root.

theca   a protective case or sheath for a part or organ.

toxins   poisons of organic origin.

tubercle   a small tuber or swelling.

Tubifex   small freshwater segmented worms that live in mud.

unisexual   having only one set of reproductive organs, either male or female.

variegated   having various colors in spots, streaks, or stripes.

variety   a subdivision of the species grouping, based on secondary characteristics; individuals of one variety can breed with those of another variety of the same species.

ventral   pertaining to the lower surface.

ventral fin   a paired fin in a ventral position in front of the anus, also called pelvic fin.

vermiculations   wavy, wormlike markings.

verruca   a small protuberance.

vesicle   a small sac or swelling.

viral   produced by a virus.

virus   an infectious organism with simpler structure than a cell.

viscera   the internal organs of the body cavities.

viviparous   producing live offspring.

whorl   a group of leaves, flowers, branches, roots, arising from the same level of a stem.

Index